AF291993

The Music and Influence of Cher

The Music and Influence of Cher

Angela Andaloro

WHITE OWL

AN IMPRINT OF PEN & SWORD BOOKS LTD.
YORKSHIRE · PHILADELPHIA

First published in Great Britain in 2026 by
White Owl
An imprint of Pen & Sword Books Limited
Yorkshire – Philadelphia

ISBN 978 1 03612 335 2

A CIP catalogue record for this book is
available from the British Library.

Typeset by Mac Style
Printed in the UK by CPI Group (UK) Ltd, Croydon, CR0 4YY.

The Publisher's authorised representative in the EU for product
safety is Authorised Rep Compliance Ltd., Ground Floor,
71 Lower Baggot Street, Dublin D02 P593, Ireland.
www.arccompliance.com

For a complete list of Pen & Sword titles please contact:

PEN & SWORD BOOKS LIMITED
47 Church Street, Barnsley, South Yorkshire, S70 2AS, England
E-mail: enquiries@pen-and-sword.co.uk
Website: www.pen-and-sword.co.uk
or
PEN AND SWORD BOOKS
1950 Lawrence Road, Havertown, PA 19083, USA
E-mail: uspen-and-sword@casematepublishers.com
Website: www.penandswordbooks.com

Contents

Acknowledgements — vii
Foreword — viii
Introduction — x

Chapter 1 — Early Life — 1

Chapter 2 — Early Talent — 6

Chapter 3 — 1962–1965 — 8

Chapter 4 — 1965–1969 — 15

Chapter 5 — 1970–1974 — 29

Chapter 6 — 1975 — 45

Chapter 7 — 1976–1979 — 52

Chapter 8 — 1980–1984 — 62

Chapter 9 — 1985–1987 — 77

Chapter 10 — 1988–1989 — 92

Chapter 11 — 1990–1994 — 102

Chapter 12 — 1995–1997 — 114

Chapter 13 — 1998–1999 — 122

Chapter 14 — 2000–2004 — 133

Chapter 15 — 2005–2009 — 146

Chapter 16 — Chaz — 155

Chapter 17   2010–2014   167

Chapter 18   Elijah   173

Chapter 19   2015–2019   180

Chapter 20   2020   187

Chapter 21   2021–2025   191

Chapter 22   Legacy   202

Bibliography   204

Acknowledgements

While I've spent just the last year writing this book, in so many ways, it's practically a lifetime in the making. I've always been inspired by strong women who march to the beat of their own drum. I'd like to thank Cher for her longstanding spot at the top of that list.

I would, of course, like to thank my family. This book's beginnings are in little me, staying up late to watch *The Sonny and Cher Comedy Hour*. For that, I would like to thank my mom, who always just let me be me. I also owe a great deal to my grandparents, who were the first to introduce me to the greats, in music and beyond. Thank you for raising me to understand that strong women make the world go round. The powerful women I saw in my own home and on TV made me who I am today.

There's no world where this book could have happened without my husband, who was endlessly understanding of my chaos along the way. Thank you for talking me off countless ledges throughout this process. Your patience and support have meant the world to me. It may even talk me into doing this again sometime.

This book wouldn't be what it is without the countless talented journalists along the way who took an interest in bringing someone as ethereal as Cher to life for mere mortals. Devouring every interview was a pleasure and reaffirms to me that entertainment journalism is important and impactful work, for which I'm endlessly grateful to be able to contribute. An additional special thank you to each and every photographer whose work is displayed in this book. These striking images tell Cher's story so beautifully.

Finally, thank you to the team at White Owl Books and Pen & Sword for their support along the way.

Foreword

"Cher always had a large contingent of kids watching her show. She was hip, cool, and everything they wanted to be."

– George Schlatter

In the '90s, I was one of those kids. Nick at Nite made one last attempt to syndicate *The Sonny and Cher Show* from December 1995 to April 1997. During that period, I religiously tuned in to the half-hour block, captivated by the power and adoration Cher commanded from an audience. Even when she was snarky or did the unexpected, she was still met with such respect. That kind of commanding presence and the reverence it received were entirely unfamiliar to me, but like so many other fans, it drew me in.

The following year, I'd find out that those reruns were a little behind the times when Sonny Bono died in a skiing accident. I was young and didn't understand divorce (or how much time had passed between those shows and the unfolding situation). I found myself worried about Cher, seeing her mournful face across TV and on magazine covers. But if there's one thing you should know about Cher, it's that though she sometimes finds herself down, she's never out. Give it another two years, and she'd be topping the charts for a new and unique sound, and a whole new lease on life.

It's been 25 years since her turn-of-the-millennium hit, 'Believe,' and Cher is still making headlines. She still has stories that resonate with listeners, old and new, and a way with words unlike any other. She's a multi-hyphenate who, in her sixth decade of fame, remains as relevant as ever and continues to collect accolades, including her 2024 induction into the Rock & Roll Hall of Fame.

I've been interested in Cher's story for so long that I thought I knew it all. However, to say that it has been an honour and a privilege to immerse myself in Cher's personal history and her meteoric rise to fame would be a true understatement. I am in constant awe, even as I write these words, of how she has moved herself forward and pivoted from moments that might have ended a lesser star's career, to triumph in some of her greatest accomplishments of all time.

I am thrilled to share the story behind the powerhouse and give insight into a woman who is inspirational to so many and has lived an unapologetic and magical life, and graciously shared so much of it with the world.

Introduction

The word 'icon' is thrown around rather loosely today. Anything from an animal meme to a pair of shoes to a movie that came out a week ago, can be determined iconic, but let's face it – there's a stark difference between the ordinary and the extraordinary.

Those who wax poetic about a bygone era will tell you that reaching that status used to *mean* something. It took true grit to claw your way out of obscurity and find your dream, making something of yourself. It took luck, timing, and determination to hustle hard enough that someone else thought something of you.

As you'll learn in what's ahead, Cher had dreams bigger than anything else. From an early age, Cher knew what she wanted from life. Those dreams became increasingly clear to her in the decade between falling in love with song and stage and setting out on her own, where she quickly met Sonny Bono.

If there was a time when anyone could attribute Cher's star power to Sonny, it is a time also bygone. Though it's undeniable that the duo made a lasting mark on the music industry and pop culture, Sonny and Cher were a mere moment, a defining but establishing chapter in an epic.

Cher is the rare figure that seems at home in every era. In a career spanning decades, there has never been a time when Cher has truly seemed out of place – though her commercial success might not always reflect it. For many years, she's likened herself to a bumper car that bounces back from every angle. Indeed, her track record proves that she has done it, time and time again, often in the face of naysayers and corporate doubt.

In a world of frivolous icons, there's a reason why Cher is the real deal. She has lived life in the public eye, dealing with the good and bad with countless spectators watching. She's always been blunt and honest, owning the moments where life has humbled her.

It's no secret that Western society is obsessed with the idea that image is everything. Despite being firmly entrenched in that world and celebrated for it, Cher has never stopped herself from doing what she does to consider her image. She's not caught up in the public perception of her. She doesn't try to rise above; she does so naturally, leading with her heart. It has shaped her as a nurturing and genuine figure in a world where those qualities are in short supply.

Cher has brought throngs of people to their feet – to dance, to believe, to celebrate. Her ability to straddle many worlds, to be both entirely relatable and entirely singular, has made her a bonafide vestige of pop culture. It makes her story one that you can't help but dive into.

Chapter One

Early Life

From the very beginning, Cher has had a big personality and big dreams. She was born Cheryl Sarkisian on 20 May 1946 in El Centro, California. The baby girl who the world would come to know as Cher was born to Jackie Jean Crouch, 15, and John Sarkisian, 21.

Jackie Jean, who the world would later come to know as Georgia Holt, was very much a teenage girl when she welcomed her first daughter. She, too, had dreams of making it big. By day, she'd waitress and take on odd jobs to make ends meet, but from her days in rural Arkansas, she knew she had talent and sought after fame. Her father, Roy, had even moved the family to California for a time, hoping that Jackie's booming voice would be the family's ticket out of a life of poverty and suffering.

Hers wasn't that linear of a journey. She spent her childhood and young adult life moving around and trying to provide for herself and her family. When she'd had enough of her chaotic home life, she struck out on her own, finding domestic care work in Los Angeles that also allowed her to go back to school. She began to excel and find a place where she felt like she belonged, only to be drawn back to her family when Roy wrote to her, informing her he had been in an accident that left him in a full-body cast. She vowed to make her way back to Los Angeles, compelled by her feeling of belonging.

Getting back there would involve a few stops along the way. She met John Sarkisian, the baby of a large family, when she was just 18. Before they knew it, their connection led them to Reno, Nevada, where the two exchanged vows when Jackie was 19 and John was 20 years old. It took just a beat for Jackie to regret the decision, but John talked her into trying out the marriage for a few months instead. Frustrated, she left after three months, only to find out she was pregnant shortly thereafter.

Jackie nearly got an abortion, devastated by being left with two choices that both seemed insurmountable at her age, in her situation. At the last minute, she had a change of heart and decided to continue her pregnancy. She welcomed her baby girl a month early.

Jackie's name wouldn't be the only one to change. Cher revealed that, although she spent her whole life thinking her name was Cherilyn, that was not the case. When she went to legally change it to the mononym she's become known by, she learned that she was actually named Cheryl on her original birth certificate.

Becoming a mother only made her dreams of attaining the perfect life as a movie star that much bigger, but there were still struggles to overcome. Six months after Cher was born, John lost his trucking business, which had only just started providing the family a truly comfortable life while gambling. He tried to turn things around by proposing the family move to New York, where his sister could help them get back on their feet. While en route through a series of Greyhound transfers, John confessed to Jackie that he'd stolen a car and driven it into Mexico to sell, using the proceeds to pay for the bus tickets.

They made it to New York, but John grew paranoid that the police were out to get him. Refusing to let the family fall again, Jackie got a job as a cigarette girl at the Copacabana. She did well there, but John's paranoia forced them to leave New York and move to Scranton, Pennsylvania.

They weren't there long before they found themselves impoverished once again and running out of options. John left town to borrow money from his sister and find work, leaving Jackie to fend for herself. As for Cher, John suggested boarding her with a Catholic children's home in the area, hoping the temporary relief would help them get back on their feet. Then, they'd go back to Cher and their life as a family.

With no other option, Jackie agreed. She got to work waitressing and paying for Cher's stay at the home, but John never returned. When the nuns at the home told her she was unfit to be Cher's mother, she feared she'd never see her daughter again. She enlisted the help of a kind-hearted customer, who happened to be politically affiliated, to help get her baby girl back. The separation was so traumatising to Jackie that she spoke of it rarely until Cher was well into adulthood.

Separations between the mother and daughter didn't end there. Jackie and Cher did make their way back to Los Angeles, but Jackie depended on the kindness of her friends and her own mom, Lynda, to help care for her toddler as she tried to get her life on track. During that time, Jackie worked on getting a divorce from John and entered a beauty pageant, both of which she had success with while in Reno. She returned to Los Angeles, entering another pageant. She went on to win titles such as Miss Reno Nevada, Miss Holiday on Wings, and Miss Bellflower. In the process, she also caught the attention of a talent scout from a bona fide Hollywood drama school who was interested in offering her a scholarship.

She also met an actor, Chris Alcaide, who would become her second husband. Their relationship was troubled when Alcaide became jealous of Jackie's rising star, booking commercials and starring in plays at school. The two split when Cher was four, opening the door for a more substantial relationship. Jackie, who officially became known as Georgia during this time, met another actor, E.J. 'John' Southall, whom she fell for. They married and settled into life as a family. John Southall became the man Cher considered a father figure for much of her childhood.

The family spent much of their time in Los Angeles but would occasionally fall on hard times and retreat to John Southall's family home in Texas. As a little girl, Cher often retreated into her imagination. During her time as an only child, she became enamuored with two things: her imaginary friends and music.

In 1950, Georgia found herself down on her luck after nailing the lead role in *The Asphalt Jungle*, only to be replaced by a then-unknown actress by the name of Marilyn Monroe. Soon after learning she'd lost the role, Georgia discovered she was pregnant. In September 1951, Cher's sister, Georganne (whom she refers to as 'Gee'), was born. Cher was initially enthralled by the idea of having a little sister, at first. However, the reality that she could only interact with an infant so much soured the deal a bit for her. Georgia and John Southall took the tag-team approach, with Cher's stepfather providing her with significant support throughout the transition. The period became one of the family's better times together and though things weren't perfect, they gelled well as a unit and navigated their ups and downs.

Throughout times of hardship, Cher kept a sense of wonder about her. She was often busy exploring her world. One day, a backyard play accident led to an injury that endangered the use of Cher's left foot, for which she had to undergo surgery. It left her in a cast for weeks and with a distinct walk that she's kept all her life.

Life was complicated for Cher during those years. There were moments when she enjoyed some of the glamour that came with being the daughter of a working actress. Georgia's singing was, in many ways, the soundtrack to Cher's early childhood.

There were other times, however, when she hid and shrunk herself down as she listened to her parents fight about finances or Southall's escalating drinking problem. The problems weren't just under their roof. When Cher was 8, she would overhear her mother on the phone discussing how her father, Sarkisian, had been arrested on a narcotics charge. He would go on to serve three years in prison at San Quentin.

The two would ultimately stay together until Cher was 9 years old. Because the couple had run hot and cold for so long, it took a while for the little girl to realise that Southall was gone for good, although Georganne remained with her and Georgia.

Bouncing between schools and having a life unlike many of her peers, Cher balanced a mischievous nature with a strong sense of wanting to be good and achieve. She struggled a bit academically, but what was thought to be boredom and disinterest would later be diagnosed as dyslexia, though not until she was an adult.

Despite her academic setbacks, Cher was well-received by various groups of people and enjoyed herself in school. She was disengaged from the work; however, teachers seldom expressed frustrations with her because her presence made her an integral part of anything in which she participated.

When Cher was 11, life would change once again with Georgia's marriage to real estate bigwig Joseph Harper Collins. The two met at a party in the summer of 1957, where Cher claims Collins proposed to Georgia after 15 minutes of getting to know each other. She wouldn't agree until weeks later, but it was still sudden for the family. One of the big shifts that came with the marriage was in the family's economic status.

Collins was wealthy and lived in Beverly Hills. Their union, though it would only last five months, would mean Cher and her sister would start attending private school.

Cher, in particular, stuck out among her peers, which included Tina Sinatra. Cher's looks were unique and striking, a combination of her father's Armenian ancestry and Georgia's German, Irish, English, and Native American ancestry. She had thick black hair that curled when she was younger until she adopted the pin-straight hairstyles of the 1970s.

As she entered her teenage years, Cher's adventurous side started to shine through. In 1959, Cher experimented with both drugs and alcohol for the first time. At 14, she tried Benzedrine with a few friends at a party. She took two pills and remembered spending the whole weekend wide awake, chewing gum as she felt the effects of the amphetamine. Terrified of what she was experiencing, Cher came clean to Georgia. While her mom was comforting, she also didn't punish her, feeling like she had learned her lesson well enough from the terrifying experience.

Alcohol wasn't as appealing to Cher, who had seen what it had done to her father and her stepfather. Still, she experimented not too long after the Benzedrine incident. She drank two tall cans of malt liquor before throwing up while out with friends at the theatre.

In 1961, Georgia found love once again, marrying Gilbert Hartmann LaPiere, a bank manager. The couple was serious about the relationship going the distance. LaPiere even adopted Georganne and Cher, with the two girls taking his last name. Their lives took on a different pace with the family moving to New York.

Her new opulent surroundings made her feel out of place at a significant time in her life, though it didn't stop her from embracing her true self. Not only was she comfortable clowning around and making people laugh, but she'd also sing. That talent would follow her back to Encino when the family made another move, and it became the beginning of the journey she dreamed of but never thought possible.

Chapter Two

Early Talent

A love of the arts coursed through Cher's veins. Some of her fondest memories from growing up involved interacting with the pop culture of her time. Like teenage girls before and after her, Cher had an acute sense of what was happening in the music and television scenes and was already dreaming of how she could fit into those industries.

Georgia's early brushes with fame continued as she raised her daughters. She enjoyed minor roles in *I Love Lucy* and *The Adventures of Ozzie and Harriet*. When she could, she would bring her daughters along to sets and even sneak them into scenes as extras. Even in the family's darkest times, they held a sparkle in their eye for something they felt was sure to come.

Singing was where Georgia got her start as a child, so it's not surprising that she carried that talent into adulthood, inspiring Cher. The star has said she shares a similar sound with her mom, surprising to many who find her deep contralto so singular. Georgia wouldn't take a stab at singing professionally until decades after her daughter skyrocketed to fame.

Cher proved from an early age that she had a singular ability to visualise and execute performances. In the fifth grade, she gathered a group of girls from her school and produced them in a performance of *Oklahoma!*, a musical she'd come to love. At just 11 years old, Cher was able to direct and choreograph dance numbers, all while taking on the male roles in the production and handling the accompanying music.

Georgia was keen to encourage Cher's creative pursuits and would laud them whenever her daughter's academic shortcomings were mentioned. This approach was great for Cher, who became intoxicated with fame as she continued to grow. Time watching television was particularly intriguing to her, with the young girl dreaming of a world where she could be a famous on-screen personality.

One of Cher's fondest musical memories comes from watching *American Bandstand* after school. One day, she watched in awe, being reduced to tears as Ray Charles sang 'Georgia On My Mind.' The moment of musical connection, made more significant because the track featured her mom's name, became a meaningful one she'd recall as a musical awakening many times throughout her career.

The more Cher considered fame, the more she was drawn to it. She always felt 'different' than her peers and destined for something greater. As a preteen, she began practising the signature she adorns things with to this day. She knew, even then, that a mononym was right for her.

'I was always "Cher"; I never thought of myself as anything but "Cher." I went by different last names as a child, but none of them seemed really me,' she revealed in her first-ever memoir, *The First Time*.

While there was desire, there was also doubt. Cher wasn't initially confident in her skills as a performer. Furthermore, she was discouraged by the fact that many of the leading ladies of the day looked like Georgia – tall, blonde, statuesque women. Outside of Audrey Hepburn, dark-haired leading ladies had yet to have their moment. Cher battled between feeling discouraged that other women with exotic or unusual appearances weren't breaking through and wanting to be the one to change that one day.

Georgia and her daughters shared a love for the musicians of their time that blossomed as Cher entered her pre-teen years. One time, an equally enthusiastic Georgia took an 11-year-old Cher to see Elvis, 22 at the time, live at the Pan-Pacific Auditorium in Los Angeles. Cher looked back at the moment fondly, recalling how she and Georgia felt more like sisters as they stood on their seats, screaming and jumping along with the masses, captivated by the King of Rock.

As she became a teen, Cher really began to understand her capacity for entertaining. She charmed her peers with her willingness to burst into theatrics, whether that was singing on top of a lunch table or delivering a monologue mid-class. As other kids considered their futures – college or marriage being the most common options – Cher sought out stardom, knowing she had her mom's support.

Chapter Three

1962–1965

When Cher turned 16, she entered a truly transformative year that began with getting her driving license. She was on a drive in LaPiere's car when she almost got into a fender bender with an up-and-coming Warren Beatty, who invited her out to lunch. Lunch turned into more, with the teen returning home after curfew and infuriating her parents. Beatty called Georgia personally to smooth things over the next day without any prompting from Cher. They'd continue to see each other despite the fact that he was nearly a decade her senior, with neither having any major expectations from the pairing.

That year, Cher also decided to leave school behind for good, floating in and out before officially dropping out during her junior year. It wouldn't be an easy road for Cher. Her parents demanded that she work in her spare time, in lieu of returning to her education. She decided that she would work and take acting classes as a way to start exploring her creative side.

Cher trained with actor Jeff Corey, who was sceptical of the teen's commitment and hesitant to take her on as his youngest student. After making her read *Of Mice and Men*, he relented and entered her into his world. Corey's method called on students to draw from their life experiences in every role they tackled. Her fellow students, in their twenties and beyond, also doubted Cher, but she showed up ready to work twice each week, enjoying herself most when they practised improv. Still, Cher took the task of honing her acting skills seriously, believing she had more potential in acting than in music. Georgia claimed that Cher was the youngest actress to ever qualify for the Pasadena Playhouse workshop, which made it that much more upsetting when she didn't stick with it.

With a creative pursuit taken care of, there was still the matter of a job. Cher did odd work, feeling traditional gigs didn't suit her. This led to another big decision: moving out of her family home. Cher moved in with a friend, Melissa Melcher. She spent her time in Hollywood networking, whether it was dancing in clubs on the Sunset Strip or introducing herself to the businesspeople behind some of the biggest stars. Cher's larger-than-life attitude – which she was armed with even in her less confident days – attracted people to her. She operated on the gut feeling that her moment was just around the corner, and she was more cogent in that intuition than she could have imagined.

The third big moment of Cher's sixteenth year came when the guy she was dating proposed a double date with his friend – described as an eccentric divorcée getting back into the dating scene – and her roommate Melissa joined them. When the quad met up at a coffee shop in November 1962, Cher's date, Red Baldwin, introduced his friend, Salvatore 'Sonny' Bono. Recalling the moment many times over the years, Cher has said she knew then that her life was about to change.

What Cher didn't know in that moment was that Sonny was already making his mark in the music industry. He wasn't new to dreaming of stardom, begrudgingly working day jobs to support his wife and daughter while pursuing the entertainment industry at night. Sonny didn't care how he got his foot in the door as long as he did. Once he started networking, Sonny relied on charming his way into connected circles. Eventually, Sonny got hired as an A&R assistant, screening unsolicited materials sent to the label with their repertoire in mind. He also submitted material of his own, paying attention to what made a song marketable. He earned writing and production credits on a number of records, but reinvested his earnings back into the label rather than his family.

Sonny would start writing and releasing songs under pseudonyms and took a few goes at running a small label himself. He kept going, wheeling and dealing until he found himself as an A&R rep for Philles Records, owned by Phil Spector. Spector was a major player in entertainment, though known as much for his musical brilliance as for his unorthodox and sometimes unethical business practices. Spector revelled in being a mad genius type, with his technique, 'The Wall of Sound,' becoming legendary in the industry. Sonny watched him intently and was in awe of him.

In meeting Cher, the two were set on the road to becoming a duo in every sense. But before that happened, Sonny played other roles in Cher's life first. At one point, he was her neighbour, unknowingly moving in next door to the apartment she shared with a friend. When her roommate later left and Cher couldn't make rent on her own, Sonny became her boss, hiring her as a housekeeper as she continued to try to work her way into the industry. She wasn't crazy about the responsibility, but she was already crazy about Sonny. It wasn't romantic, however. His magnetism appealed to her, and although it wasn't romantic at first, her fascination with him ran deep and eventually evolved into a teenage crush.

To Sonny and the rest of the world, Cher seemed both whimsically childlike and grown up. When she wasn't chasing dreams of stardom, she was on a softball team with her friends. Cher was inspired by Sonny's hustle and considered their relationship a form of tutelage in what it took to succeed in the entertainment business, although Sonny was still figuring that out himself. Moving in with Sonny would solve her immediate problems, and at the moment, that's as far as she was thinking it through.

Making the living arrangement work would require a little fibbing on Cher's part, telling her family she had a stewardess roommate, so that it made sense they never met the roommate. It was in trying to keep up this charade that Sonny learned Cher's true age. He thought she was already 18 when, in reality, she was still two months away from turning 17. Sonny was angry at first, then understanding. That was, in part, because he realised his singing, live-in teenage "housekeeper" could *sing*.

At that point, however, Georgia had figured out what was going on. She also realised that Sonny was still a legally married man who had a child. Uncomfortable with the relationship between the two, she moved Cher back to Encino to see if the distance would put an end to the relationship.

Cher wouldn't tolerate living at home, so Georgia agreed to letting her live in a girls' residence. It was better than home, but not by much when it came to her freedom. Though Cher insisted nothing was romantically going on between her and Sonny, Georgia sensed the chemistry between them. She was so distressed that she consulted a therapist, who told her not to make too big of a deal about the pairing and let it blow over.

In one last desperate attempt, Georgia took Cher and Georganne down to Arkansas for an extended stay. Again, she hoped the distance would help Cher forget about Sonny. While they were there, Georgia learned that her own husband, LaPiere, wanted to end their marriage. He was moving on with a close friend of Georgia's, which was a particularly crushing blow.

When it didn't and Cher stood her ground in being miserable, she relented in letting the two see each other. Georgia had big concerns; however, as a mom she worried that Cher was headed down a road too similar to her own with Sarkisian. It would cause strain in the mother-daughter relationship that recurred throughout Sonny and Cher's relationship.

In the time Cher wasn't around, Sonny realised he missed her and what that meant to him. When Cher was finally able to come back around, things were great for a while. There was a brief breakup, however, when Sonny voiced his opinion on Cher's acting. He felt it was time for her to leave acting lessons behind and focus entirely on music. Cher wanted to try pursuing both, which Sonny felt lessened the likelihood of success in either field.

Cher didn't have to wait long until Sonny introduced her to Spector. She, too, would land a job with the famed talent – minding his girlfriend, Ronnie Bennett. Ronnie was the lead singer of the Ronettes. Spector wanted to keep a close eye on Ronnie, as both talent and his partner. Cher was supposed to hang out with her and keep her from engaging in behaviour he would disagree with. It wasn't hard work for Cher, who hit it off with Ronnie pretty quickly, developing a genuine friendship.

The Ronettes were working on 'Be My Baby,' with both Sonny and Cher in the studio. Spector pulled Cher aside and said that Sonny suggested she step in for a backup singer who was running late. It was the first time she'd sing into a microphone in a professional recording environment, with Sonny there to coach her through it.

The budding singer would go on to lend her voice to the background vocals on several songs. She was an unnamed contributor on 'Da Doo Ron Ron' by the Crystals and the Righteous Brothers' 'You've Lost That Lovin' Feelin'.'

While Cher was having fun providing backup vocals, Sonny believed she was capable of more. He spoke to Spector a number of times about recording Cher. Eventually, he convinced the producer to do just that. Sonny was elated, while Cher was nervous that she wouldn't rise to the occasion. Her very first single, 'Ringo, I Love You,' was credited to Bonnie Jo Mason. Spector believed that Cherilyn LaPiere wouldn't work commercially, with down-home American names being the trend of that time.

The track was a love letter to The Beatles' drummer, recorded in February 1964. The recording session came just weeks after songwriters Pete Anders and Vinnie Poncia submitted the track to Spector. It was released about a month later, on 4 March.

The single didn't make it far after DJs expressed concerns that her low voice made her sound like a man professing his love for Ringo Starr. Some people questioned whether the single was really a gag. Cher was crushed, but Sonny didn't think that was the end for her. He was resentful of the fact that he felt they were set up to fail with the song, but he was ready to press forward.

The 18-year-old also had a lot going on in her personal life. John Sarkisian reappeared in a newly-single Georgia's life with an interest in meeting his daughter. Georgia asked Cher, and though she knew she wouldn't find a dad in her biological father, she was curious enough to agree. The meeting was uncomfortable and unexpected, though Cher saw some of her qualities that frustrated Georgia originated with her father.

She thought that would be the end of it, but fate had other plans. Sarkisian and her uncle Mickey, who was living with them at the time, struck up a friendship that would bring him more regularly into their orbit. He managed to charm Georgia once again, and in 1965, they remarried.

Though Cher wasn't a fan of the pairing, she understood at that point that, societally, her mother felt more secure as a married woman. Cher also got the opportunity to connect with the Armenian side of her family during that time, something that felt special as they were relatives she didn't share with Georgia or Georganne. Sadly, Sarkisian fell back into both drugs and gambling. It all came to a head when he fell asleep while on a bender with a lit cigarette in his mouth. Cher and Georganne woke up to smoke filling the house, and they rushed to get their mom and get out as Georgia cursed Sarkisian for what he'd done. From then on, Sarkisian also stopped seeing Cher.

The chaos in her family life was almost expected by the newly minted adult. Cher tried not to get caught up in it, with her sights set on her future. Romantically, things also continued to develop between her and Sonny. The two dedicated themselves to being a couple, riding out the good times and bad as they each tried to find their way.

In November 1963, Cher found out she was pregnant. The news was both exciting and daunting. She and Sonny were in love, but he already had a daughter from his first marriage. She was just starting to gain some footing in music and was unsure of her path forward. She ended up miscarrying 16 weeks into the pregnancy.

From that point on, Cher decided to go on the pill. The added hormones resulted in a nearly 20 lb. weight gain, which she struggled with. It was the first time in her life that Cher had ever felt heavy. She wanted her usual body type back and found it would take more work than ever before. It would mark the beginning of an up-and-down pattern with her weight that would persist throughout her relationship with Sonny.

Although it was painful both physically and emotionally, the couple took a short time to process their feelings before getting back to work. They would refer to themselves as being married before Cher turned 18, but decided to do something to mark their commitment once she was. In a bathroom ceremony in their Tijuana, Mexico hotel room on 27 October 1964, the two exchanged vows and rings engraved with each other's names. From that point forward, they considered themselves husband and wife. Cher kept the milestone close to the vest, deciding not to share the news with her family.

Acting as her manager, Sonny began booking Cher at local venues. Paralysed with stage fright at her first performance at a roller rink, she convinced Sonny to join her on stage. He sang harmonies with her and tried to distract her from her fears. Noticing the intrigue in them as a duo, they began to work together. Sonny's Julius Caesar-style haircut, paired with Cher's long, black hair, helped the two to achieve their new identities – Caesar and Cleo. Sonny also hoped they could capitalise off of the scandal surrounding *Cleopatra*, the 1963 movie starring Elizabeth

Taylor and Richard Burton, who became a couple themselves in the process of filming.

As Caesar and Cleo, Sonny and Cher released a number of singles. Their first was 'The Letter,' followed by 'Love Is Strange.' The singles weren't successful, but as they worked on their sound together, Cher signed a separate deal with Liberty Records to record an album of covers. As she continued to develop both, Sonny and Cher were introduced to the Rolling Stones, who were in the United States as a band for the very first time. Mick Jagger and Keith Richards were just 19 at the time, with older members Bill Wyman and Charlie Watts still having fun hanging out. Brian Jones and Cher hit it off, as did Sonny and Jagger. They suggested that listeners in the United Kingdom were more ready for their sound than those in the United States.

The result of their work together was 'Baby Don't Go,' originally intended as a solo song for Cher. Her stage fright crept up again, this time in the recording studio. She coaxed Sonny into supporting her through it once again. He took the recorded song to Spector, who agreed to pay £380 for half the royalties.

In September 1964, 'Baby Don't Go' was released. Executives at Frank Sinatra's Reprise level, unaware that Sonny and Cher were already working with them as Caesar and Cleo, released the single attributed to Sonny and Cher.

The two took the stage for their first-ever engagement, opening for Ike and Tina Turner at the Purple Onion, a nightclub in San Francisco, in November 1964. Being their first live performance, they didn't have a band of their own yet. As a result, Sonny found himself arguing with the band he had pieced together in the lead-up to the gig. He didn't feel confident about the sound and grew furious while Cher mostly ignored him and complained of boredom. The performance was a low-grade disaster, but taught the two a lot about what this journey would take.

After completing work on The Righteous Brothers' 'You've Got That Lovin' Feelin',' the two finished their time with Spector and were ready to embark on a new chapter. Cher was well on her way. With Sonny by her side, her confidence as a performer and an adult blossomed, putting her on the path to stardom.

Chapter Four

1965–1969

Sonny and Cher were laser focused on developing their budding music career in 1965. It began with *Baby Don't Go*, the album building on the single's success. The album was credited to 'Sonny and Cher and friends,' a compilation of singles by the duo, The Lettermen, and Bill Medley of The Righteous Brothers. In the interim, they also released 'Just You' as a single, which Cher has proclaimed one of her favourite songs of theirs together in the years since.

That year, Sonny also began working on a song that would change everything for the pair. After buying a £65 stand-up piano and getting it into their cramped living space, he started working day and night on different songs. He eventually presented the song to an initially unimpressed Cher, but he didn't give up when she wasn't sold on it. He continued to tinker with it, writing lyrics and notes on the cardboard that came with his dry cleaning. Cher suggested using a modulation in a song after hearing one in a song by Jackie De Shanon. Sonny took the suggestion and applied it to, 'I Got You Babe.'

Brian Stone and Charlie Greene became the duo's managers and roommates during that time. The duo knew to bring the regional success of 'Baby Don't Go' to Reprise's attention, letting the label know that Sonny and Cher wanted to be signed elsewhere. They worked on securing the next step for both Cher as a solo artist and Sonny and Cher as a duo.

Just weeks after *Look At Us* was released, Cher's solo covers album, *All I Really Want to Do* was released by Imperial. The single of the same name was one of the covers featured. It came out just after The Byrds had released their own cover of the song. The band wasn't thrilled about the timing, at first. After a few listens, they gave credit where it was due, especially when Cher's version began seeing radio play and wider success. It became a top-twenty record that summer.

All of these exciting developments led up to Sonny and Cher recording 'I Got You Babe.' It was recorded from 7–9 July 1965. However, the record executives weren't convinced. In fact, they believed the song's B-side, 'It's Gonna Rain' was the real hit. Sonny argued with Ahmet Ertegun about the studio's desire to release that as the single, with 'I Got You Babe' as the B-side. The conversation concluded with Ertegun demanding that his way be the final say. Sonny defied him, leaking 'I Got You Babe' to KHJ radio in Los Angeles. They started to play the track as an exclusive teaser for the album.

The song took off like a rocket. Ertegun was furious, but Sonny was smug, knowing his instincts were correct. Audiences loved the song and called in requesting it. By 14 August 1965, 'I Got You Babe,' had hit the top of the Billboard pop chart. That same week, it would become the number one song in America. Fans began coming out as the duo joined The Beach Boys on West Coast tour dates, enamoured with both their sound and their look. Cher had been experimenting with Sonny's outfits and gaining more confidence in putting together her own, and people were captivated.

Their growing popularity found a momentum they'd struggled to achieve before, and the two were in agreement that they needed to make the most of it. They reconsidered Mick Jagger's suggestion that British audiences may be more receptive to their act and decided to head overseas. It wouldn't be easy, of course. To afford their trip and stay in London, Sonny and Cher would have to sell off just about everything they owned. By August, the couple, along with Stone and Greene, flew to London.

Somehow, the two managed to make headlines within hours of entering the UK on 31 August 1965. The two landed and headed to their stay at the Hilton hotel, only to be turned away when they went to check in. Sonny was dressed in a ruffled shirt and fur vest, while Cher wore knit red, white, and blue bell-bottoms and a matching blouse. Their outrageous outfits put off the hotel manager, who insisted they had no record of their reservation and had them escorted out of the hotel. It just so happened that two members of the press witnessed them being seen out and talked to them outside the hotel.

The story took off like wildfire and sparked an intrigue into the husband and wife pair. They were approached for appearances on both TV and radio, proving Jagger's theory to be correct early on. It helped 'I Got You Babe,' released in July, to soar on the British charts. Days after their arrival in the UK, they were set to perform the single across the media platforms of the time, appearing on popular shows like *Top of the Pops* and *Ready Steady Go!*.

A gruelling schedule was key to Sonny and Cher's early success. Not only were they finding many opportunities in the UK, but they were also making the most of social time. In their time in London, they encountered Rod Stewart, Dusty Springfield, John Lennon, and Paul McCartney. They even knocked The Beatles out of the number one spot briefly, replacing 'Help!' with their smash single.

'I Got You Babe' also started seeing success in the States. The demand for them in venues across the country made it clear their time in the UK was coming to a close.

Sonny and Cher returned to mobs of screaming fans, although not everyone knew the duo were Americans themselves. Because of their initial UK success, some mistakenly regarded them as part of the British invasion of the music scene in the mid-1960s. The popularity also increased demand for an album, which left the pair with little time to enjoy the spoils of their newfound fame. They returned to the studios at Atlantic Records, working on what would be the first Sonny and Cher album, 1965's *Look At Us*. The album featured previously recorded tracks, as well as a few covers. It spent eight weeks at number two on the Billboard 200.

Like many of the popular acts of the time, the pair also appeared in a surfer movie. The two made a cameo appearance as themselves in *Wild on the Beach*, which starred Frankie Randall, Sherry Jackson, Sandy Nelson, and Cindy Malone. They can be seen performing 'It's Gonna Rain,' as the characters party on the beach.

The buzz around the two only grew, with people being interested in the fact that Sonny and Cher, the married couple, were one project and Cher, the solo act, was another. TV came calling, with the couple making a memorable appearance on *Hullabaloo* in September 1965. They got the chance to perform with Sammy Davis Jr. The Lovin' Spoonful and the Supremes also appeared in the episode.

That opportunity was followed up with an even bigger one: CBS' *The Ed Sullivan Show* reached out to ask them to perform. The ask was monumental for Cher, who had grown up watching some of her favourite acts and early inspirations perform on that very show. The pair performed 'I Got You Babe,' 'Where Do You Go?,' and 'But You're Mine' in their appearance on 26 September 1965.

After some time living with Georgia, the two bought their first home in Encino. The £56,000 property was more than she'd ever imagined. Cher was in disbelief about the life she was suddenly living. For the first time in her 19 years, she found herself financially comfortable, with a house of her own and a promising career ahead of her. Cher wanted to enjoy that moment, but clashed with Sonny over work and finances. He believed they had to maintain momentum by continuing to work hard. He was open to breaks, but they were sparing.

The work was hard, but there were opportunities Cher would throw herself into, like the couple's fashion line with Gordon & Marx of California. The goal of the line was to bring Sonny and Cher's fans key pieces like the ones they wore. The pieces ranged in size from 5 to 15 and retailed for £15, targeting the younger demographic. They had a pulse on what the fans wanted, in part because Sonny believed in keeping close relationships with them.

When fans would appear at the gates to their home, adorned with an 'S' and a 'C,' Sonny would sometimes invite them in. Cher was surprised by the visits but not averse to them. Sonny even landed Cher a column with *Teen Beat*, where young fans wrote to the singer for advice. Cher admits she was only able to keep up with it for a while before having to hand it off to someone else. Still, she was intrigued by the responsibility her fans presented her with as they increasingly confided in her during encounters.

Cher also caught the attention of another notable woman in pop culture, Jacqueline Kennedy. When the former First Lady was honoured at a society event, she requested that Sonny and Cher perform at the swanky gathering. The two women may have seemed worlds apart to the public, but Cher hit it off with Kennedy when the two met later that night.

At that party, Cher encountered *Vogue* editor Diana Vreeland, although she didn't know it at the time. The next day, Vreeland's team called with an offer for Cher to be featured in the magazine. And if that wasn't enough, Princess Margaret asked for Sonny and Cher to perform at the Hollywood Palladium. The moments, deeply meaningful and increasingly absurd all at once, stunned Cher over and over. She noted that while she was always trying to catch up to the moment, Sonny kept his cool, showing up with his ever-present charm at every opportunity that called for it.

While Cher enjoyed the success the duo found, she was also very hesitant about it. Having an upbringing where she veered into and out of poverty made her aware that circumstances could change at any time. As a result, she admits to making some unnecessary purchases, like buying two of things in case she couldn't afford a new one when the original was worn out. Still, Cher was very young and had no preparation for the attention or the money that would come their way. Sonny talked a good game, but he, too, had little idea how to manage what was happening as their star rose.

Sonny and Cher kicked off 1966 by performing at the Hollywood Bowl, with the support of The Righteous Brothers, Jan and Dan, and the Mamas & the Papas. The performance was made even more special by some special guests in the audience – Georganne, Georgia, and Cher's Grampa Roy, the latter of whom was taken by Cher's resemblance to her mother as she took the stage. The beginning of the year would have many moments where enthusiastic audiences encroached more and more on her space, something that was fascinating and terrifying for Cher to process.

Another project Cher was trying to process was *Good Times*. Inspired by other artists who were reinterpreting the stories told in their songs for the screen, Sonny wanted them to make a movie, believing they had the potential to make good money on a film. Looking for a way to pivot their relationship with audiences, Sonny revisited the idea he'd first considered just before their trip to London and subsequent success in the UK. This time, Sonny shared his ideas with some friends in the film industry, Francis Ford Coppola and William Friedkin. Coppola was still a student at UCLA at the time, while Friedkin was working on documentaries.

Sonny enlisted Friedkin, who would later direct *The Exorcist*, in what would be a first for both of them. The two came up with a meta concept, a movie about a movie getting made. The concept saw a musical couple agreeing to do a film, only to discover they hate the premise and have just days to come up with something better.

They began filming on 24 January 1966 at the couple's Encino home. At first, everyone was excited about the idea and this new approach to engaging in the creative process. Just days into shooting, however, Cher found herself getting increasingly frustrated with the ego Sonny had built around the film. As the material unfolded, it seemed more geared toward launching Sonny as an actor than telling a story that equally highlighted both.

Still, Cher went along with it. They filmed in the Africa USA wildlife park, encountering some of the park's majestic animals in the time between takes. It was a memorable time for the couple despite the struggles.

Cher was cautious in her approach to the film. She loved the opportunity to use her acting skills. When she considered a future in acting, however, she wanted to go after dramatic roles. She harboured concerns that the roles crafted for her by Sonny wouldn't get her there. It was one of the first times she was concerned he'd steer them wrong.

Cher worked on her music with Sonny, as well as her solo career. In March 1966, Cher's second solo album, *The Sonny Side of Chér*, was released. The album was full of covers arranged by Sonny to suit Cher's voice, as well as some original compositions like 'Bang Bang (My Baby Shot Me Down)'. That May, the couple released their second album as a duo, *The Wondrous World of Sonny & Chér*. The album brought forth two hits, 'But You're Mine' and 'What Now My Love,' both of which enjoyed success in the US and UK.

It was during this time that Cher had a significant run-in and one of her only truly star-struck moments. While Sonny worked on some music at a recording studio in New York, Cher accompanied him. Waiting outside for him to finish, Cher was near the building's service lift. She was shocked when the doors opened, and Bob Dylan stepped out. He introduced himself and complimented Cher on her cover of 'All I Really Want to Do.' He moved on to greet Sonny, leaving Cher truly in awe.

As 1966 continued, rock audiences began exploring acid rock. The shift in the culture, gradual at first, changed the very definition of what was cool at the time. Sonny and Cher were perceived as 'square' as a married couple who didn't engage with drug culture. For all the assumptions made about the artists because of how they dressed, neither had much interest in drugs or alcohol. Artists such as Jimi Hendrix and Led Zeppelin brought rock to the forefront, and while Cher was eager to explore it, Sonny was not. He had the last say, and at the time, she let it be so.

January 1967 saw the couple making some unexpected appearances. The first was on New Year's Day, when they were invited to ride a float in the Rose Bowl Parade in Pasadena, California. They were the first pop duo ever to have the honour.

Then, the two were offered a private audience with Pope Paul VI in Rome. They accepted. The occasion would call for them to ditch the clothes that helped them make headlines across Europe, with Cher opting for a modest black crepe dress instead. It was nerve-wracking, but awe-inspiring for the both of them. Sonny, in particular, felt the magnitude of the moment, raised in the Catholic faith.

In March 1967, the duo released their third album, *In Case You're In Love*. It featured one of the duo's biggest European hits, 'Little Man.' The album also featured one of their most beloved tracks, 'The Beat Goes On.'

Weeks later, *Good Times* premiered in Austin, Texas. The governor of the area even changed the city's name to Good Times, Texas, for 24 hours as a promotional event. They'd do interviews and perform songs from the film's soundtrack at each stop.

The movie wasn't as successful as Sonny and Cher had hoped, in part because of the lengthy production time. That said, the couple made the most of it on their seven-city tour in support of the film. The promo they could do was no match for some of the bigger titles the film was up against, such as *In the Heat of the Night* and *The Dirty Dozen*. Critics weren't too harsh on the film, but they were perplexed by all the different elements that came together in it. If anything, they were harder on the soundtrack, which they felt chopped the movie up into what felt like segmented skits rather than a continuous story.

That said, it didn't deter Sonny from exploring the myriad of film ideas he had in mind for himself and Cher. His next film idea was one for just Cher, and he also had ideas for an animated film in mind. Sonny was also fleshing out his musical concept, *The Beat Goes On*.

Sonny surprised Cher with a special gift for her twentieth birthday in May 1966. The ring featured a nine-karat sapphire lined with eleven karats of marquise-cut diamonds. The massive ring seemed out of place with the couple's style, but Cher adored it. She wore it on her right index finger, leading many to believe it was a piece of costume jewellery.

While this was going on, Cher was quietly experiencing fertility struggles. She and Sonny learned she was expecting in the summer of 1967, but she'd go on to have a miscarriage. It came before the two were due to perform a big show in Minneapolis. Worried about the impacts of the cancelled performance, the team talked Sonny into performing alone. Then, they got the idea to spin the situation into a promotional opportunity. They publicised Cher's miscarriage news and allowed a few select fans the opportunity to stand in for Cher.

There were conflicting reports on whether Sonny was on board with the promotion or if he had been coerced into it, but some fans questioned him for making the move. Still, a crowd of young women, many of whom dressed as Cher lookalikes, showed up. Of that group, 21 girls were auditioned, and five girls between the ages of 14 and 18 were chosen, each performing one song with Sonny. It was the first time he ever performed without Cher. She has never commented publicly about how the promotional stunt made her feel.

That September, Cher's third solo album, *Chér*, was released. The album included a cover of Burt Bacharach's 'Alfie' from the film of the same name, starring Michael Caine. Her version appeared on the soundtrack and received decent circulation in Europe, although it was later overshadowed by a Dionne Warwick cover of the track.

At this point, Sonny had made it clear that he didn't like the direction of Cher's solo album. He thought they relied too much on covers and wanted to insert more of his own original writings, which he believed could rise to the same level when paired with Cher's vocal abilities. Cher sat a bit on the fence on the issue. She loved performing her Bob Dylan covers and was interested in taking on more original material, but at the same time, she didn't want to be shackled to Sonny's ear, still tuned to Spector's influence despite the changing times.

Sonny and Cher would get another thrilling invitation in November 1967 that would provide insight into their future. They were asked to appear as guests on the first season of *The Carol Burnett Show*. The variety show, hosted by a woman, was remarkable for its time. The world was already enraptured with Burnett, and Cher was no exception.

It was during her first professional wardrobe fitting for the show that Cher met someone else who would become an important figure in her life and a close friend. Bob Mackie was the wardrobe designer for the show. He and Cher hit it off immediately, beginning one of the most significant relationships of her life that continues to this day. Mackie quickly found that he understood Cher's innate sense of style and was willing to help her meet the moment.

Sonny pushed himself and Cher creatively while she yearned for a break. Cher sought out different hobbies but found that in doing so, she frustrated Sonny, who wanted her to focus more on music and acting. He was intent on making Cher a star and found opportunities for himself in every iteration of doing so.

At the same time, the cultural shift was continuing. Sonny and Cher's image was always centred on a mix of the conservative – the two being married and working together – and the progressive, such as being kicked out of hotels and joining picket lines. However, as Sonny's star rose and he was presented with more opportunities to share his views, he appeared more traditional than their look originally suggested.

People wondered if the same was true of Cher or if Sonny was taming a wild spirit. The two appeared in anti-drug and pro-education PSAs that were shown in high schools around the country. It made some of their youngest fans look at the couple in a new light and question what they truly stood for. Cher's backstory wasn't widely known at the time, and therefore, people didn't understand her stance on substances. She was even seen as a hypocrite by some, who pointed out that the high school dropout-turned-pop star was lauding the importance of a traditional education.

October 1967 would bring Cher's fourth solo album, *With Love, Cher*. The album was notable because Cher recorded some Italian renditions of the original singles from the album. She also continued her tradition of including a Bob Dylan cover on the album, this time singing, 'The Times They Are A-Changin'.'

In the autumn, the couple learned they were pregnant once again. Sadly, it also ended in miscarriage. Cher suffered both physically and emotionally with each loss. At 21, she questioned if she would ever get to carry a child to term. Starting a family was one of the areas where Sonny and Cher were always on the same page. Their difficulties felt like a significant drawback to each of them in their own ways.

Sonny and Cher continued to tour in the early part of 1968. Cher's solo career was getting good traction, however, and Sonny wanted to capitalise on her marketability. Once again, he looked to film as a means to help her star rise. Inspired by the story-driven singles Cher was releasing that fans gravitated toward, he wanted to create a film that connected with Cher's image as a young woman who grew up on the rough side of town.

His initial ideas were all considered scandalous, even for the changing times. He warned Cher to explore different partners throughout the film, including a lesbian love scene. He believed the controversy would drive the views, so much so that he took out a mortgage on the Holmby Hills home to finance the movie. Sonny tried getting William Friedkin on board, but he was already working on *The Night They Raided Minsky's*. He moved on to Alessio de Paola, who really saw his vision and was happy to take the story on.

In May 1968, *Chastity* began filming in Phoenix, Arizona. They didn't have a studio attached to the film yet, but Sonny remained confident in his abilities, continuing to pour more of his and Cher's money into financing the film. Meanwhile, Sonny continued to work on *Chastity*, Cher's solo film, which was filmed in the second half of 1968. He wrote it without the intention of appearing in it. The idea was a young transient woman trying to find the meaning of life and her various encounters as she navigated her world.

While working on the film, Sonny hired a secretary with whom he had allegedly had an affair. In the midst of the miscarriages and the stress of their career, it was crushing for Cher. She surprised herself with how quick she was to forgive him. Distressed by Sonny's cheating, Cher turned to her mom, who had admitted to hearing rumours about him herself. While Cher could forgive Sonny, Georgia couldn't. It led to a period of estrangement between mother and daughter.

Another huge moment occurred as they filmed *Chastity* in 1968. Robert F. Kennedy, whose campaign the duo supported, was assassinated in Los Angeles. The two were due to join the campaign for an event when they completed filming. Instead, they would perform at the Madison Square Garden benefit concert in Martin Luther King Jr.'s honour. The civil rights leader was assassinated just weeks before Kennedy met the same fate.. It was the first time the two would perform at the esteemed venue, and it was a moment that was unforgettable, although they were a minor note to bigger acts of the time, including Jimi Hendrix and Aretha Franklin.

They returned to Arizona after the benefit, with the intention of finishing the movie. The tension on set was high, with Cher aware of Sonny's indiscretions and his growing fear that she would give him a taste of his own medicine. They made it through the completion of the film, and when they got back to Los Angeles, they learned that Cher was pregnant once again. After four miscarriages, Cher was apprehensive and struggled to be optimistic about the news. Based on her experiences, doctors advised her to take a break from her busy schedule. Cher obliged, but it did add to the financial pressure facing the couple.

Things didn't come to a halt altogether for the pair. On 4 August 1968, Sonny and Cher made a move toward repairing their 'square' image by appearing as one of the headliners at the Newport Pop Festival in Costa Mesa, California. The duo performed as part of a lineup that included the Grateful Dead, Jefferson Airplane, and the Byrds. These acts exemplified the drug culture Sonny held such disdain for.

In September 1968, Cher's fifth solo studio album, *Backstage*, was released. It was as serious an indicator as anything else at that time that musical interests were shifting. Cher didn't have a single rise above the rest on the album despite exploring different genres and sounds.

During the pregnancy, Sonny decided the couple should make their marriage official. The two had friends come over, as well as their attorney and a justice of the peace. It wasn't as meaningful to Cher as the Tijuana ceremony that bonded them, but it felt like a logical next step with their baby on the way. Sonny, already father to a daughter, hoped for a boy. Cher was so worried about the baby's health that she hoped only for their child to be born in good health.

Although Sonny was busy trying to dig the couple out of their financial struggles, he was doting when he was around. He enjoyed documenting Cher's pregnancy, taking countless photos of her, sometimes to her ire. She was cautious throughout, worried with thoughts of the pregnancies that had gone wrong before. Things went better this time. There was a false alarm on Sonny's birthday in February 1969, but their baby wouldn't arrive until 4 March. The couple welcomed Chastity Sun Bono at Cedars Los Angeles, named after Cher's character in the film. The healthy baby was born 7 lbs., 10 oz.

While Cher was in the hospital, Georgia quietly snuck in to see her grandchild but didn't visit her daughter. It deepened the wound at the heart of their rift, especially because Sonny had to be the bearer of that bad news. Georgia would pop up again three months later, unannounced and supposedly critical of her daughter's parenting. Her words upset Cher and deepened Sonny's distaste for his mother-in-law, putting the new mom in a no-win situation at a time when she wanted and needed them both.

Despite a scary incident with excessive bleeding shortly after giving birth, Cher knew she had to get back to work. Three weeks postpartum, she travelled to Arizona for a *Vogue* shoot. Although she enjoyed the shoot, Vreeland, who was once again responsible for putting it all together, was fired amid the shoot. As a result, the prominent feature was cut down into a shorter spread that wouldn't be published until August 1970.

Now parents raising a baby as they tackled the music scene, Sonny and Cher had even less in common with younger acts. The two continued to run in very famous circles but particularly enjoyed the friendships they had with folks older than themselves. Between Sonny's industry contacts and the actresses Cher knew from their work with her mother, they had a support system of folks who knew how they felt because they'd been there.

The family's bliss was interrupted three weeks later, when Sonny informed her that they were in debt to the Internal Revenue Service (IRS) for over a quarter of a million dollars. He sincerely believed he could get them out of the hole in two years, and while stressed by the news, Cher didn't blame her husband. She genuinely believed their fame had reached a point neither was prepared for and that they weren't equipped with the tools to succeed.

In hopes of turning things around, Cher agreed to appear on *This Is Tom Jones*, performing a number of duets with the singer that concluded with Sonny pretending to be mad that she had sung with another man and dragging her off the stage. After the London appearance, they briefly stopped in New York before travelling to Alabama. There, Cher would work on her sixth studio album, *3614 Jackson Highway*. The album's title reflected the street address of Muscle Shoals studio, where she recorded it.

Cher was set to work on the album with Jerry Wexler of Atlantic Records. Sonny, who was there with Chas and was only supposed to be supporting his wife and documenting the process, continuously chimed in with his thoughts on production. The two frequently butted heads. Sonny would later admit to feeling slighted by the fact that he was ousted as producer, although the decision was that of the label and not Cher personally. Cher would later say that Sonny's arguing with Wexler led to the Atlantic producer being hospitalised, although Wexler claimed he missed the recording sessions due to being hospitalised with pneumonia.

3614 Jackson Highway was released 20 June 1969. Fans didn't flock to the album, resulting in disappointing sales. What it lacked in popularity, it made up for in critical acclaim. People admired the changes in Cher's vocals, marking a newer, more mature era for the now 23-year-old.

When it came to *Chastity*, released just four days after the new album, critics weren't so kind. Reviews found the film to be poorly put together with too weak of a plot. Sonny and Cher both came down with the flu and were unable to attend the film's premiere. Cher felt the film's R-rating, a decision she felt was nonsensical, was to blame. Their young audience would have to find a willing adult to take them to the film in order to see it, presenting a sizable barrier to entry considering how older people often looked down their noses at the duo.

The results didn't bode well for Sonny, who was trying to develop himself as a screenwriter. Cher did score some critical acclaim, with people recognising some talent in her ability to take on the guileless, directionless character. Still, both felt like their luck was floundering when all was said and done. The couple was unable to recover the £380,000 they had mortgaged their home to invest in the film, which was another crushing blow.

It was time for reinvention, with the two deciding to give the casino and hotel circuit a try. Beginning with a month-long stay in Ontario, Canada, the two played to much smaller crowds. They also underwent a visual transformation, leaving behind their 'hippie' style in favour of tuxedos and evening gowns. While it wasn't what they were hoping for, Cher was grateful that the evening-centric schedule left her plenty of time to watch Chas continue to grow. She'd taken to motherhood despite their unconventional circumstances, with help from sister Georganne, as well as a number of babysitters at different points.

Sonny and Cher worked on their act, which consisted of ribbing each other in a loving spouses sort of way that made crowds roar with laughter. They built up a following, and demand for the shows incrementally grew. It allowed the two of them the kind of creative banter that also helped the relationship offstage, which was strained due to stress. By the end of 1969, the two were finding new footing to lead them into a new decade.

Chapter Five

1970–1974

Cher began the 1970s by dedicating herself to getting Sonny and Cher back to their prime. That meant long days and nights on the road, trying their new act in different areas. The banter between them pulled in crowds, much like the allure of the pair as a married couple did in the first leg of their career together.

During their time on the road, they honed the act to perfection. Cher felt that, for the first time, the snarky, 'smart' attitude that Sonny spent so much time trying to curb was coming to their benefit. She wasn't taking all the credit, however. She was impressed with Sonny's capability to be charming and meet her barbs with equally sharp ones. They felt in sync in a way that was reminiscent of their early creative years.

Happy with how the act was going, the two got more support from the William Morris Agency, which helped spread the show across the country. Their hard work was eventually rewarded. During a stretch of shows at Los Angeles' Century Plaza Hotel, the couple had an opportunity to perform to an audience of comedians, with their act coming just before Bill Cosby's. Despite the fact that neither walked away from the performance with a sense that it went well, they were offered a television special as a result.

The Sonny & Cher Nitty Gritty Hour was taped in Toronto in 1970 and shopped around for months before it aired on CBS in 1971. While it was received well, the duo was unhappy with the fact that it was more planned out and less spontaneous than their live show. They figured it would be a one-off, but they continued to get invitations to appear on TV, with Sonny selling executives on their potential.

In January 1971, both Sonny and Cher appeared as guest stars on *Love, American Style*. A few months later, CBS's head of programming, Fred Silverman, came to see the duo perform in New York. Impressed with the act, Silverman contacted the William Morris Agency to book the two as substitute hosts on an episode of *The Merv Griffin Show*. The two subbed in for the late-night star in April 1971. It wasn't a format they were familiar with, but they went along with it and were well received. The CBS team was impressed enough to develop a show that was based on their live act.

The two were officially approached to film a summer pilot for *The Sonny & Cher Comedy Hour*. There were two months between the offer and the beginning of filming, giving Sonny and Cher a chance to wrap up their scheduled dates on the road. The initial offer was for just six episodes, but when the show premiered on 1 August 1971, it was a clear hit.

Cher had one major stipulation for doing the show – she wanted costumes by Bob Mackie. She requested such from the network, which informed her Ret Turner, head of wardrobe for NBC, was already assigned to the show. Mackie was outside of their budget. Not one to quit, Cher took a break from the meeting to step out and call Mackie herself. It was then that he agreed to work with Turner, a friend of his. Turner handled Sonny, guest stars, and any other talent, but when it came to Cher's wardrobe, it was all Mackie.

At their height, Cher's Mackie originals cost nearly £4,000 per dress. The investment proved well worth it when she was named one of the ten best-dressed women in America that year. Justifying the wardrobe budget, especially as the show progressed, proved to be difficult. Executives at CBS took the time to recognise the fact that it wasn't just the talent drawing in viewers but also the costumes, which ranged from hilarious and zany to breathtaking.

What she indulged in for wardrobe, she made up for in glam. Cher was happy to do her own makeup, as she found herself dissatisfied with how she looked when wearing professional makeup. The early days of the show marked the first time she'd have her makeup done professionally. At first, she enjoyed it. Later, she'd find that wearing significantly more makeup than she was accustomed to resulted in severe adult acne.

It would take a lot of work for Cher's skin to recover. She had to cut back on the greasy foods she enjoyed and up her water intake. She also had to try to find a way to manage her stress and anxiety, which wasn't something she'd ever made an attempt to consciously control up until that point.

This project was unlike anything that Cher had tried before. Where she sometimes struggled with feeling insecure in her musical abilities, TV was where she flourished. Recalling all the seminal moments in her own life where she connected with a star's television presence, she was assured as ever when it was her turn to take that stage.

Cher's confidence was through the roof, but she was aware that the act required the same effort it did on the road. The first few shows were experimental, with her and Sonny trying to find their groove. Noticing Sonny seemed stiff when reading the cue cards, Cher provided constructive criticism, relying on their trusted bond to get her message across effectively. She handled him in a way that she needed to so that she could provide direction without hurting his pride. In doing so, she helped Sonny develop his own signature comedic style, one that genuinely made her and audiences both laugh.

One of Cher's favourite parts of the show was her solo. Each show included a song she sang alone, dressed in an immaculately crafted and fitted Mackie creation. The songs she chose were personal favourites, songs that meant something to her at different points in her life. To make sure those solos were flawless, she'd practice with Sonny watching, careful to take any notes he gave her.

The work was difficult, but it was fun. Sonny and Cher were enjoying a period of connectivity that felt more positive than ever before. With Chas toddling around the studio with a nanny not too far behind, the two were blissful at the way they handled their work-life balance in the early days of *The Sonny & Cher Comedy Hour*. Their palpable happiness is part of what drew crowds to the husband-wife duo. When they weren't working, they were taking time for family and spending quiet weekends at the beach with Chas.

Despite spending her days with stars, at night, Cher held the schedule of the average wife and mom. Knowing it wouldn't last, she soaked up those times. She was just starting to get noticed on the rare occasions she did go out, a phenomenon she hadn't fully considered until she was experiencing it. It was both gratifying and overwhelming, a mix of feelings she'd continue to feel during big moments throughout her career.

Sonny thought the time was right to capitalise on their success with new music. While Sonny worked on a new act for their upcoming concert tour, Cher worked on recording her seventh solo album, *Chér*. The stylisation, which appeared in a number of her recordings throughout the 60s and 70s was inspired by one of the variations on her signature she tried on for size as a little girl at home, dreaming of fame.

The first single, 'Gypsies, Tramps and Thieves,' was released in September 1971, just a month after the show's summer premiere. It proved that the tides had once again turned in Cher's favour. The experimental pop track was her first solo single to reach the Top 10 and would later earn Cher her first Grammy nomination. Despite the song's commercial success and significance within her career history, Cher has admitted that the storytelling track isn't one of her favourites. It was for that reason she wasn't too heartbroken when the Grammy ended up going to Carole King for 'Tapestry.'

That same month, CBS confirmed they were ordering a second season of the show, this time with thirteen episodes airing between December 1971 and March 1972. Among the additions to the writing staff was an up-and-coming writer and comedian named Steve Martin, who was coming off the success of *The Smothers Brothers Comedy Hour*. In fact, a number of *Smothers Brothers* alumni found work at *The Sonny and Cher Comedy Hour*.

The amplified comedy on the show didn't just make it fun to watch for viewers. It also drew in guest stars. Guests ranged from fellow musicians like Elton John and Tina Turner to notable celebrities of the moment, such as Twiggy, Hugh Hefner, and Muhammad Ali.

The prospect was exciting and an indicator that things were really working out the way Sonny and Cher had always hoped. The two even worked on a new album, released in February 1972. *All I Ever Need Is You*. It was well received, reaching number 14 on the Billboard 200. The single, 'A Cowboy's Work Is Never Done,' would be the pair's last hit record together.

The more their star was rising, the more the two started experiencing a disconnect in their relationship. Cher was uncomfortable with how entrenched Sonny became in business, noting he was morphing into the kind of person they used to make fun of for taking themselves too seriously. While the two were still having fun on stage, behind the scenes, their life had lost the lustre they both fell in love with. They wouldn't fight on the job, but a sense of their unhappiness would eventually begin to drift into their professional environment.

In an effort to reignite the spark, the two purchased friend Tony Curtis' home in Holmby Hills, something Cher had dreamed of half a decade earlier. It was the definition of luxe, with nine bedrooms and ten bathrooms, spanning over 1100 sq. m. From the moment they could first call it their own, Cher dreamed of entertaining family and friends at the house and celebrating special occasions there. However, Sonny became even more reclusive in that sense.

In June 1972, Cher found friendship in Paulette Betts, an Armenian woman with a chaotic back-story who had begun dating Sonny and Cher's road manager, Jerry Ridgeway. She ended up joining them on tour, thus beginning a decades-long friendship between the two. Paulette admired Cher's life and believed what most of the public did – that she was at the top of her game and things were perfect. Cher's increasingly slim frame told another story, however, with the star neglecting her dietary needs as she grappled with immense stress.

That summer, Cher made a heartbreaking realisation. She loved Sonny and the life they had built together, but she was no longer in love with her husband. In part, that stemmed from the feeling he no longer cared the way he once did. Sonny no longer sought her out in a room and provided her with the feeling of safety that solidified their pairing. Yet, she truly didn't feel she had other options. For all her fame and access, she still felt unsure of what her life would look like without a man by her side. Furthermore, she wasn't just thinking about herself. Cher had deep concerns and reservations about how any decision she made would impact Chas and their family dynamic.

The pain of a loveless marriage and the draw to stay put started taking a toll. During a span of shows in Las Vegas, Cher contemplated taking her own life. In her darkest moments, she kept her mind on Chas, Georgia, and even her fans, concerned for how such a tragedy might impact them all.

It was that incident that made Cher really consider what life beyond her marriage to Sonny would be like. She began to spend more time away with Paulette, which Sonny didn't mind much. He was feeling the disconnect as well but focused instead of keeping their success going. They were able to pay back the IRS, but Sonny was forever fearful moving forward that a wrong move could land them back at square one.

At the same time, Cher was still pursuing her solo career. In July 1972, she released her eighth studio album, *Foxy Lady*. The show gave Cher an opportunity to promote the album, which tailed her most successful release to that point. Getting to the release wasn't easy, however. Once again, Sonny was overstepping his predetermined involvement. He was often at odds with producer Snuff Garrett.

Cher spent more time trying to hang out with the band after shows, going with them to see other performers on some nights and hanging out in a hotel room having drinks on other nights. In doing this, she started developing a flirtation with her own band's drummer, Bill Hamm. The young Texan sparked something in Cher, and she found herself spending more time with him, though she was unsure of herself and what she wanted out of the situation. When she went on a walk with him, where the two talked about the band's perception of her marriage, Hamm kissed Cher. Within half an hour, Sonny was on the phone, summoning her back to their own hotel suite. Cher returned with Hamm in tow, making a potentially volatile situation a little more explosive.

When Sonny confronted her, Cher surprised both of them by admitting she was attracted to Hamm. She was blunt, prompting Sonny to leave the suite. It delivered Cher the ultimate confirmation that he no longer cared what she did or who she did it with.

Instead of anything physical happening between them, Hamm inquired further into Sonny and Cher's dynamic and when things had gotten so uncomfortable between the two. Hamm left after hours of Cher's tearful admissions. Sonny returned hours later, and believing his wife was asleep, he walked over to her side of the bed and slipped her wedding ring off of her hand.

The next morning, Cher was upset. She focused on going to see Chastity, only to discover the nanny had taken the child back to Los Angeles at Sonny's instructions. Annoyed at his exertion of power, Cher wandered around Las Vegas, trying to clear her head and make sense of what was happening. When she returned to the hotel to find Sonny, he was furious, even telling Cher that the public would blame her for their breakup.

Cher took refuge in Paulette, but when she realised that Sonny slept with Hamm's girlfriend as payback, she knew things were damaged beyond repair. As it turned out, the two bumped into each other in the casino. Sonny was playing blackjack while Hamm's girlfriend was looking for him. Sonny told her the whole story and spared no details. The star stayed the night with Hamm's girlfriend and only left when the drummer returned to the room the following morning. There was no confrontation between the two men despite what they each believed the situation was.

Cher skipped out on her performance and left town with Hamm to compose herself. When they tracked her down, she begrudgingly went back and faced the rumours of physical violence between the two that led to the cancelled performance. Officially, representatives for the couple claimed Cher was suffering from exhaustion and was too ill to perform.

With intermediaries involved, Cher agreed to continue performing with Sonny in exchange for a Malibu beach house to call her own and a monthly allowance of £4,500 to be set aside in her own bank account. Sonny was agreeable, focused on keeping the public out of their private turmoil. He had professionals explain the ramifications of skipping out on a show to Cher again, determined to continue their marriage as far as the public was concerned.

Years later, Cher would reflect on the split in her 2024 memoir, writing, 'Years later somebody asked me if I left Sonny for another man, and I told them, "No, I left him for another woman. Me."'

The two had just days before they went back to filming *The Sonny and Cher Comedy Hour*, dazzling audiences as well as they ever had. On stage, they could still pull off being Sonny and Cher. Offstage, she'd continue to find herself as an independent woman, all while continuing to see Hamm whenever her schedule would permit. Her weekdays were still spent at the Holmby Hills home she shared with Sonny, where his assistant Connie moved in. They all got along, with Chas continuing to bring everyone together. It was the bond developed during this time that made Cher genuinely enjoy Connie's company, something that wouldn't change once it became clear that her and Sonny's relationship was more than a professional one.

The unusual set-up led to more positivity in Sonny and Cher's relationship, allowing the two to rediscover the friendship that started it all. The two even took a spontaneous weekend trip to Paris together. What would have looked to the public like a romantic marital getaway was actually an opportunity to redefine their friendship and connect without married life, family life, and business life all hanging heavily over them.

In January 1973, Sonny and Cher attended the Golden Globes together. *The Sonny and Cher Comedy Hour* had been nominated for Best Musical or Comedy Series, though it wouldn't take home the award that night. It hardly mattered to Cher, who was a movie lover interested in rooting for her favourites at the ceremony, including her and Sonny's longtime friend, Francis Ford Coppola. She had stars in her eyes as she watched Liza Minnelli's win for *Cabaret* and Diana Ross being celebrated for her role as Billie Holiday in *Lady Sings the Blues*. It was then that Cher knew she wanted to have a similar moment one day on that very stage, accepting those kinds of awards.

The next month, Sonny and Cher released what would be their final album together, *Mama Was a Rock and Roll Singer, Papa Used to Write All Her Songs*. Aside from the title track, the original, which clocks in at over nine minutes, was written by Sonny. Cher also worked on and released her ninth studio album, *Bittersweet White Light*. Cher worked with Sonny on the album, recording reimagined renditions of popular songs from the 1920s-1940s. The idea was to highlight Cher's vocals in a similar way that her solos on the show did. It didn't achieve the heights they'd hoped, propelling Cher to put out a second album later in 1973.

While things were going well professionally, Cher's relationship with Hamm fizzled out. Enamoured with the star, he had dreams of marrying her himself. The newly independent Cher was just discovering who she was, what she enjoyed, and what her life as a single woman looked like.

She wasn't in a rush to marry and even felt at times like she wouldn't have a desire to marry again, no matter what kind of love she found. She didn't feel like there was a future for her and Hamm, which was upsetting for him to come to terms with.

The artist enjoyed an emotional moment on stage on her 27th birthday while performing in San Antonio, Texas. Between her two last songs, her crew brought out a huge cake. The audience of 10,000 or more people sang 'Happy Birthday' to her as she teared up. A lone heckler could then be heard chiding Cher for being 'over the hill.' When she sniped right back at him, her fans gave her a standing ovation.

Cher was trying to undergo self-exploration at 27 while also trying to understand her place in her creative partnership and the industry at large. There were many firsts for her. She got her first tattoos – matching bouquets of flowers with butterflies among them on each side of her rear end. She also tried therapy for the first time that year at Sonny's suggestion. What she didn't know at the time was that the therapist was reporting what she shared back to Sonny, a crushing violation of trust that deeply upset her.

What was more upsetting for Cher was learning that Sonny had his share of indiscretions with other women throughout the entire duration of their relationship. Not only did he get involved with different women they met along their travels, but he allegedly even paid for sex and brought some of these women to their family home. As some women who contacted Cher supposedly informed her, Sonny would tell others he and Cher were in an open marriage. Though not common at the time, the perplexing response was enough to keep most from bringing the subject up around his wife.

It was a lot for Cher to wrap her head around. She'd genuinely believed he only stepped out on their marriage one time. As she discovered, nearly everyone else in her orbit was aware of Sonny's ways. She felt like that made them complicit in keeping those secrets from her, deepening her feeling of betrayal. Sonny would also continue to find ways to exert his power over her. After she flirted with a band member on the road, Sonny ordered the band and everyone else on the tour not to speak to Cher for its duration, including her friend Paulette. Terrified of Sonny and his increasingly angry outbursts, they complied, isolating one-half of the starring duo with whom they worked.

In September 1973, Cher released *Half-Breed*, her tenth studio album. With his understanding that Sonny was no longer in the picture, Snuff Garrett was excited to work with Cher again. The album received mixed reviews, but it contained a sentimental track. Cher re-wrote Seals and Crofts' 'Ruby Jean & Billy Lee' and retitled it, 'Chastity Sun' in dedication to her child.

When the tour was over and they returned to work on season three of *The Sonny and Cher Comedy Hour*, Cher could feel a shift in their dynamic. Things were still working well and audiences were still entertained, but she sometimes felt Sonny's supposedly off-the-cuff comments were pointed. It made her self-conscious and sometimes put her in her head in a place where she'd always operated fearlessly and on instinct.

In December 1973, Cher was invited to Lou Adler's Christmas party. Having agreed to only step out in professional settings with Sonny, the two attended. It was there that Cher met David Geffen, manager to artists including the Eagles, Joni Mitchell, Carly Simon, and Elton John. The founder of Asylum Records invited her on a date, which she accepted. While Geffen was honest about his interest early on, Cher wasn't sure if getting involved with someone in the business while she was keeping up appearances with Sonny was the best idea. She hesitated at first, but their friendship grew closer and their bond grew stronger.

Cher and Geffen had a small circle that they could be open about their relationship with. Geffen first told his best friend, Sandy Gallin. Later, they'd start hanging out with more of his close friends. Anjelica Huston, Jack Nicholson, Warren Beatty, and Julie Christie became their group. They were happy to share laughs in their quiet circle. Geffen adored Cher, who was his first significant partner. He was the first man who ever tried to romance her, making for some memorable moments, like her first-ever Valentine's Day celebration and gift. Geffen paid the kind of attention to her that she'd long accepted Sonny never would.

When the news of their pairing got back to Sonny, he wasn't happy, and it furthered the wedge between the two. As his attitudes changed, Geffen became concerned with what the dissolution of Sonny and Cher's business relationship would look like. As the two started discussing season four of *The Sonny and Cher Comedy Hour*, Cher admitted to Geffen that she knew nothing about her contract or how she was paid. He, in turn, got a copy of the documents and informed Cher that she worked for Sonny, by way of 'Cher Enterprises.' He owned ninety-five per cent of the company, gifting the other five per cent to his attorney, Irwin Spiegel. Aside from the £4,500 a month she had received since the split, she didn't have the authorisation to access any Sonny and Cher-related income without Sonny or Spiegel's permission. Cher couldn't even pursue other avenues to make money without one of them giving written consent.

At the core of the conflict was a difference in perspective. All along, Cher believed that all things Sonny and Cher were a fifty-fifty effort. Sonny, however, believed that he put a lot more time and effort into making their success happen than Cher ever had. Cher was beside herself when she saw it spelled out on paper. She consulted Lucille Ball, whom she'd known for most of her life. Lucy's complicated divorce from her own creative partner, Desi Arnaz, gave her important insights that she shared with Cher. With Ball's advice and Geffen's help, Cher obtained Mickey Rudin as her attorney. He advised her it was time to file for divorce, but Cher couldn't bring herself to do so.

Cher made one more attempt to reason with Sonny, going to talk to him at his office. She asked him to acknowledge her as an equal partner in all they had built. She appealed to him to be fair. And as passionate as she was in what she told him, Sonny shut it down. He told her he wouldn't renegotiate their terms. Cher threatened to walk away from season four of *The Sonny and Cher Comedy Hour*. Sonny told Cher she would be sued and ultimately believed she would fall in line when called to do so.

Geffen supported Cher through the time, allowing her to move in until he rented her a home in Malibu. It gave her refuge from the spotlight, which she would need after 18 February 1974, when, to her surprise, Sonny filed for divorce. It was while they were filming and just four days before they had to play a show in Houston together, on the lineup with Elvis and the Jackson Five.

When Rudin filed a countersuit against Sonny's divorce petition two days later, he claimed Sonny violated Cher's Thirteenth Amendment rights by holding her in 'involuntary servitude' with the terms of their business holdings. It would begin a series of back-and-forth lawsuits, including one by Sonny against Geffen. Sonny accused Geffen of interfering in his and Cher's contractual affairs and even sought a temporary restraining order against the music executive. At that point, the friendship between Sonny and Cher truly ceased, with the two only talking to discuss matters of co-parenting Chas.

Cher appealed to Fred Silverman, explaining her situation and vowing not to go ahead with any deals with any other network. She asked for the network to drop the show for a fourth season. To everyone's surprise, it worked. *The Sonny and Cher Comedy Hour* would end at the completion of season three in March 1974. Furious, Sonny kicked Cher out of the Holmby Hills home, where they enjoyed the height of their life as a family. She left with just a bag of clothes.

The cancellation of the show was a blow not just to the duo, but the people who loved their husband-wife act. They still had to finish filming season three. At their final show, a speech by producer Chris Bearde alluded to the pair's split to the live studio audience. Both Georgia and Georganne came to support Cher, tearful at the end of the partnership and the marriage. The finale aired on 29 May.

Despite the fact that both Cher and *The Sonny and Cher Comedy Hour* were nominated for Golden Globes, they did not attend the 1974 ceremony. Cher didn't feel confident she would win the award for Best Actress in a Musical or a Comedy Television Series, but that's exactly what happened. It was the moment she'd been hoping for, but she couldn't be present to take it in. Further, she wasn't in a place where she could see the achievement beyond the irony of its timing.

Cher was determined to keep control of her own life and decided to go public with her relationship with Geffen. On 2 March 1974, the two attended the Grammy Awards together, whipping up a media frenzy as Hollywood's hottest new pairing. He accompanied her again a month later, this time to the Academy Awards, where she was asked to present the award for Best Original Dramatic Score.

Meanwhile, custody was proving to be harder to figure out than either Sonny or Cher had hoped. At a time when divorce was still uncommon, the world was still trying to wrap its head around the concept of the single, working mother. Cher's commitment to parenting came into question. Though at first, Sonny was okay with splitting time with Cher, in his anger, he filed for full custody of their only child.

He went to great lengths to prove Cher as an unfit mother, a move that deeply hurt her. Sonny was aware of how troubled Cher's childhood was and how important it was to her to get things right with Chas. The basis of his argument was Cher's friendship with Hugh Hefner and the fact that she'd brought Chas to lunch there to get to meet pet monkeys Hefner had on his infamous Los Angeles property. It was harmless, but Sonny allowed his legal team to spin it.

The family Cher shared with Sonny wasn't the only one to take a blow in 1974. Her family of origin was also experiencing a tough time. In March 1974, they learned that John Southall, Georganne's biological father and the only man Cher ever considered a father was seriously ill. They went to visit him weeks later, seeing the physical effects of the liver failure that would be his demise. He died less than a week later.

Cher was going through the emotional gamut, but she kept pressing forward. Spending time with people at the top of their game and being seen with new eyes as a separate entity from Sonny made for an exhilarating and creative time for her. She worked on *Dark Lady*. The moody album cover featured a black and white full-body shot of Cher, dressed in a sheer black full-length dress while holding a black cat. It was photographed by Richard Avedon, her *Vogue* photographer, and began her involvement in the design and production of her album covers.

The title single went straight to number one after its release in May 1974. It was her third American number one hit and also charted in the UK, where it topped out at thirty-six. Cher wouldn't have another single chart in the UK until the late 80s.

After finishing work on *Dark Lady,* Geffen suggested to Cher that she continue meeting the creative moment by working with some of the biggest names in songwriting. Among his suggestions was Phil Spector, whom Cher knew through her and Sonny's time working with him. At the time, Spector was working on John Lennon's *Rock n' Roll*. After hearing from Cher, Spector asked if she'd be interested in recording backing vocals on the album with Harry Nilsson. When they got there, Spector and Lennon were fighting, and Lennon stormed out. Spector asked the pair to lay down a guide vocal Lennon could use to understand what he was looking for.

Cher thought nothing of it until learning from her label weeks later that Spector illegally released the single overseas. Determined to confront him, she went to his home and found Spector's demeanour unusual. She was shocked to find him attempting to intimidate her. He refused to put an end to the song's circulation, telling her to have her label sue him. As he did, he allegedly started to twirl a revolver in his fingers as he paced the room. Cher was scared but reminded Spector he'd known her forever and it wasn't right to treat her this way. He apologised as she made a quick exit, unnerved by the experience.

With Geffen, Cher made another bold move – to take back her Holmby Hills home. She expected resistance from Sonny and Connie, who still lived there. Having just gotten through the thorniness of their brief custody battle, he agreed, and the two retreated to the former couple's St. Cloud home, which Cher had signed over.

Cher was concerned about her professional future, but had a great support system in Geffen, who talked to CBS about getting Cher her own show. They were panicked at losing the viewership that *The Sonny and Cher Comedy Hour* had enjoyed. The last episode, aired in May 1974, was the eighth most popular show on television that night. There were pleas behind the scenes for Sonny and Cher to patch things up professionally, but Cher stood her ground. Those close to Sonny believe he took the professional split worse than the end of the relationship. He was up to something, however, as Cher would later discover. Sonny brokered a deal with ABC for his own show, *The Sonny Comedy Revue*. The format was essentially the same, with different female celebrities stepping in to co-host where Cher once stood.

Amid the negotiations, she enjoyed a girls' trip to Paris in September 1974 with Paulette and Georganne. From that whirlwind adventure, she vacationed with Geffen and friends in Aspen. When that trip was through, Geffen started raising the idea of marriage. Though Cher wasn't divorced, the two ended up getting engaged, with the idea they'd marry late the following year in Aspen. Though she loved Geffen, it was a little overwhelming for Cher, who was not yet divorced, to feel like she was jumping into another marriage. Her experience with Sonny made her question whether there were sacrifices to her freedom and artistry that would come with the arrangement.

That same month, her adventurous nature led Cher to find herself in a dangerous situation. She was at Los Angeles' The Troubadour watching Average White Band perform. Afterwards, she was invited to a party with the band held in Hollywood Hills at the home of wealthy stockbroker Ken Moss. Cher was at the party when she saw people passing around a white powder. Uninterested in drugs herself, she passed. She watched people doing it, believing it to be cocaine. It wasn't until people started passing out that someone admitted it was a combination of heroin and morphine.

At one point in the night, drummer Robbie McIntosh was removed from the party and taken back to his hotel in the area to sleep off his high from the party. He would die before morning. Bass player Alan Gorrie also had an adverse effect. This time, Cher jumped into action. She called her doctor and when she couldn't get in touch with anyone else, she consulted her gynaecologist on how to help him. She was instructed to induce vomiting in Gorrie, and it ultimately saved his life.

In November 1974, Cher was invited to an event that would prove to be a pivotal moment – both in the history of fashion and in the singer's personal history. Diana Vreeland, who was working as a consultant for the Metropolitan Museum of Art's Costume Institute, was redesigning the organisation's annual gala. Under Vreeland's direction, the Met Gala became a moment for fashion and pop culture to intersect in the heart of New York City. The theme of that first year was 'Romantic and Glamorous Hollywood Design.' Cher opted to team up with Bob Mackie for the occasion, once again. The designer also served as her date for the night as she stepped out in arguably one of her most iconic looks.

The feathery 'naked' dress Cher wore to the event was from a *Vogue* layout she shot with Mackie, focused on fashion throughout the decades. The spread, titled '60 Years of Cher,' featured her in looks from the 1920s to the 1970s. The dress was sprayed with water to further the rare material's sheerness. A photo of Cher from the evening ended up being selected for the cover of *Time*'s March 1975 issue.

During the same trip, Cher met with Andy Warhol for an interview with *Interview Magazine*, his publication. While she spoke about her split from Sonny in depth during the interview, many were surprised to see she didn't trash her ex. Instead, she spoke fairly about the split and admitted that she didn't resent Sonny in any lingering way. Even when their custody battle was referenced in the interview, Cher mentioned that though she'd been awarded a greater share of custody, she had no intention of keeping Chas away from Sonny.

At the end of 1974, Cher was cautiously optimistic about what the future had in store. What she didn't know was that one of the most eventful years of her life was just ahead of her.

Chapter Six

1975

Cher kicked off 1975 with a new project on her plate – her very own show. With Geffen's help, she secured guests Elton John, Flip Wilson, and Bette Midler. Cher was nervous to set out on her own, and for that first show, she was truly out on a limb. CBS agreed to air the pilot as a special to gauge the audience's interest. In the time it had taken *Cher* to get into production, *The Sonny Comedy Revue* had been cancelled. Though Cher knew she was talented outside of her professional relationship with Sonny, the show was an avenue where she was particularly used to leaning on his guidance and support.

When it was time for the special episode on 6 January 1975, the 28-year-old stepped on stage and tried her best to ooze confidence in herself. With Mackie and Turner returning to bring her looks to the next level, she'd pull that confidence from her outfits to get her through. She even gave her dress its own moment, prompting the audience to clap for both the front and the back of the nude rhinestone look. All the costumes from the night had an ethereal quality that drove home Cher's otherworldly stardom. Audiences agreed, with 21 million viewers tuning in, securing the show a regular time slot.

Being herself within the confines of the show seemed like the perk of being the star, but Cher would find navigating those waters difficult without a partner. It wasn't due to a lack of talent or know-how in business. Rather, it was because her freedom as a divorced woman was one that still made some audiences of the era uncomfortable. Particularly, her revealing outfits, which had been a staple of *The Sonny and Cher Comedy Hour*, were now coming into question by network censors. Cher felt that the network suddenly saw her sense of style as inappropriate simply because she wasn't spoken for. In ways, it seemed like everything was suddenly looked at through a sexual, male gaze in situations where sex appeal wasn't even central or thought of in achieving a particular creative vision.

The way that the world and the entertainment industry regarded her as a single woman added to Cher's conflicted feelings about marrying Geffen. She couldn't deny the love she had for him, but she felt uneasy about the decision, noting that she'd only had a few years of experience making decisions for herself, by herself. In early 1975, she came to the conclusion that she couldn't marry Geffen. The two didn't immediately break up, but he did move out of the Holmby Hills home. He stayed at the Beverly Hills Hotel and continued to try to work on the relationship, including continuing to contribute to the show.

After Geffen moved out, Paulette moved into the home with Cher and Chas, entering an era of freedom and positivity. Cher felt that she could let her guard completely down and be herself and embrace in a sort of girldom she'd missed out on in her early 20s.

It was during this time that Paulette introduced her to the music of the Allman Brothers, praising the duo's take on southern rock. When Cher saw Gregg Allman was opening for Etta James at the Troubadour, she decided to go check the show out. Paulette, Geffen, Georganne, and 12-year-old Tatum O'Neal joined her in attending the show.

Cher was impressed by Gregg's set but surprised when his friend came over to her and gave her a note from the performer, offering to come back and play another night if she'd come out to see him. At first, she just kept the note and didn't do anything with it. Days later, she decided to give him a call and agreed to dinner. To mark the occasion, he'd gotten Cher a tiny pink carved elephant. Despite his intentions, an awkward dinner followed by a night out at a party where everyone was different forms of intoxicated wasn't what Cher had in mind. When he made a hasty move, she asked to be taken home. He made a snide comment about saying hi to her 'assistant', Paulette, which made Cher write the night off as a disaster. As one of the very few dates she'd ever been on, she grew worried this was what dating would be like.

Gregg didn't give up, calling her back to apologise for the lousy date and proposing a do-over. It took Cher a while to agree, but when she did, she found that he had dropped the rock star act and tried being his genuine self. That worked better for Cher and, though their professional commitments would keep them physically apart, they talked frequently on the phone and began to fall for each other. Geffen took Cher's move from him to a 'bad boy' as an offence and decided he couldn't continue a friendship with her any longer. This was a deep blow to Cher, but not enough to keep her from continuing her relationship with Gregg.

The two performers got a chance to physically spend time together during a lull in the Allman Brothers' touring schedule. Anytime that Cher wasn't working, she was with Gregg. As the relationship progressed, those who knew Gregg warned Cher that he had a substance abuse issue. Looking back, Cher acknowledges that she didn't want to see the signs and the problem for what it was, but she also still had some naivety about it because she hadn't had much experience with drugs, let alone long-term addiction.

As she went down south to Macon, Georgia, she'd get a better idea of who Gregg was. While she wasn't a fan of many members of his band, meeting his mom was a positive experience that gave her insight into the man she loved. Gregg's father had been killed when he was just 2 years old after picking up a hitchhiker who was violent. He was very close with his mother, Alice, and brother Duane as a result. The two brothers started the band in the 60s and enjoyed success together until Duane was killed in a motorcycle accident in their hometown in 1971.

The trauma of those losses and their impact on his mother stayed with him. At the end of their visit, Gregg confessed to Cher that the chatter about his drug use was true. He was a self-professed heroin addict, but wanted to get help in that moment. Cher, who knew her father was a heroin addict, turned to her mom for guidance and support. Knowing she loved Gregg, Georgia told her to see it through.

Professional help for addiction wasn't as prevalent in the 70s, so Cher took it upon herself, with the help of her inner circle, to get Gregg clean. It wouldn't be easy, especially because both artists were facing scrutiny from fans for their relationship. Allman Brothers' fans saw Cher as too mainstream and straight for him. Cher's fans felt that it was a destructive choice for her and went against who they'd known her to be at that point. There was a large contingent of fans who still hoped that Cher and Sonny would get back together. When Cher convinced CBS to let Gregg appear on her show and perform with her, both their fans gave them a good deal of slack for it. If she attended one of his shows, fans would treat her badly and continue to make advances at Gregg as though she wasn't there at all.

In April 1975, Cher released *Stars*, her twelfth studio album. It didn't perform well commercially, but meant a lot to her. She worked with Jimmy Web on the album, which featured tracks that she picked herself, from Jackson Browne's 'These Days' to Neil Young's 'Mr Soul.' It was undoubtedly a departure from Cher's other work and her first real dabbling in rock. It marked the beginning of a tough stretch for Cher musically. She tried not to take it too hard, knowing that she herself was trying to figure out where her sound would go next. She had the last laugh, with the album achieving cult-classic status later in her career.

Similarly, she tried not to take the downturn in *Cher* too personally. After Geffen's departure, CBS became more contentious about what was and wasn't allowed. She put her all into the performances and her relationships with guests like The Jackson 5, The Osmonds, and Jerry Lewis. She knew, however, that being at odds with the network would mean the show would only go on for so long. The show would ultimately conclude at the end of 1975 after two seasons.

That April, Cher also had to deal with an unwelcome re-emergence of her father, John Sarkisian. He filed a £3 million lawsuit against his daughter, as well as several publications after Cher made remarks about him during interviews with both outlets. Sarkisian reasoned that by publicly speculating he was up to no good as a person with public influence, Cher was causing harm to his personal and professional life. While he conceded to being troubled in his past, he claimed that he'd lived a clean and sober life for 9 years and didn't want his daughter dredging up his past. The matter was handled quietly, but the already-strained relationship between father and daughter would not recover.

Cher celebrated her 29th birthday that May at a party thrown for her by her by former manager Joe D and best friend Paulette. The guest list included Carole King, Joni Mitchell, and even Sonny. Things felt like they were in a genuine amicable place between the two.

On 27 June 1975, Sonny and Cher's divorce was finalised. While it felt like the end of an era, knowing she was still connected to Sonny through Chas and their newfound friendship came as a comfort. At this point, she felt like that chapter of her life had finally come to a close.

Things wouldn't stay quiet for her for long. She soon learned that she was pregnant with Gregg's baby. Despite the fact that she wasn't entirely sure about the relationship, she agreed to marry him. The two, accompanied by some close friends, went to Las Vegas, and tied the knot on 30 June 1975, just three days after her divorce from Sonny was completed. She was the third Mrs. Gregg Allman, while he was her second husband. She later admitted that she felt more comfortable being married to the man whose baby she was having, despite her hesitations about their connection in general.

At this point in her life, Cher was being hounded by tabloid magazines. Every move the star made led to scrutiny. It was for that reason that to help keep the sudden wedding private, former manager Joe D started the rumour that Frank Sinatra and Barbara Marx were getting married elsewhere in Las Vegas that day. Knowing the press would flock to that area, Cher was able to move around unnoticed and unscrutinised at that moment.

Immediately after the wedding, the two had to part ways for work obligations. The way Gregg left told Cher they weren't in a good place. She started to question what she'd done. Further, she had to grapple with a pregnancy, not knowing where she stood in the relationship. When her doctor offered her the option of terminating the pregnancy, grateful for the choice, she accepted.

There was more scrutiny in store days later. Cher got a call and learned that Gregg, whom she'd barely heard from since he left, had filed for divorce. This came after she'd heard a rumour he was doing so and confronted him about it. He denied everything. She had no choice but to file her own petition for divorce, citing irreconcilable differences. She believes it barely registered to him when she told him she would do as much, because he was under the influence.

While Cher was telling the press the marriage had been a mistake she was hoping to quickly correct, Gregg told reporters the divorce wouldn't go ahead. He then travelled from Georgia to upstate New York to seek treatment from psychiatrists specialising in addiction.

Looking for guidance, Cher reached out to Sonny, who was happy to be a friend in her time of need. He gave her some suggestions on how to move forward. He also mentioned he was slated to appear on *The Tonight Show* and suggested she join him for the second half of the interview. Though she wasn't sure about how it would go over, she accepted. Though she was legally married to Gregg, people were charmed by the fact that Sonny and Cher still had their banter and bond. Host George Segal joked with Cher about her headline-making month, which helped Cher weather the media firestorm. Later that night, Cher would grab a bite with Sonny and his girlfriend, Susie Coelho. The media couldn't believe it and questioned what was going on.

When Cher heard from Gregg's therapists asking for her participation in his therapy sessions, she was unsure. She genuinely didn't believe he would get better, but Sonny said she should go and try to help either way. He agreed to keep Chas with him so she could take whatever time was needed. She went to Buffalo, New York in July 1975, and did feel there were some breakthroughs with Gregg in therapy. He admitted to feeling pressure from the constant analysis of their relationship in the press and worried he wouldn't live up to her expectations of a husband. She doubled down on wanting his sobriety more than any relationship goalpost, and so they continued together. She dropped the divorce filing on 1 August 1975.

The man she saw in these sessions was one she loved, but she worried how he'd hold up his sobriety once he got back to familiar stomping grounds and touring. Her instincts were correct, and Gregg did relapse.

The two were on and off when Cher found out she was pregnant. She knew that she'd have to keep at work, not only for the sake of her career but for the sake of her family. She met up with Sonny once again, this time proposing they reunite for a new TV show. He agreed and got negotiations underway.

Once the deal was secured, she confided in Sonny about the pregnancy, telling him before even Gregg knew. Sonny was nervous about how it would play out with executives. After all, it was a momentous feat to have two ex-spouses co-hosting a TV show together in the first place. Factoring in her on-again, off-again marriage to a rock star publicly battling addiction and a pregnancy seemed like a lot for the public to learn to swallow.

Sonny did what he did best, however, and managed to get CBS on board. *The Sonny and Cher Show* was announced in a press conference on 4 December 1975, to begin airing in February 1976. The contract they were given helped resolve some of the legal issues between the two, further sweetening the deal. The season would run through April, and Cher would welcome her second baby in July. With Mackie's creative designs, they felt they could minimise the look and make it palatable for TV.

In the meantime, *Cher* continued to air. The 8 November 1975 episode featured the US network television debut of David Bowie. He sang with Cher while also performing his own beloved single, 'Fame.' LaBelle, fresh off the success of 'Lady Marmalade,' was also there for a sensational performance that featured some of Bob Mackie's most creative outfits of the series.

Cher's next task was informing Gregg of her plans. The pregnancy news had him return to Los Angeles, but the two weren't spending time together. When *The Sonny and Cher Show* was announced, the press began questioning if Sonny and Cher could be platonic. They questioned why they'd reunite, especially when they publicly traded barbs. Aside from *The Tonight Show* appearance together, Sonny and Cher's friendship post-divorce wasn't what the public was familiar with. The question of ulterior motives swirled as the reunited duo prepared to take the stage in February 1976.

Chapter Seven

1976–1979

The last of *Cher* began airing in January. On 1 February 1976, *The Sonny and Cher Show* debuted. The first two shows received mixed reviews. On the one hand, longtime fans of the pairing were happy to see them take the stage together and that after all the bad blood, things were peaceful again. On the other hand, some people couldn't be convinced that they could keep things platonic.

Critics may have been torn, but fans were all in. The show was the seventh most viewed of the week across different networks. Among the programs it came in behind was a new sitcom, *Laverne and Shirley*.

Gregg grew increasingly resentful as the press started to paint a love triangle between him, Cher, and Sonny. He worried that the speculation around Sonny and Cher was true and that, in the end, he'd be the one left out in the dust. It couldn't have been farther from the truth, with Cher focused on work and her pregnancy while Sonny was quietly dating Susie Coelho.

Sonny and Cher's on-screen banter once included them trading insults about each other. Added to that was the two making zingers about their divorce. Executives worried it was too modern a set-up for audiences to welcome into their homes and normalise. Still, the two pressed on, having fun together and enjoying themselves with a slew of guests.

Though Sonny succeeded at smoothing over their unusual, modern dynamic with the network, he had more reservations behind the scenes. It was no secret to anyone who spent time with them that Sonny was always the more conservative of the two of them. As a result, he often worried that the things Cher did would reflect poorly on them. Though he no longer had a say in her personal life beyond their child, he had a hard time not worrying that Cher's personal choices were going to hurt their shared business.

Cher was also back in the studio, working on her thirteenth studio album, which would be titled *I'd Rather Believe in You*. The album didn't produce any commercially successful singles. Cher didn't feel as connected to the body of work as she did her other albums, in part because it was pieced together over months, in between other items on her packed schedule. The only single released was 'Long Distance Love Affair,' which she performed twice on *The Sonny and Cher Show*.

Once the show wrapped for the season, Cher retreated to Hawaii for quality time with Chas and to focus on her pregnancy. She was also worried about Gregg, having given him an ultimatum to go to rehab. Shortly after she got the mid-June phone call that he was keeping up his end of the deal, she began to feel contractions. Panicked due to her medical history, particularly with pregnancy, she went to a hospital while Paulette called Gregg, Georganne, and Sonny.

Sonny offered to come be by her side, but Cher declined. She'd later find out Gregg was leaving rehab and on the way. When he arrived, the contractions had been slowed, and they cleared Cher for release. They wanted her to take it easy for the remaining weeks of her pregnancy. She worried that she would have her baby prematurely, but ended up having to be induced when she got back to Los Angeles, just one day after finishing her album.

On 10 July 1976, Cher welcomed son Elijah Sky Blue Allman. The second that Cher looked at her son, all she saw was Gregg. The little boy found an enthusiastic older sibling in Chas, who would sneak into his room and hold him as an infant. Gregg himself was captivated with his son, happy to have been there to support Cher through the birth.

The next month, Cher would visit a plastic surgeon to have her breasts done. As a result of her previous botched surgery, she would have to get them touched up a number of times over the years.

The family graced the cover of a September 1976 issue of *People Magazine*. Despite the fact that his band broke up just before the birth, Gregg did everything he could to maintain his sobriety and figure out the next steps for the relationship and their family. It was made difficult, however, by fans who blamed this new life for the band's dissolution.

In January 1977, Cher stepped out with Gregg in an unexpected setting. After his fellow Georgian and friend Jimmy Carter got elected

President of the United States, he invited the couple to a post-inaugural reception at the White House. He credited the Allman Brothers with campaigning for him in the state before he'd garnered national interest. The two were even invited for dinner with the President and First Lady after the reception, to Cher's surprise.

Cher got another special invitation on 27 April 1977. Club owner Steve Rubell invited Cher to be one of 4,000 people to experience the opening of Studio 54 in New York City. The night was marked with a fashion show by Antonio Lopez's Fiorucci. Alvin Ailey dancers also helped entertain guests on what would be a legendary night. She arrived for the night in a casual look, pairing jeans with a knit tunic-style top and a straw fedora. The outfit was comfortable for a night of dancing and catching up with friends. Cher was photographed dancing with writer/director Howard Himmelstein and enjoying a conversation with Andy Warhol. Nights out with friends and time with her kids helped restore Cher through this difficult time.

For a time, Gregg was fiercely dedicated to his sobriety. He was carefully following a methadone program and was enjoying the spoils of sobriety for the first time in a long time. Gregg got a taste of family life and, in turn, gave Cher a taste of what their life as a married couple raising their kids could be.

Then, Gregg hit the road with his new band, the Gregg Allman Band. Back in the spotlight, Gregg once again found himself becoming conflicted about how the world perceived his relationship with Cher. Though they were vastly different artists, he was tired of comparisons and correlations.

When they were together, they worked on an album together under the name Allman and Woman. *Two the Hard Way* was a fun project for the couple to make. What they lacked in cohesiveness in their relationship, they made up for in respect for each other's artistry. They also hoped they could introduce each other's fanbases to new sounds and foster some more mutual respect. The album featured a rendition of 'You've Really Got a Hold On Me,' which Cher performed with Sonny on their first album together. Fans took note of the similarity and didn't appreciate it. Some male fans, in particular, believed Cher was willing to fit whatever man she was romantically involved with into her career.

The album was, in a sense, reflective of their rocky relationship. It didn't perform well commercially after its November 1977 release. Even in discussing its failure, Cher would say that it was because her voice couldn't keep up with Gregg's. She lauded his vocal talent and hated that he jeopardised it with drinking and drug use.

The first part of the year included filming for what would be the end of *The Sonny and Cher Show*. In August 1977, *The Sonny and Cher Show* was officially cancelled. After filming concluded, the two hit the road for their reunion tour. It was an eerie parallel for Cher, who had raised Chas on the road at another pivotal moment in her career and found herself doing the same with Elijah. During that time, Sonny helped entertain both the kids.

With the help of her road village, Cher was also able to enjoy individual time with each of the kids. On one outing, she and Elijah visited a working farm. Cher thought it would be a cute outing with an opportunity for her little guy to see farm animals. That wasn't the case, however, with both her and Elijah horrified by the realities of farm life. From that point on, Cher rarely could bring herself to eat meat.

Cher also worked on her fourteenth studio album, *Cherished*. Warner Bros. wanted Cher to return to the pop music that had made her famous, while she wanted to explore more of the rock side of her sound. She teamed up once again with Snuff Garrett. Despite the best efforts, she wasn't happy with the finished product. Fans and critics agreed. The song would be the end of her Warner Bros. contract.

Cher and Chas briefly joined Gregg on the road, first in Japan and then in Europe. It was there that she learned Gregg had quietly picked up drinking again. Exhausted, she left and went back home, preparing for her last few tour dates with Sonny. As a cheeky mind game, Sonny had hired Cher's ex, Bill Hamm, to play the closing string of dates with them. Cher and Hamm briefly reconnected, but it didn't last. The last performance with Sonny (and Bill) came on New Year's Eve, when hours before 1978 rang in, the two sang, 'I Got You Babe.'

Cher returned home after the tour was through, focused on a now toddler Elijah and an almost 9-year-old Chas. Sonny moved to Palm Springs. As Cher and his friendship progressed and his own relationship struggles occurred, he apologised to her for his many infidelities and the way their relationship ended. She accepted and was happy to have the acknowledgement.

Gregg would come in and out of the picture, enjoying stretches of sobriety with his family before leaving again to use. After a particularly paranoid episode where he believed gunmen were hiding around the outside of their family home, Cher realised his antics were becoming unsafe for the kids. She decided to call it quits in January 1978, filing for divorce.

The decision wasn't easy for Cher, who had to hire an armed guard to keep him out of her Los Angeles home. While Gregg initially became concerned that Cher or the kids were in danger, he became irritated when he realised that security was there to protect them from him.

It didn't take long for Cher to realise her approach to business needed to change as a single mother of two. She managed to make a deal with ABC for a special that combined skits and music, in the style she felt comfortable with. Titled *Cher…Special,* she performed alongside guests Dolly Parton, Rod Stewart, and The Tubes. Those big names were joined by some other very special guests – Georgia, Chas, and Elijah would all make appearances. It was also the special where Cher would perform a fifteen-minute skit where she played all of the characters in West Side Story, a call back to her childhood.

Cher was invited to a Gerald Ford event by Neil Bogart, the head of her new record label, Casablanca Records. There, Bogart offered her the opportunity to meet Gene Simmons. Cher misunderstood, thinking it was an opportunity to meet British actress Jean Simmons, of whom she was a fan. Still, she knew who Gene was, as Chas had an interest in rock. She got something signed for her and got a chance to get to know the rocker, the child of a Holocaust survivor who endured unthinkable atrocities at a Nazi concentration camp.

Cher learned Gene led a sober life, which was majorly appealing to her after what she went through with Gregg. The rocker's earnestness after letting down his guard intrigued Cher. He gave her a ride home that night, dropping her off and then returning with Kiss merchandise for Chas, who also got to meet him. Cher was touched by his effort, especially just hours after meeting her. It caught her attention, but so too did his flirtatiousness with other women. The two would frequent the same company for a while before Gene called her from Japan to profess his love for her. Cher was compelled to give him a chance, and the two started dating.

The pairing seemed odd to many people. However, those people were looking at the artists based on their stage personas. What they shared was the fact that they were comfortable being larger than life in front of an audience of thousands, but were more reserved in any other setting. He made her feel safe in a way she hadn't in a long time.

This relationship was different than Cher's previous ones because, despite being involved with an entertainer, she had no interest in collaborating professionally. It was also for the sake of their fans, who the two joked would never tolerate such a musical pairing.

At the same time, she became involved in building what would be known as 'The Egyptian House,' her biblical-era-accurate North African-inspired home built in Benedict Canyon. The project was unique and the concept was hard to get building professionals on board with. She didn't give up. The home was meant to be a safe haven for her, Chas, and Elijah. Though Gene was in the picture, he was living at the Beverly Hills Hotel when he was in town from New York. There, he had a plane skywrite, 'I Love You Cher' on her 32nd birthday, which was followed by a performance by a full marching band and choir. A fan of the grand gesture, he staged a mini-parade filled with loved ones for Cher on Sunset Boulevard, followed by dinner with all her favourite people.

Gene integrated himself into Cher's life. He had a great relationship with her children, growing to become an extra father figure for both Chas and Elijah. He introduced his Kiss bandmate, Paul Stanley, to Georganne, and the two started dating.

Cher was comfortable with the pace of life during this time. She got to focus most of her time on the things that mattered most to her. Knowing that her mother and sister were both consumed with their own relationships, she enjoyed a casual schedule with Gene that made her feel appreciated but still free to do her own thing. She spent most of her time with the kids at their home in Malibu. She enjoyed watching the relationship between Chas and Elijah bloom as the younger of the two grew up. It was especially important to Cher that the two had a close bond. She hoped they'd be able to be there for each other, especially in moments when her busy schedule wouldn't allow her to be.

When push came to shove, Gene was uncomfortable with Los Angeles' celebrity culture. A New Yorker, he was used to being able to blend into the crowd when he ventured out without his stage makeup. In Los Angeles, however, he was leered at for doing the same. There was no avoiding press while stepping out with Cher, leading him to avoid those situations where that might happen. It presented a difficult roadblock to the relationship, but the two continued seeing each other.

Gearing up to return to the studio, Cher was met with a proposal. Her label suggested disco to introduce her to audiences in a new light. It wasn't a genre she saw her sound aligned with, and worried it would play inauthentic to both her fans and disco fans. She objected in hopes of pleading her case further. Bogart stayed firm in his position and wanting to start on a good note with a new label, Cher ultimately agreed to the disco album. She began work on her fifteenth studio album, *Take Me Home*.

The different musical process challenged Cher vocally. This, in turn, made her question whether the album was the right move again and again. Once she settled into what the dance sound required, her nerves eased. The content also differed from much of her work to that point because the music was so sexually driven. Disco and dance were all about getting physical, on the dance floor and off. Though there are plenty of other feelings explored on the album, it felt like a maturing moment in Cher's career.

Cher was surprised to get a call while working on the album from Chas's school. She was called in for a meeting where faculty told her that they felt Chas was emotionally disturbed and needed a psychiatrist. Cher panicked, immediately blaming her own busy schedule for whatever might be going on. After the meeting ended, Chas's teacher pulled Cher aside and shared that she felt the other professionals were reading the situation incorrectly. She recommended Chas be tested for dyslexia, unaware Cher struggled with the same for most of her upbringing. Relieved that the problem was one she was familiar with, Cher emphasised to Chas that there was no shame in their differences.

Take Me Home was released in January 1979, at the beginning of a year that would be remembered for the power of disco. The titular single helped propel the record to the charts, with strong follow-up releases 'Wasn't It Good' and 'It's Too Late to Love Me Now.' On another fan favourite, 'Git Down (Guitar Groupie),' Gene lent his talents.

There was also the deeply personal 'My Song,' which was inspired by Cher's relationship with Gregg. It discussed communication struggles and lamented the family life he'd miss out on. When she played it live, she played it with photos of Elijah projected behind her, driving the point home. Gregg was, of course, hurt by the move, but Cher reserved her right to discuss the disappointment the relationship – and countless others like it that other people experienced – could make a person feel.

The reception energised Cher, who decided she wanted to work on the rock album she'd been dreaming of. It would become her sixteenth studio album, *Prisoner*. She tried to make the transition smooth, with her first single, 'Hell On Wheels' being a punchy ode to her love of roller skating.

While Cher worked on realising that dream, she was also trying her best to work on another – acting. Throughout her networking in the industry, Cher had put it out there that she wanted to get back to her acting roots on a number of occasions. Her mentions were often dismissed because her image was so strongly aligned with music. At the time, crossing over between industries wasn't as typical as it has become today.

Eventually, Jack Nicholson agreed to introduce Cher to Oscar-winning director Mike Nichols, with whom he was working with on *The Fortune*. The meeting left Cher with the sense that she wasn't seen as the right type of woman to be a leading lady. That shored her determination to prove otherwise. She was briefly in consideration for the lead in *A Star Is Born*, which would ultimately be played by Barbra Streisand. After that, she continued to find doors closing to opportunities and turned her attention to the 'Take Me Home' tour.

The prospect of touring without Sonny for the first time was daunting for Cher. Even at this point in her career, she still struggled with stage fright and imposter syndrome. By her side was her new assistant, Deb

Paull, who continues to work with her to this day. She supported the idea of Cher opening the show as her old *Sonny & Cher Comedy Hour* character, Laverne. Laverne made a number of appearances at live shows throughout Cher's career, a comfortable place for her to return amid the uncertainty of newness and change.

She would need the reassurance for her first tour date in Reno in June 1979. Coming out as Laverne was a hit, and when she re-emerged in a Bob Mackie creation, the crowd went wild. When she started singing, however, the fire alarm went off in the venue. She tried to joke her way out of it and kept going. Things were fixed, but only for a while. Later, the mic cut out, leading Cher to joke Sonny was at the venue, sabotaging her.

The tour was a great success and led to some residency gigs for Cher, with dates in Las Vegas, Lake Tahoe, Atlantic City and Washington D.C. The show also incorporated comedy and drag, giving the audience different types of entertainment to enjoy and keeping the lighthearted and fun environment that Cher so craved when she found herself amidst serious industry types.

In Vegas, Cher found herself in good company. Other acts performing on the Las Vegas Strip at the time included Diana Ross, Tina Turner, the Eagles, Johnny Cash, and Willie Nelson. The acts playing brought a new energy to the town, which Cher appreciated. In most cities, the residency involved two shows a night. It was exhausting, with Cher taking any opportunity possible to nap in between. Still, the gruelling schedule allowed her to keep up her time with the kids when she wasn't working. When the kids weren't around, she'd go out and enjoy nightlife with her cast and crew.

In July 1979, Cher was performing at the Kennedy Center Opera House in Washington, D.C., when a fan rushed the stage, trying to jump on it. Police, security, and FBI agents present immediately tackled the boy. The situation was upsetting for Cher, who told them to take it easy on the teenager. Security continued to stay with Cher, both when she was on stage and in her free time. She'd later learn there was a death threat made against her that was called into the venue. It was for that reason that they needed to keep a particularly close eye on her and take any threats seriously. Other artists would have been rattled to learn the same, but it didn't stop Cher from continuing to tour and take the stage unabashedly.

October 1979 brought the release of *Prisoner*, an album that was most highly anticipated by Cher herself. It was the first time her solo albums featured songs written especially for her. Originally, the title was set to be *Mirror Image*, a play on her rock persona versus her disco persona. When it ended up going full rock, the change was made.

The cover was designed to push the envelope and play on what it was for Cher to feel imprisoned. The vision was to depict Cher as a sex slave, a metaphor for how the media continuously portrayed her as helpless to the power of the men in her life. It was a way to take back the power and control the conversation about her that raged for so many years in the press, often without any of her own say included. Some people appreciated the powerful message Cher was looking to deliver with the image. There were a lot of people who were outraged, however, by what they felt was a vulgar display.

The single, 'Mirror Image,' was made to address Cher's life in the spotlight. Particularly, it was a commentary on how the tabloids had become fixated on every area of her life. The song talked about what it was like to wonder if people believed who you say you are versus who they read you are.

Cher also took back power in another important way in 1979, making her mononym her legal name. Though Cher believed she was born Cherilyn Sarkisian, during this process, she discovered the name on her birth certificate was actually Cheryl, which also came as a surprise to Georgia. The young mom had gone through a very careful process choosing her daughter's name. She combined Cheryl – the name her favourite actress, Lana Turner, gave her own daughter – with Lynda, which was Georgia's mom's name, somehow the 19-year-old's wish was lost in translation.

The name change wasn't just a matter of paperwork, however. In foregoing to use a surname, Cher had to prove that her first name was recognisable enough that she didn't need one. After beginning life as Cheryl Sarkisian and becoming Cher Bono, then Cher Allman, and later Cher Allman Bono, the judge granted her wish. She was 'just plain Cher,' as she'd put it to people looking for something more formal to call her.

Chapter Eight

1980–1984

The 1980s ushered in an era of change for Cher. She began the year by considering a move to New York with Gene Simmons. Their relationship consisted of them seeing each other between Cher and Kiss's respective busy schedules.

While people thought it was more of a fling than a relationship, Cher and Gene deeply cared for each other. They didn't demand each other to live by rules in their relationship, driven by emotion more than anything. The public perception didn't match the reality, in part because the two made a concentrated effort to keep the relationship private. Gene didn't want to see his fans turn on him for the association, the same way that Gregg Allman had experienced. Cher also didn't want anyone else's career to be slighted for her involvement in their life.

Simmons, a through-and-through New Yorker, thought an East Coast home base would help make it easier for the couple to see each other. They picked out a beautiful Fifth Avenue apartment near the Central Park Zoo, but by the time it was fixed up for the couple, they had split. They remained friends, however. Cher considered the relationship one of her more pleasant and genuine ones of all.

Cher didn't have too much time to dwell on the breakup because her schedule was jam-packed. When she wasn't on the road, she was finally able to move into her Egyptian-themed Los Angeles home. The money sunk into the specific aesthetic, combined with the costs of life on the road and the nearly £1.1 million settlement that she paid Sonny left her in dire financial straits. Cher knew that she needed a new team around her to ensure she wouldn't find herself in this situation again. They helped where they could, but she was still facing Chapter 11 bankruptcy until she unexpectedly cashed in on a business deal outside of music. Earlier in her career, Cher had purchased apartment buildings in Los Angeles.

She later sold them to a man who had been paying her in instalments until he learned he could get a tax break for paying in full. His timing saved Cher from hitting financial rock bottom.

The new house had been a costly investment, but it started paying off immediately. Cher finally had the home she'd always dreamed of for hosting family and friends. There was one scary incident when Elijah, ever the daredevil of a child, managed to get out of the house on his rideable electric toy car. He started driving on the property's long driveway, which he and the staff both knew he was expressly forbidden from doing. The driveway contained a hill that Cher was coming down in her Jeep, returning from an outing. She tried slowing down on the downhill when she spotted her son and his tiny car and swerved to avoid him. Elijah crashed into the wheel, thankfully, and was safe, but Cher was horrified at the fact that she'd nearly run him over. In a hysterical rage, she fired many of her staffers for not keeping an eye on the rambunctious 4-year-old but later apologised and welcomed them all back.

When the family wasn't home together, Cher had no problem bringing the kids on the road. Cher tried timing international tour dates during the summer so the kids could join her in places they'd never seen before. Having grown up around everyone involved in her career, Chas and Elijah were well taken care of and looked out for wherever their mom's music took them. If it was going to interrupt school, Cher made sure to hire a tutor to join them on the road. She had reservations at times about the unconventional way the kids were growing up, but noted the kids knew no different and were happy with how they lived at that time.

1980 was also when Cher decided to embark on a side project. She became interested in putting together a rock band. She consulted Les Dudek, a singer/songwriter and guitarist that she first met during his work with the Allman Brothers. Since that time, Dudek has played for the Steve Miller Band and Stevie Nicks, as well as doing session work with countless other artists. He was open to being part of Cher's band and agreed to help her build out from there. Together, they recruited Gary Ferguson, Mike Finnigan, Warren Hamm, Rocket Richotte, and Trey Thompson.

The band worked on their eponymous album and began playing small clubs around Los Angeles in the early part of the year. They hoped to get recognition on merit rather than because of Cher's involvement in the project. Because their sound differed so much from Cher's norm, there wasn't much overlap between her core fan base and fans of the band.

They recorded their record with Casablanca Records, which was the label Cher was signed to at the time. It ended up being her last album with the label. *Black Rose* combined elements of new wave and hard rock. It was released in August 1980. To promote it, the group did a mini-tour along part of the East Coast called 'The Black Rose Show.' Though Cher tried to disguise herself with her best rocker transformation during shows, the select audiences who took in the shows felt it was easy to tell it was her.

The band even appeared on *The Merv Griffin Show* without tying themselves to Cher's identity. She'd later explain that she just needed someone to shake the image of her in their heads for long enough to take her seriously as a rock act. The album wasn't commercially or critically well-received. For Cher, however, the project was never about money or fame. In many ways, it was a necessary step in her evolution as an artist. Black Rose served as an escape from the Cher who was still taking the stage in the 'Take Me Home' tour. As she broadened her repertoire, she'd often take some losses with the wins, and this situation was no exception.

The band only lasted a year, during which she dated Dudek on and off. They opened for Hall and Oats on a few East Coast tour dates. The two enjoyed making music together, however, and one of their creations would go the distance. The two co-wrote a song called 'Don't Trust That Woman' that was never recorded by Black Rose. Dudek would later record the song himself and release it in 1981. Five years later, a song by the same name with the same lyrics appeared as a track on Elton John's *Leather Jackets*. John and Cher would later explain that the three of them actually wrote the song together, with John using his writing pseudonym, Lady Choc Ice.

It was also during that year that Cher would finally make some progress on her acting dream. After getting offstage after one of her Vegas shows, she was delighted to discover her old friend, Francis Ford Coppola, waiting for her. Since their days hanging out as scrappy young artists, Coppola had become one of the biggest names in Hollywood. At the point he approached Cher, he had already won Oscars for *The Godfather* films and *Apocalypse Now*. The two caught up for a while, during which Coppola brought up Cher's desire for acting. She explained the different avenues she'd tried in the nearly five years since Elijah was born and how none of them had gone anywhere.

Coppola gave Cher some advice – to prove those who had already turned her away wrong. It was time for her to find the role that would prove to her she could be a serious contender in the world of acting. Though Coppola himself didn't have a role for her, he recommended she do what it took to get her foot in the door. She recalled a piece of advice she'd once received from Shelley Winters, advising her to move to New York if she wanted to seriously pursue acting. Coppola agreed, and with that, Cher started to work on venturing east.

Cher moved to New York in 1981, ready to take up study with the Actor's Studio's Lee Strasberg. She went alone, at first, living in the apartment that Simmons had set up for them before their split. She stayed there as she looked for a more permanent place to call home, which would allow the kids to join her.. Cher also admitted she needed the dedicated time in order to really sink her teeth into the craft. She was also coming to terms with the fact that pursuing acting wouldn't guarantee her the big deals that music did, and what that might mean for her next chapter. It all seemed very serious, but there were moments of levity, too. She'd step out around the city, spending many nights at Studio 54 with friends like Liza Minnelli and Carly Simon.

After being turned away from roles in *Bonnie and Clyde* (1976), *Camelot* (1967), and more, Cher was confident that returning to acting as a student would help bring back the spark that other acting coaches had previously seen in her. She would never get to be under Strasberg's tutelage, however. She only reportedly attended two classes with the legend before another opportunity presented itself.

Georgia wanted to call Cher to check how an audition went one day. However, she accidentally dialled her friend Kathryn Reed instead. Reed didn't answer the phone, but her husband, Robert Altman, did.

Altman was a brilliant filmmaker, known at the time for *Nashville,* *Popeye,* and *M*A*S*H.* He was fresh off of selling his production company, Lion's Gate. The call let him know, by way of fate, that Cher was available for acting gigs. It so happened that Altman was beginning work on his newest project, a Broadway show called *Come Back to the Five and Dime, Jimmy Dean, Jimmy Dean.* The next time Reed and Georgia chatted, Reed mentioned the project. Georgia passed the word back on to Cher, who was immediately interested, though she'd never given much thought to acting on Broadway. While Georgia got word of Cher's interest back to Altman, Cher got ready to work on the part.

Jimmy Dean was written by an unknown playwright, Edward Graczyk. The play is about a group of six people, all of whom belonged to a James Dean fan club, meeting up again twenty years after the star stopped in on their small Texas town. The play looks back at the shock that came with Dean's death during that trip, where he was filming *Giant,* in part a reflection on the emotion that collective loss brings. Altman did see the appeal to upping the play's profile by adding Cher.

Initially, Altman pictured her as the lead, Joe. She ended up falling for and being cast in the role of Sissy, a flirty and fun girl working behind the counter at the dime store where the action unfolds. The cocktail waitress never spares a sideways comment, with her charming snark being a perfect place for Cher to shine. When Cher called William Morris Agency to tell her agents she'd landed the role and find out about joining the actor's union, a confused agent told her he couldn't get her an audition for *Jimmy Dean* because Altman was only interested in serious actors. That's when she informed him that she already got the part they thought she wasn't cut out for.

Working with Altman was a bit of a dream for Cher. She learned a lot during the experience and benefited from the fact Altman had a similar personality to her own. He, too, knew what it was to be underestimated by his peers. He was striving to make a mark that made his capabilities unquestionable. Some of his most beloved work by fans, like hers, was the work that critics held most disdain for. The two ended up gelling well together professionally, finding understanding in one another.

Altman proved he had her back from day one. On the first day of rehearsal, Cher was nervous. She tried taking a multivitamin while talking and started choking on it. She was gasping for air when a terrified Altman grabbed her and performed the Heimlich manoeuvre. Not only did he save her life, but it also solidified their bond.

The play also starred then-newcomer Kathy Bates, as well as Sandy Dennis, Marta Heflin, Karen Black, and Sudi Bond. They reportedly all got along well, except for Black, who felt them both too different to find much common ground. In particular, Dennis and Cher became close. Bates loved Cher but didn't appreciate that her fans weren't always well-versed in theatre etiquette, sometimes taking flash photos during performances.

Jimmy Dean opened in February 1982 at the Martin Beck theatre. Cher's first performance led to another encounter with her stage fright. She made it through the first half of the play when, just before intermission, she began to feel it. Dennis encouraged her to push through and finish. The initial reviews were mixed, with many critics unimpressed by the production. Altman believed in the talent and the story, so he sank his own money into the play to float it through a few tough weeks. Word of mouth began to spread, and audiences were filled once again.

Cher adjusted well to life while working on Broadway. She got to prepare in a dressing room that used to be Elizabeth Taylor's. She really felt like an actress, though she didn't always feel like she fit in right away. She enjoyed working on her character, finding the little nuances she could change from one performance to the next to keep the character fresh. Matinées were her creative playground, and the practice paid off. Though she didn't always feel confident in her performances, she delivered during the play's run, which ended that April after fifty-two performances.

Cher felt empowered in her first step and that there were some positive mentions of her work within the mixed reviews. Despite the mixed feedback, Altman decided to go ahead with a film version of the play, which was shot in 17 days on a modest £600,000 budget. The dramatic role would elevate Cher in the movie world, just as the play had done for her theatre work.

The play also led to another big opportunity for Cher when she got a knock on her dressing room door from none other than director Mike Nichols. Nichols had previously turned Cher away, and she vowed he'd be sorry for it. Now, he was coming to her with a role, not on Broadway, but in film. The movie was *Silkwood*, which would pair Cher with the already-legendary Meryl Streep. Cher jumped right in, ready to take on the role. She got to enjoy some time at home in Los Angeles with her kids before filming would begin.

The timing was also right. Cher had decided on a break from music after her only album with Columbia Records, *I Paralyze*. Released in May 1982, the album was another go at new wave rock. It didn't get the attention Cher hoped for from fans, and critics ranged from indifferent to unaware.

The album's two singles, 'I Paralyze' and 'Rudy,' were given little promotion, with Cher making a few appearances in support of each due to her busy schedule around *Silkwood*. Though she never officially declared it, the end of *I Paralyze* promotion marked the beginning of her hiatus from music. By shifting her attention to acting, Cher could still make use of her frenetic creative energy but take some pressure off of herself where singing and songwriting were concerned.

May 1982 was also when Cher celebrated her 36th birthday. Friends threw her a birthday party that was a mix of those nearest and dearest to her and the who's who of Hollywood. Among the guests was a then 25-year-old Val Kilmer. The two met for the first time that night and hit it off. When he reached out to her to hang out, it was strictly platonic. Kilmer and Cher became fast friends, and the chemistry between them was palpable. Still, Cher was hesitant to take things the romantic route because of the 14-year age gap between them. Part of her thought they could overcome it, but she was also familiar, at this point, with how outside sources could interfere with even the strongest relationships.

Right before she left for the set in Dallas in June, Cher broke down. She was paralysed by feelings of inadequacy. She confided in Georganne, who encouraged her that she could handle the role and work with Streep. Meanwhile, Streep would later admit that she was intimidated by the idea of working with Cher before the two women met and quickly hit it off. While Cher was expecting a serious and straight acting environment for the heavy film and the talented actress, Streep greeted her with a big hug when they first met. From there, they had a bond that was natural and would really translate on film, the beginnings of a friendship that continues to this day.

Cher would play Dolly Pelliker, roommate of Streep's Karen Silkwood. Ironically, Cher had briefly met Karen Silkwood years prior when she and her boyfriend, Drew Stephens, visited backstage at a Sonny and Cher concert. Though she didn't remember the encounter, Cher was stricken by the twist of fate.

Nichols asked Cher if she'd have an issue playing a lesbian woman, and she reassured him she didn't care. The film, based on a true story, focused on Silkwood's journey, sounding the alarm after discovering that her employer was putting her and her co-workers at serious risk. For her attempt to bring awareness to the issue and get justice, Silkwood was run off the road and killed in the ensuing crash. The significant proof she had against her former employer was never recovered.

Pelliker's character was a composite character, telling the story of Silkwood's sister and best friend. The character is far more than just a roommate, serving as the realistic but supportive confidante who helped Silkwood find her strength. In a film where there's a lot of serious, buttoned-up business, Pelliker provides a warm and human side and immense support amid Silkwood's journey. Cher excelled at playing a compelling secondary character.

The role put Cher far out of her element. From a public perspective, Cher's life as a glamorous pop star wearing custom dresses as she dazzled on stage with stars seemed worlds away from Dolly's stripped-down vulnerability. She never seemed out of place in the setting, however.

Being makeup-free in much of the film boiled Cher back down to her roots. That doesn't mean it came easily, however. Nichols also asked Cher to put on weight for the role. She tried her best, eating all the foods she knew better than to pursue. She cut back on her usual exercise, and yet, it still wasn't quite what Nichols envisioned. They ultimately padded Cher's pants to make her look heavier throughout the film, in addition to whatever weight she gained.

She was self-conscious about her gritty look in the film, and that feeling was intensified with a comment from Kurt Russell. In one of their first days on set in September 1982 when he allegedly asked her, 'What the fuck are you supposed to be?' The question sent Cher back to her dressing room, where she cried about her insecurities. It took her a while to settle into the look, especially because her co-stars didn't have to appear as raw or earthy.

In reality, she had more in common with her character than people would expect. Cher knew what it was to feel like you didn't belong. She knew what it was like to have to live out of one's element and make it work. It seemed she channelled all the uncertainty she ever experienced into the role. She also took advantage of her proximity to seasoned talent. Cher credits Streep with teaching her a lot about the acting game, both as an art form and as a business. Georganne, who had become a star in her own right with a role on *General Hospital*, was also there when she could be, to lend her support. During the months-long shoot, the two women developed a ritual of spending the day out to lunch and catching movies.

Silkwood finished shooting in November 1982, just in time for the holidays. That month, Cher would also enjoy the premiere of the film adaptation of *Come Back To the Five and Dime, Jimmy Dean, Jimmy Dean*. It debuted at the Chicago Film Festival that September, on the 27th anniversary of James Dean's death, and received a ten-minute standing ovation. The film earned Cher her very first solo Golden Globe nomination for Best Supporting Actress in a Motion Picture.

After completing filming on *Silkwood* and losing the Golden Globe, Cher was once again struggling with uncertainty. She knew the movie was good and that the story it told was important, but she didn't know how audiences would feel about her performance. She got a taste of their response when she went to see the trailer with her manager and Georganne. People reacted to the stars' names on screen. When Cher's name came up, the audience laughed. While Georganne and her manager started to cry, Cher kept a stiff upper lip and focused on not taking it personally. She was deeply hopeful the full story would change audiences' minds.

In January 1983, Cher was invited to speak to students at UCLA about her career journey to that point. The students were mesmerised by Cher's honesty, from the fact that Black Rose was a 'huge flop' to the fact that her Las Vegas shows were a means to an end. Cher also shared updates on her kids during the interview, admitting that a now-teenaged Chas enjoyed life in New York City more than life in Los Angeles. Cher was happy to see her kids thriving and enjoying childhood in a way she didn't get to.

During the discussion, she credited Sonny's help with Chas for making it possible for them to have a good relationship. She also acknowledged that Gregg wasn't part of Elijah's life, noting that she didn't let either circumstance stop her from bonding with her kids and exploring her career to the fullest. Still dating Kilmer at the time, she noted, 'If I had a husband, it would be better, but I don't know if a husband's worth it.'

That February, Cher had lent her support to Sonny as he opened the second of his Bono's restaurants. Other special guests that evening included Donna Mills, Tony Curtis, and Valerie Perrine. It would later become a chain across Palm Springs and West Hollywood, and become the career move that paved the way for his entrance to politics. At that time, however, Cher was just happy to see the sparkle in Sonny's eye that came when he thought he was on the brink of something quite wonderful.

The following month, *Cher: A Celebration at Caesar's* was filmed at the famed destination. The concert special was derived from Cher's Las Vegas act. In the special, she performed some of her favourite covers along with a set of six dancers and a number of drag queens. The nearly hour-long set made for a fun and energetic display that put Cher front and centre, entertaining as she did best. Fans responded well when it aired on TV in April 1983.

Cher almost signed on to another role in 1983, a failed film that was supposed to be called *Road Show*. She was made to believe she would star in the film alongside Nicholson and Timothy Hutton. The intended director, Marty Ritt, told Cher he thought she was perfect for the part. However, she'd discover while she was out celebrating her 39th birthday in New York that she had mentioned the part to someone who urged her to contact her agent. No one answered Cher's calls, and she said she no longer wanted the role. She'd later learn the same part in the same film was also promised to Mary Steenburgen and Debra Winger.

She also flat-out turned down some roles. For example, she was offered another wrong-side-of-the-tracks character in Randal Kleiser's *Grandview USA*. It was appealing because it offered a relatively light role, an easy shooting schedule, and a decent pay cheque. They struggled to cast a male lead, however, which made Cher uncertain. She wanted to be sure she'd be working with someone whom she had chemistry with on camera and would be respectful off-camera. The longer the role stayed in limbo, the more Cher had her doubts. She ultimately passed on the role, which was later given to Jamie Lee Curtis.

As Cher considered different roles, she realised she was drawn to characters that were everyday people. Though a few more glamorous roles were floated her way, she considered that part of her stage act something for a Las Vegas performance or a red carpet rather than a way of honing her acting chops.

That summer, Cher enjoyed spending time in Los Angeles with the kids while also enjoying her own private life. She continued to see Kilmer. The two, who nicknamed each other Ethel and Sid, had a lot of fun together, but both of their busy schedules allowed her the flexibility to spend plenty of time with friends as well.

Cher also turned within during this time, starting to explore spirituality in a way she hadn't before. She was introduced to transcendental meditation. At first, the star found the practice futile. Her mind was too busy for her to turn off the noise and tune into something deeper. She found it helped not just in acting but in music, too. She was able to come down after being on stage and transition from an entertainment mindset to being in the moment as herself.

When she found something that worked for her, she didn't hesitate to share it. Ever the open book, Cher introduced other people to the practice as she continued to enjoy the summer of 1983. In August, Cher and Georganne went to see David Bowie's 'Serious Moonlight' tour at the Forum. The two were photographed backstage hanging out with Bowie, Michael Jackson, Bette Midler, and more. Cher seemed at ease and enjoyed the star-studded event.

Before she knew it, it was time for the world to see *Silkwood*. Hard work on this serious role paid off for Cher. The film premiered in December 1983 to rave reviews from critics. People were starting to admit they'd underestimated Cher's acting abilities. Suddenly, other people saw that special something her earliest acting instructors had told her they spotted. It was her biggest dream realised, and she did all the work to make it happen on her own. Though she didn't understand the magnitude of it at the moment, this was more than just a career goal achieved for Cher. It very much influenced the direction of her career and her life in the years to come.

With the critical acclaim came the award nominations. Cher was nominated for Best Supporting Actress by a number of organisations – the Golden Globes, the Academy Awards, the British Academy Film Awards (BAFTA), the Los Angeles Film Critics Association (LAFCA) Awards, the National Society of Film Critics (NSFC) Awards, and New York Film Critics Circle (NYFCC) Awards. Of those six nominations, she came in runner-up for LAFCA, NSFC, and NYFCC.

While all of Hollywood was once again abuzz about Cher, she didn't always want to participate in the high-visibility, always-available nature of the business. It was something she and Kilmer could agree on. When neither of them liked their options for how to spend New Year's 1984, the two decided on a quiet night that Kilmer took to the next level. He showed up at Cher's home with art supplies, and the two spent the night making art with the kids. Kilmer clicked with Chas and Elijah quickly, particularly Elijah. He appreciated that male presence in his life, though the fact that Kilmer was such an alpha would later cause problems between him and Cher.

The new year came with so many big moments for Cher. The first was when Cher won the Golden Globe for her portrayal of Pelliker on January 28, 1984. The film was also nominated on other fronts – Streep for Best Actress, Best Motion Picture Drama, and more. While Cher was elated at the accolades, she wasn't quite ready to consider that she might win. Particularly, she thought Linda Hunt was a shoo-in after seeing *The Year of Living Dangerously*. It was before she ever realised the two could be facing each other in any competitive sense. Cher was truly moved by

Hunt's performance. It was for that reason that she was in shock when she won. She walked up, joking with the audience as she told them, 'Just look at my dress 'til I can think of something.' Cher may not have taken home the Oscar win, but she had arrived as a serious actress. Further, she delivered a gracious acceptance speech that acknowledged her underdog status and thanked everyone who took a chance on her in spite of it.

Cher's arrival in acting meant that she was a true contender. Offers for different films began to come in. The offers were widely varied – some lucrative, some artsy, some light-hearted. Of course, the bigger the names attached, the more traditionally appealing the films should have been. Other actors might have snatched up any of the roles that came early on in hopes of keeping up the momentum. But like in all other areas of life, Cher's approach to acting wasn't traditional. She took the time to field offers before landing on her next project. It was months before she found what felt like the perfect match.

That next project would, once again, be based on a true story. *Mask* is based on the experience of Roy Lee 'Rocky' Dennis, who lived with facial malformation after he was born with craniodiaphyseal dysplasia. The film focuses on the last months of his life, which was a remarkable three times longer than the prognosis his family was given when he was born. Cher was cast in the role of Florence 'Rusty' Dennis opposite actor Eric Stoltz. Rusty was a devoted mother but also a drug-addicted biker. Once again, Cher would be called to bring warmth to the film through a complicated character. It was, in ways, even more complex than Silkwood. This time, she walked in with a tad bit more confidence in her ability to rise to the occasion. Still, she knew she wasn't the first choice for the studio, which was rumoured to have opened up auditions after pursuing Jane Fonda for the role.

Once again, Kilmer was helping Cher build that confidence behind the scenes. He went over lines with her and helped her with her screen test for the film. When she would end up with the role, she recommended Kilmer for the role of Gar, which was ultimately played by Sam Elliott. Kilmer was turned away for being too young. In April 1984, the two attended the Academy Awards together, this time with an almost 8-year-old Elijah in tow. The public was seeing Kilmer's natural way with Elijah and, for the first time, it seemed people took the pairing more seriously. Sadly, their relationship was heading into its final stages, with the two splitting before the year's end.

Production began on *Mask* in May 1984. There were some inherent challenges for Cher in working with Peter Bogdanovich. The two had set off on the wrong foot nearly two decades earlier. The director had previously written a scathing profile about Sonny and Cher in *The Saturday Evening Post* in 1966. When they reconnected to work on *Mask*, she didn't feel that his perspective about her had changed much. She believed that Bogdanovich didn't agree with the kind of woman that she was on a fundamental level.

Cher noted that while she did have similarities with the character she portrayed, it seemed like the director would sometimes conflate her with Rusty. Rusty was fierce and wonderful in so many ways – a protective mother, a loyal friend, and a bona fide badass biker. However, she coped with life's difficulties through drugs and promiscuity. She was also misguided in some of her attempts at a powerful mom moment, like when she attempts to hire a sex worker to help quell Rocky's concerns that women won't be attracted to him because of his differences. During one argument, she angrily rips up one of Rocky's prized baseball cards and even slaps her son. All those instances where she didn't meet the moment melt away, however, when she loses her son. The complexities of Rusty were markedly different than those of Cher, but it was the inability to be anything but an enigmatic, many-faceted woman that the character and the actress shared.

Filming allowed Cher to keep her life somewhat normal. The film was made in and around Los Angeles, which allowed her the work/life balance she'd come to love, although part of her still yearned to make New York her more permanent home. There was a downside, however. Cher had to dye her hair red for the film. The result was awful and damaged her hair. Little by little, she'd cut more of her real hair off and work with her hair team on hair pieces and, by the end, a wig to remedy the situation as Cher's hair recovered.

Cher was nervous about going against Bogdanovich's direction, at first. As she sat with Rusty's character, however, she started to get a sense of what felt organic to her and what did not. Her ideas and suggestions sometimes caused the director and actor to butt heads. Cher did worry that she was making a mistake, but she also couldn't ignore the voice telling her to speak up, for herself and Rusty. At times, he allegedly even threatened to cut Cher out of the movie.

Eventually, she struck a balance. At the suggestion of Stoltz, Cher learned to hold back from engaging in the argument with Bogdanovich. She realised that she was committing too much of her energy to having the last word. That didn't mean she'd just comply, however. She learned that the other part of resisting the fight was to continue to quietly follow her instincts when the cameras rolled. The conflicts were fewer with this technique, but there was no questioning that the damage was done. The wounds of that damage would reopen in 1985 during the promotion of the film.

/

Chapter Nine

1985–1987

As Cher went into 1985, things in her life were changing. She and Val Kilmer quietly split at the end of 1984, with the star admitting that her younger beau left her, though she's never shared his reason why. The two continued a friendship, however, and Cher wasn't without love in her life for long. She began dating Joshua Donen, the film producer son of revered director Stanley Donen. The two appeared to run in similar circles toward the end of 1984, though it's unclear when they went from acquaintances to an item.

Cher's acting career was centre stage in her life at this point. In February 1985, she was honoured by Harvard University's Hasty Pudding Theatricals. She was named their Woman of the Year honour. The theatrical society bestows the honour on a woman who has made a significant impact in entertainment that year. It was an honour for Cher to visit Cambridge and accept her accolade. In her acceptance speech, which followed a parade and a number of performances in her honour, Cher joked she'd turn the pudding pot given to her to commemorate the moment into an earring.

As she geared up to promote *Mask*, other offers were coming in. Cher was exhausted after the movie wrapped and hadn't figured out her next steps. She was offered the female lead in *Baby Boom* but passed on it. The role would go to Diane Keaton, whom Cher felt was the best pick for it when she later saw the film.

On 8 March 1985, *Mask* was released in theatres. Cher attended the Los Angeles premiere with Donen by her side. While usually, the first signs of a new relationship would be the headline-making moment, Cher's performance in the film far overshadowed the happenings in her personal life, perhaps for the first time ever. Commercially, the film was an overwhelming success, bringing in over £30,000,000 at the box office.

Critics were touched by the story and praised the cast's work across the board, with many highlighting the true talent Cher displayed as Rusty.

Cher wasn't just effective in the role of Rusty; she was deeply impacted by it. Cher connected with the National Craniofacial Foundation, an organisation dedicated to helping children with craniofacial conditions. It's a relationship that Cher has continued to this day, not only donating to the cause but developing relationships with kids growing up with these differences that continued as they came into adulthood. In the decades since the film, Cher has invited kids she's met through NCF backstage and on stage at her shows.

The following month, Cher appeared on *The Tonight Show*, where she chatted with guest host Joan Rivers, who announced to the audience that the film would be screened at the Cannes Film Festival the following month. During the sit-down, the two friends joked about a failed attempt at a garage sale. They also discussed the movie and Cher's struggles breaking into acting, followed by a clip from the film where Rusty is frantically trying to write Rocky a letter at camp while Gar helps her. Rusty's apologetic tone and genuine desperation in realising she can't reach her son the way she wants to at that moment translate into a heartfelt moment that both audiences and critics are touched by.

In May, *Mask* played at the Cannes Film Festival, and though the moment was major for the film, its significance as a milestone wasn't what caught the attention of the public. Instead, it was a disagreement that broke out between Cher and Peter Bogdanovich. While Cher was there, as expected, in the promotion of the film, Universal Studios did not include Bogdanovich in the event because of their differences. The director had fought with the studio over the soundtrack and had swapped Bruce Springsteen's music for Bob Seger's, as well as six minutes of footage cut from the film. Bogdanovich showed up anyway, making comments to the press that disparaged Cher. He felt she ignored direction often throughout the film and suggested it, along with the editorial decisions made without his consent.

In response, Cher admitted she didn't expect the director to put the film's interests above his own. The actress pointed out that what Bogdanovich claimed the studio had done to his vision of the film is what directors and executives do with actors' work. They, too, have no say in the finished product and aren't always happy with the result, she pointed out. She was open about the fact that they didn't see eye to eye while filming, but stopped short of further condemnation, noting it wasn't doing anyone or the film any favours.

Despite the obvious tension between the two, Cher got the ultimate win when she was named Best Actress alongside Norma Aleandro for *The Official Story*. She won the award on 20 May, her 39th birthday. She called it 'the best birthday present' in her acceptance speech, where she also thanked her mom for making the special moment possible. Donen was also there, quietly cheering her on. Their relationship still made headlines for the age gap between them, but it was among Cher's tamer pairings, as the public saw it.

Amid the buzz around the film, Cher was doing a lot of press. One of her more notable interviews was a sit-down with Barbara Walters. In it, she opened up a lot about her personal life. Walters drew comparisons to Sonny's role in Cher's life as a pseudo-father figure and how that compared to her relationship with Gregg Allman, who was like a child. She asked where Donen fell in her life in those terms, and Cher described him as being a multifaceted presence in her life. She felt an understanding she hadn't experienced before, one that came without the highs and lows. Cher doubled down on the fact that Gregg wasn't active in Elijah's life during the interview, noting he hadn't spoken to his son in two years.

On the subject of Donen and the possibility of marriage, Cher revealed that the couple had discussed it before. Cher admitted to being more hesitant about it than Donen because of her two failed attempts at marriage. She said that part of her hesitance comes from the fact that the world could be so hard on her in the moments where she did seem to 'fail,' particularly in her personal life. Having gone through two very public divorces coloured her perspective on what a third could look like.

In a *Los Angeles Times* profile that same month, it was revealed that the couple was living together in Malibu, although Cher wasn't as forthcoming with details as she'd been in other relationships. She seemed focused on keeping her professional life the subject of conversation, but handled it with the same candour she'd previously used in discussions of her personal life. Her head-on approach to anything that had people talking earned her a lot of respect, though it wasn't always met with a great deal of understanding.

Despite the focus on acting, Cher made a special exception in July 1985, when the opportunity to perform at Live Aid was presented to her. While she was thrilled to be part of the special moment, she wasn't originally meant to be in it. Like many things in Cher's life, it came up on a whim. Cher was flying Concorde. Phil Collins, who had recently established his own solo career, was also on board. He was on his way to making history at Live Aid, having performed on stage in London and quickly travelling to Philadelphia to do the same.

Cher, busy in her own world, was unaware of the event. The event, which was held in both London's Wembley Stadium and Philadelphia's John F. Kennedy Stadium, was a benefit concert to raise money for Ethiopians struggling after a years-long famine. Cher immediately wanted to get involved, so Collins suggested she just show up, confident they'd use all the star power they could get. When the two disembarked from the flight, Collins noticed a previously casually dressed Cher was done up as if she was prepared to take the stage. She followed his suggestion, and Collins was, indeed, correct. Cher was invited to join and sang in the chorus of 'We Are the World,' closing out the momentous event.

During that summer, Donen and Cher went through some struggles in their relationship and briefly split. They reconciled, and he accompanied her when she attended Madonna's wedding to Sean Penn in August 1985. Cher and Penn were good friends at that point despite her mixed feelings about the 'Like a Virgin' singer. Cher dressed in a demure black pantsuit but balanced it with an outrageous purple wig.

It was there that she first met Tom Cruise, whose star was still on the rise after 1983's *Risky Business*. The two got to know each other a bit and would encounter each other again two months later, when both were invited by First Lady Nancy Reagan to the White House. Both dyslexic celebrities, as well as Caitlyn Jenner, were among several invited to a reception. They were deemed recipients of the Outstanding Learning Disabled Achiever Award, also celebrating President Ronald Reagan's declaration that October be National Dyslexia Awareness Month. While

Cher says that this was the first time that she noticed a connection between the two, she also said it wasn't until later that they had briefly dated. Cher even admitted to Cruise being one of her best lovers, though she's never said much about how long they were together or what their relationship was like. She and Donen did later reconcile.

In December, Cher was once again accompanied by Bob Mackie to the Met Gala. The theme was 'Costumes of Royal India.' Cher wore a gorgeous, jewel-encrusted long-sleeve bodice that had feather-like black and gold wisps across it, with a low-slung black skirt that drew attention as it hung from her hips. Giant cuff earrings that sat on each side of her slicked-back hair brought attention to the star's face, which looked almost statuesque with stonelike makeup. It was very different from her 'naked' dress years prior, but it felt like it suited Cher in the moment and showcased Mackie's immense talent once again.

Cher kicked off 1986 with big hopes for awards season. After taking home Best Actress at Cannes, the whole industry thought that the Golden Globes and Academy Awards were sure to follow. She did snag the Golden Globe nomination for Best Actress in a Motion Picture - Drama. She attended the January 1986 event with Donen. She wore a black gown that was sheer with two slashes through the chest and a black bandage skirt underlay. Sadly, the award would ultimately go to Whoopi Goldberg for *The Colour Purple*, but she still had her eyes on the Academy Award.

That, too, would end up being a letdown. Cher was not nominated for her role in *Mask*, which confounded her and many of those who lauded her performance. Of course, there was talk about that decision throughout the industry between the time that the nominations were announced and the awards ceremony itself. Through that talk, Cher learned it was her music persona, not her acting abilities, that kept her from being nominated. People found her to be frivolous in a way that didn't belong in the acting industry. Some members felt that because she dated different men and didn't dress as a 'serious' actress might, giving her the honour might say something about the Academy itself. It was upsetting to Cher, who initially thought of boycottingthe awards. Then, she was asked to present the award for Best Supporting Actor.

Immediately, she turned to Mackie for an outfit that would be perfect for the occasion. The two worked together on what would become a memorable creation that's among the highlights of each's career. Cher's inspiration was the look of a Mohawk tribesperson. Of course, Mohawk hairstyles were being co-opted by the punk movement, so it wasn't unusual altogether. It was a look, however, that Chas begged Cher not to try herself. Cher met her halfway with a Mohawk-inspired headpiece that was remarkable but not the centrepiece of her look for the night.

Mackie made Cher a dress to fit her request for something 'outrageous.' The black satin two-piece outfit consisted of Native American symbols embossed in the dress's pattern. The top, made in the likeness of a breastplate, had chunky black diamonds and beading in a grid neckline that fell into a chain of chunky diamonds with beaded fringe. The matching pants had a zig-zag waistline that sat low on Cher's waist, with a loincloth-style overlay. A matching full-length coat brought the whole look together. It was an astonishing sight among the usual award show fare. Not only was Donen happy to walk the carpet by her side, but when his executive father, who was producing the show, saw the outfit, he also gave his seal of approval.

Jane Fonda was so surprised to see Cher's look backstage that she begged her to wait to come out until she was seated in the audience and could see everyone's reaction. She was the one to introduce Cher and couldn't help but quip about the look. When she got on stage for her presentation gig, Cher joked, 'As you can see, I got my Academy handbook on how to dress as a serious actress.' The crowd roared with laughter, with the elephant in the room being acknowledged as only Cher knew how.

In May, Cher made crowds laugh once again with an appearance on *The Late Show with David Letterman*. Cher was a fan of the show but thought that the late-night host was sometimes unfair to guests he felt were beneath him. She was invited on the show a number of times but always declined. Cher eventually relented and threw a crazy offer at them. She told production that if they paid her £28,000 hotel bill in the city, she'd come on the show. She wasn't sure how they made it happen, but they did. When producer Robert Morton met her, he wondered aloud why she'd never been a guest before. Cher candidly admitted she thought Letterman could be 'an asshole.'

In introducing her, Letterman teased that they'd tried for four years to get her on the show, reaching out 81 separate times. The host chided her, but Cher also wasn't shy about admitting what she thought of him. The crowd laughed after she called him an asshole, with a few boos intertwined. The two laughed it off, but Cher was honest about her opinion, and Letterman respected her for it. He later admitted it took a few years to shake the shock of the exchange off.

Donen and Cher split shortly after the Oscars, but once again, her next love wasn't too far off. On the eve of her 40th birthday, Cher was in New York. The women were enjoying a night at a club called Heartbreak when Cher first laid eyes on Rob Camilletti. Camilletti, just 22 at the time, and only spoke to the star briefly that day. Months later, she'd go back to the club and bump into him again. He mentioned that he was acting outside of his day job at a bagel shop in Queens, so she took his number down. Initially, she wanted to keep him in mind for a music video, with the idea of a new album starting to brew. There were other feelings there, though she wouldn't acknowledge them until later on.

Cher's 40th birthday would be momentous, not just because she was entering a new decade in her life. She also learned she'd be taking on a new acting project. The actress woke up to a call from director George Miller about his upcoming project, *The Witches of Eastwick*, based on the novel by John Updike. The novel would only be a really loose outline for what the film became. Miller was coming off of the *Mad Max* trilogy and eager to plunge into a new world.

The film centres around three women, Alexandra Medford, Jane Spofford, and Sukie Ridgemont. The Rhode Island small-towners are disappointed and bored by their lives, but things are shaken up when they unknowingly form a coven. When a charming man shows up in town, they are intrigued until they learn he is the devil himself. The film intertwined the supernatural and fantasy elements with comedic elements.

The good news was that she was being considered for a part. The bad news was it wasn't the one she'd hoped for. The dark comedy project had quickly become the interest of many in Hollywood. Jack Nicholson became attached to the project after his then-partner, Anjelica Huston, informed him that Bill Murray had dropped out of the project. Huston was auditioning for a role herself, having screen-tested for Alexandra Medford. She did her screen test with Michelle Pfeiffer, who was cast as Sukie.

Huston didn't get the role, but Susan Sarandon did. It was the one Cher wanted, but Miller claimed Nicholson was opposed to her playing it. She would later learn it was Miller who had objections, not just about Cher in that role, but in the film overall, due to the incessant tabloid attention surrounding her personal life. She stood her ground on feeling she most aligned with the role, and eventually, Miller and the studio agreed to cast her as Alexandra. They told Cher they would move Sarandon, who wasn't attached to any particular role, so long as she was in the project.

Sarandon was recast as Jane, but was not told of the change until the day she showed up to begin filming. Cher admitted it caused Sarandon to start on a sour note with her, until the two women compared notes and realised the studio was to blame, not either of them. Pfeiffer, Sarandon, and Cher had a lot of fun together, both on and off the clock. The three women would share guilty pleasure snacks across their trailers during the day. After weeks of a junk food kick, they moved on to health food, microwaving sweet potatoes and making salads between scenes.

Cher's differences with Miller also eased as filming began in July 1986. While Cher often worried she'd run into another contentious situation, feeling as though she didn't understand Miller, she wasn't alone. Production also clashed with the director, making for an unusual feeling on the set. Cher recalled no one seemed certain that theirs was the right move, but the cast got along so marvellously that it all started to even out. It was a long shoot, however, in various locations throughout Massachusetts.

It was fun making the film, but there were also moments that called for more from the actress. In a scene where she's supposed to wake up panicked after finding herself in a bed of live snakes, Cher was struggling to find the right anxiety to suit the moment. She had no genuine fear of snakes, which they used in their first attempt to make the scene happen. Cher was uncomfortable with the snakes slithering into her clothes as she lay there and worried her exaggerated movements from the camera

Advertisement for Cher's debut single, "All I Really Want to Do" from June 1965. (*Cashbox Magazine*)

Sonny and Cher leave the Netherlands from Schiphol Airport in Sept. 1966. (*Joop van Bilsen/Anefo*)

Sonny and Cher in 1966.
(*Tony Gale*)

Cher filming with Sonny in the
background for Swedish TV in 1966.
(*Roger Tillberg/Alamy Stock Photo*)

Sonny and Cher as guest stars on the television comedy show *Love, American Style* in 1971. (*ABC Television*)

Cher performing on *The Sonny & Cher Comedy Hour* in 1971. (*Columbia Broadcasting System (CBS) / Album*)

1970s publicity photo of Cher.
(*Light Show, Casablanca Records*)

Sonny Bono and Cher perform together in *The Sonny & Cher Comedy Hour* in 1971. (*Columbia Broadcasting System (CBS) / Album*)

Gregg Allman and Cher in 1976. (*Unknown Author*)

Cher at the 1974 Met Gala in an iconic
Bob Mackie creation. (*ZUMA*)

Farrah Fawcett and Cher in Bob
Mackie gowns on *The Sonny &
Cher Show* in 1976. (*CBS Television*)

Cher with toddler son Elijah Blue perched on her lap in 1977. (*ZUMA Press*)

Cher and Gregg Allman in London in Nov. 1977. (*KEYSTONE Pictures USA*)

Georgeann LaPiere, Georgia Holt, a young Chaz Bono, and Cher share a laugh. (© *Globe Photos/ ZUMAPRESS.com*)

Georgia Holt, Cher, Chaz Bono and Sonny Bono in April 1983. (*Ralph Dominguez/MediaPunch*)

Cher at Solid Gold, 1983. (*Ron Wolfson / Rock Negatives / MediaPunch*)

Cher and Elijah Blue backstage at Solid Gold in 1984. (*Ron Wolfson / MediaPunch*)

Cher wearing a Bob Mackie original at the 58th Annual Academy Awards, 1986. (*PictureLux / The Hollywood Archive / Alamy Stock Photo*)

Rob Camiletti and Cher at the premiere of *Torch Song Trilogy* in Dec. 1988. (*Laura Luongo/ZUMAPRESS.com*)

Cher performs to benefit the Pediatric AIDS Foundation in Washington, D.C. in June 1989. (*M Abancourt*)

Tina Turner and Cher share
a laugh in a 1990 meetup.
(*John Barrett/PHOTOlink*)

Sean Hayes as Jack McFarland with Cher
during her *Will & Grace* cameo in 2000.
(*Chris Haston*)

Cher and Elijah Blue at a red carpet event in 2007. (*Image: Tsuni / USA*)

Cher attends an Oct. 2007 event. (*Tsuni / USA*)

Cher at the premiere of *Burlesque* at the Empire Leicester Square in London. (*Ian Smith*)

Cher performs at London's O2 Arena in 2010. (*Raphael Pour-Hashemi*)

Cher performs at London's O2 Arena in 2010. (*Raphael Pour-Hashemi*)

Cher at the 2010 MTV Video Music Awards. (*Sara Cozolino/Everett Collection*)

Cher and mom Georgia Holt at Cher's Hand and Footprint Ceremony at Grauman's Chinese Theatre in Nov. 2010. (*Michael Germana/Everett Collection*)

Cher performs at London's O2 Arena in 2010. (*Raphael Pour-Hashemi*)

Cher and Chaz Bono smile at Cher's Nov. 2010 Hand and Footprint Ceremony, held at the Mann Chinese Theatre. (© *Lisa O'Connor/ ZUMAPRESS.com*)

Cher and Chaz Bono at the 23rd GLAAD Media Awards in 2012. (*DVSROSS*)

Alexander Edwards and Cher at *The Bikeriders* LA Premiere at the TCL Chinese Theater in Hollywood, California in June 2024. (*Faye Sadou/ Media Punch/Alamy Live News*)

Alexander Edwards and Cher at the Versace F/W 2023 event in Los Angeles in March 2023. (*UPI/Alamy Live News*)

might put them in danger or make them feel threatened. They decided to accomplish the look with special effects, so in subsequent takes, there were no actual snakes on set to even try reacting to. When she couldn't get the hysteria right, she turned to a substance she knew she didn't tolerate well – caffeine.

The scene was shot at night, and in the bit of time ahead of the scene, Cher quickly downed about four cups of coffee. She made it about halfway through filming the scene before she broke into an intense panic. The impact of the caffeine made her both physically jittery and emotionally anxious. Cher felt out of control, to the point that they shut down shooting for the night and sent her home. Once she went home, she found herself still unable to relax and felt the jittery feeling well into the next day.

Cher and Donen were involved in an accident while she was leaving filming one day. The driver of their car, a station wagon, was bringing them back to their hotel. Their car was hit by a drunk driver, with the hit propelling them into the car that was in front of them. Thankfully, no one was seriously hurt. Cher was brought into the hospital to be sure, however, leading some local outlets to report on the crash.

While shooting *Witches*, Cher started to experience some unusual symptoms. She found herself more fatigued than she usually was. She had a feeling that she was sick or recovering from illness constantly. At first, she thought it was a combination of her busy schedule and the fact that she'd maintained a pretty non-stop lifestyle. She started paying more attention to her diet in hopes it would make a difference, but she found it did not. Concerned about what the issue could be, Cher underwent medical testing. It was during this time that she was first diagnosed with chronic Epstein-Barr virus, known as the 'yuppie flu' at the time.

The illness, a type of herpes virus that's spread through bodily fluids, presents with cold or flu-like symptoms. The chronic nature of the virus made the symptoms recur after a period of dormancy. Cher wouldn't fully understand what this would mean for her health until years later. However, it was at this point that she was starting to feel its impacts.

During that time, Cher thought again about Camilletti. She invited him out to a play, where they were joined by Melanie Griffith. They went out afterwards, all platonically. She saw him again the next night, going to Heartbreak before moving on to China Club. It was in that setting that Cher felt the age gap was too great for them to be anything more than friends. After all, he was just five years older than Chas. She did eventually have to go back to Los Angeles to conclude filming on the studio's lot. The two stayed in touch, and when Cher had a few days off, she snuck away to New York to visit him.

Eventually, she got an apartment there. Cher enjoyed the simplicity of the relationship. On its face, the two didn't have much in common. They were able to get out and about and appreciate the world together in a way that Cher cherished. The two would do couple's activities that were mundane by Hollywood standards – long walks, days at the movie theatre, checking out local haunts, or playing board games and card games. Still, she was thrilled by the romance and by him.

Cher closed out 1986 by enjoying her relationship, spending time with her kids, and preparing for new projects. She had shifted into a new phase, with Elijah beginning to attend boarding school while Chas faced young adulthood. The new stages her kids were at allowed her to maintain the non-stop schedule that was ahead of her. Not only was she set to have a busy year in acting, but she was also determined to get back into music. It had been almost 5 years since her last, and she finally felt that she musically had something to say and a sound in mind for it. More importantly, the prospect of making music felt exciting and not like a means to an end.

The year began with *Moonstruck*. The film follows Loretta Castorini, a widowed woman in her thirties who agrees to marry a man she's seeing, Johnny Cammareri, even though he wasn't what she had in mind for herself. It's only after the fact that she meets a man who makes her heart race – Johnny's brother, Ronny. The romantic comedy included a cast of characters designed by playwright John Patrick Shanley to bring the laughs. While Hollywood still wasn't entirely sold on Cher, who noted the studio once again had reservations about her casting, director Norman Jewison thought of her as he envisioned the character of Loretta. Shanley initially pictured Sally Field for the role, but her prior commitment left Cher as the duo's top choice.

Cher fell for the character and had someone in mind to play her Ronny, Nicolas Cage. She was impressed with his work after seeing him in *Peggy Sue Got Married* and felt he could bring a unique energy to the role, which countless actors, including Tom Cruise and Ray Liotta, had auditioned for. The studio wasn't into the idea at first. Cher claims they were interested in Peter Gallagher for the role, and while she appreciated his talent, she felt he lacked the edge that Cage could bring to the character. She did a screen test with both actors. The studios picked Gallagher, but when Cher threatened to pull out of the production, they agreed to go along with her recommendation.

Cage got the role, but the chemistry between the two was off when production began in December 1987. Cher was her usual mellow self, focused on the work at hand. Cage's unique ways of preparation were, at times, amusing to her. But at times, he went to a place that was off-putting. It was hard to bring sexual tension to their roles when things were so hot and cold behind the scenes. The two also had the added element of Danny Aiello's Johnny, which at times brought balance and, at other times, a different chaos. It felt like a challenging shoot for everyone involved, driven to varying points of frustration, they were able to make it magic on film.

Filming took place over about twelve weeks. There was no time for resting and recuperating, however. Cher had just five days to herself until she began filming on *Suspect,* which had to delay production to accommodate Cher's completion of *Moonstruck.* In exchange for the concession, MGM agreed not to release *Moonstruck* until two months after *Suspect*'s premiere.

During the short few days she had to herself, Cher went to Los Angeles with Camilletti. While there, he presented her with a puppy in celebration of their anniversary. The sweet gesture is illustrative of the way that he was different in the way he looked at and perceived Cher and her place in the world. She was touched and delighted by the gift.

That window also saw Cher appear with Georgia on a special called *Superstars and Their Moms.* The special highlighted the mother-child relationships of some of the time's biggest stars. It was hosted by Carol Burnett and her daughter, Carrie Hamilton. Other guests included

Whitney and Cissy Houston, Bill and Anna Pearl Cosby, Cybill and Patty Shepherd, and more. It was a sweet moment for Cher and Georgia, who gushed with pride as she recognised her daughter's many achievements.

The law thriller sees Cher as a Washington, D.C., public defender for a homeless man who is revealed to be a veteran. Played by Liam Neeson, Carl Wayne Anderson was charged with the murder of a law clerk who had found a breakthrough detail in a cold case. With the help of a juror, Eddie Sanger (Dennis Quaid), they find true justice in the misunderstood crime.

The role required Cher to get in touch with her inner plain Jane. It was a smart role that made great use of her ability to quip and elevated it to an art form, fitting of a scrappy attorney. She was a little intimidated by the jargon around the role, with no particular knowledge of the legal system. The role was another step into 'serious actress' territory, yet still, a departure from the style maven or Vegas performer audiences associated her with. It played on the emotions cerebrally rather than in the more animated and theatrical way other roles did.

Playing Kathleen Riley allowed for the suspension of disbelief and wasn't as draining a production process for Cher as some of her other roles, which worked out well for her after making three movies back-to-back. Cher liked the challenge and even spent time in the Washington, D.C. Public Defender's Office researching her role. The fast-paced environment was a little difficult to grasp because of her dyslexia, but she didn't let it stop her.

Once again, Cher's dedication to the grind and honing her acting skills paid off in a major way. *The Witches of Eastwick* premiered in June 1987. The unusual comedy with literary roots received mixed reviews from critics. Much of the praise went to Nicholson, with the coven of women acknowledged as a collective rather than for what their individual performances brought to the film when combined. Audiences were much more into it, with the film grossing over £75 million worldwide.

It was shortly after the film's premiere that Cher teamed up with David Geffen and producer John Kalodner for her new, self-titled album, Cher. Kalodner reached out to Cher about an album just before her film commitments began. Cher knew she didn't have time for an album at that point, but didn't expect Kalodner to be available by the time she was able to focus on music. She was surprised when he was, admitting he was more than happy to wait to work with her. Kaldoner was working for Geffen at the time. In fact, Geffen introduced him to Cher during the years when the two dated.

Geffen wasn't just lending his help for the album. He signed Cher to Geffen Records, having just as much faith in her as he always had. Even though she was unsure after years out of the scene, she was surrounded by a team that deeply believed in her. They began recording in the summer of 1987. Once again, Cher was looking to make the rock album of her dreams happen. She was well aware that her last few attempts at rock hadn't gone as planned.

At the time, Geffen was tuned into the rock scene, working simultaneously with Guns 'N Roses on *Appetite for Destruction* and Aerosmith on *Permanent Vacation*. He wasn't sold on Cher making another rock album, but, as always, she stood her ground. Geffen wasn't entirely sold on the vision, but it didn't stop him from enlisting the best of the best to achieve the sound she was looking for. In turn, Cher took a step toward mastering the art of the power ballad.

Cher herself was excited to return to music, though she'd find that, like her already busy schedule that year, she wouldn't have much time to linger in it. In October 1987, *Suspect* was released. Critics had mixed feelings about the crime aspects of the film, arguing there were major plot holes and, in parts, too much reliance on tropes. The end of the film was something discussed by both viewers and critics who didn't quite feel it met the mark.

November 1987 was a busy month for Cher. She performed on *Saturday Night Live* for the first time. In the episode hosted by Candice Bergen, she appeared as the musical guest. She performed 'We All Sleep Alone' and 'I Found Someone.'

A few random projects would also come to pass. Cher was the narrator of an audiobook that was released that month. The singer narrated 'The Ugly Duckling' for Windham Hill Records, set to music by Patrick Hall. It was the second book in an audiobook series titled 'Rabbit Ears: Storybook Classics.'

The first fragrance by the singer-turned-actress, Uninhibited, was first released that month. The idea started in January of that year when

Michael Stern, the chairman for Parfums Stern, approached Cher asking why her name wasn't on any products yet. He suggested a fragrance, an idea that appealed to Cher. The scent was developed by Francis Bocris. Uninhibited is described as an 'aldehydic floral fragrance for women,' combining cedar, musk, sandalwood, and vanilla elements. The crescent moon-shaped bottle topper was inspired by an earring she wore during the filming of *The Witches of Eastwick*. The line was later expanded to include other bath and body products.

Cher was also released in November 1987. The album included songs written by Desmond Child, Diane Warren, Richie Sambora, Jon Bon Jovi, and Michael Bolton. The album included a redone version of 'Bang Bang (My Baby Shot Me Down).' She made the interesting decision of dedicating the album to Sonny.

The first single was 'I Found Someone,' written by Bolton and Mark Mangold, which was the album's first track. Cher released a music video alongside the single and kept true to her previous vision. She starred in it alongside Camilletti, who happily obliged her. The single did well commercially, as well. It was her first to chart in nearly 15 years. *Cher* also charted, reaching No. 10 in the US and No. 15 in the UK.

Three days after the album was released, Cher agreed to appear on *Late Night with David Letterman* once again to promote both the album and *Moonstruck*. Joining her was Sonny, who had recently announced that he was entering the realm of politics, running for Mayor of Palm Springs, California. Sonny was also having a little musical fun, teasing some performances where Chas would step in to sing her mom's parts. The two joked around with Letterman, who asked if they'd be willing to sing together on the spot.

Chas had warned Cher backstage that it might happen, which she was aware of. She and Sonny had discussed the possibility beforehand. Cher admittedly had some reservations. For one, it had been six years since she had last sung in front of a live studio audience. It was also nine years since the two last publicly performed together.

The chemistry between them was truly heartwarming. Audiences watched two people perform a song that told the story of their young love. Now, it told the story of everything they'd overcome to get to that moment, both individually and as a duo, to get to this place – where they were friends who could pal around and were raising their now adult child together. Chas and Elijah were both there to witness the performance, which made Chas emotional. There was also an equally weepy Mary Whitaker, Sonny's wife, also watching from the area off-stage. Mary was seven months pregnant with the older of their two children. It was the first time she'd ever seen Sonny and Cher perform as a duo for herself. People both in the audience and working at *Late Night* were in tears watching the pair, each with a goofy smile plastered across their faces as they sang together.

At the end of the performance, Cher remembers Sonny looking a little teary-eyed. She was also fighting tears, but didn't want to be emotional about something so private on live late-night television. They got through the song, with neither knowing it would be the last time they'd ever perform it together.

As if that wasn't enough action, Cher enjoyed the premiere of *Moonstruck* on 18 December 1987. Camilletti was Cher's date for the evening, dutifully standing by as she posed with her co-stars. Also in attendance were Sonny and Chas, who were happy to root Cher on for the special occasion. Cher beamed and her confidence in the moment felt stronger than ever before.

Critics were taken with the film and with the warmth and laughter that Cher brought to the dark but dreamy romantic comedy. They particularly celebrated Cher for her performance as Loretta, particularly charmed by how funny she came across. It came without the edge that her public image always entailed, and it softened her to a new audience.

The press's interest in the relationship between Cher and Camilletti was growing, and admittedly, the twenty-something struggled with it. The star-studded event was full of celebrities and press, and while Camilletti posed with Cher, he appeared in the background of other photos from the evening looking uncomfortable. It wasn't Cher's moment in the spotlight that bothered him. Rather, it was what her continuously rising star meant for their lifestyle and ability to have the private slice of life their relationship once offered them.

Chapter Ten

1988–1989

Cher and Robert Camilletti would only spend more time in the spotlight in early 1988, with *Moonstruck* receiving rave reviews from both audiences and critics. It was the fifth highest-grossing film of the year of its release. Awards season kicked off on 23 January 1988 with the Golden Globe Awards. Cher was nominated for Best Performance in a Motion Picture – Comedy or Musical. The competition was stiff. The other nominees were Jennifer Grey for *Dirty Dancing*, Holly Hunter for *Broadcast News*, Diane Keaton for *Baby Boom*, and Bette Midler for *Outrageous Fortune*. Cher knew there was a lot of buzz around her performance, but she was still surprised to have won. The win once again ignited Oscar buzz around Cher, but her previous disappointments held her back from getting her own hopes up.

In a profile for the January–February 1988 issue of *Film Comment*, Cher appears to be a little wary of all the attention coming her way. She warns Camilletti that 'the press' is there and not to say anything, to which he jokes the same back to her. Later in the interview, she talks about hating how the press regards him as a 'bagel maker,' as if it were embarrassing to work a job outside of the entertainment industry. She noted he'd worked plenty of 'regular' jobs, and it's never been an issue for her, but the press regarded it as the single notable thing about the relationship, aside from his age.

January 1988 was also when Cher released the second single off her self-titled album, 'We All Sleep Alone.' Two versions of the music video were also released. The original video begins with Cher, dressed in all-black lingerie, rolling around a moodily decorated, canopy-draped bed. After she sings the first chorus, the focus changes. Cher has a silk robe on over her outfit, and the camera zooms out slightly to show Camilletti in the bed behind her, also dressed in all black. As the video progresses, scenes with Cher alone are inter-spliced with scenes of her and Camilletti kissing and feeling on each other. The second version of the video only contains a portion of the original, with scenes where a group of dancers masterfully move around each other as Cher works through the crowd.

Cher appeared on the February 1988 cover of *Cosmopolitan*, though she'd later admit that she didn't like the magazine's direction at that time. She was open, once again, about being ambivalent about the press after her recent experiences. She felt frustrated that her life was often boiled down to what she was wearing and who she was dating. Even in a moment when her career was getting so much attention, she felt her essence was constantly being diminished. Worse, she saw the toll it was taking on Camilletti to feel the same.

March involved a trip overseas to attend the British Academy Film Awards. The couple went to the event, where Cher was nominated for Best Actress in a Leading Role. She didn't take home the award, furthering her nerves for the Oscars just a week later.

Cher's big night came on 11 April 1988. Camilletti dressed in his finest to join Cher at the Academy Awards. Chas and Elijah also joined them on the major night. That fateful day started with a call from Sonny, who told his ex he was confident she'd take home the coveted award. He was awaiting a fateful day of his own, with the awards taking place just 24 hours before his mayoral election day. She equally assured him he would walk away with a big win.

As for many of her big moments, Cher turned to Bob Mackie for the perfect dress for the occasion. The showgirl-inspired gown was sheer black with rhinestone embellishments. The bust featured rhinestone fringe, while the jewels splayed out along the skirt, complementing her curves. Her hair was in a messy, curly updo, with a wrap-style headband that matched her gown. She stunned in the custom look, which fit like a glove.

The night started on a chaotic note, with the couple abandoning their ride to hustle on foot when they got stuck in traffic en route to the Shrine Auditorium. She appeared on stage as a presenter first, alongside Nicolas Cage to present the Best Supporting Actor Oscar to Sean Connery for *The Untouchables*. Ironically, Cher presented him with the same award at the BAFTAs the week before.

Once again, the competition was fierce. Cher faced Glenn Close for *Fatal Attraction*, Holly Hunter for *Broadcast News*, Sally Kirkland for *Anna*, and Meryl Streep for *Ironweed*. Cher described hearing herself announced as the winner, comparing it to a sort of out-of-body experience. She hugged Camilletti and her kids before making her way to the stage. When she shouted out Chas and Elijah in her acceptance speech, the camera panned to a truly excited pair looking very proud of their mom. Cher also thanked her fellow nominees and remarked on what being in their company did for her own self-esteem as a performer. She particularly shouted out Streep, who she called by her actual name, Mary Louise, as she always did.

After the win, Cher went to the media area for interviews, where she ran into Audrey Hepburn. Hepburn had been one of Cher's idols growing up, so she was elated to meet her and learn that Hepburn had been rooting for Cher to win the award. After she finished all the press, Cher deviated from what many winners did. Instead of relishing her win at the after-parties, she went home for a pizza party with the kids, Camilletti, Georgia, and Georganne.

In the days following the big event, Cher was horrified to realise some key figures she'd forgotten to thank. She took out a full-page ad in *Variety* to right her wrong, thanking Norman Jewison and John Patrick Shanley for helping make her dream of being an Oscar-winning actress come true.

Media attention for Cher would skyrocket in the months following her Oscar win, just as she was enjoying downtime with Camilletti and her children. She had a number of attempted break-ins at her Los Angeles and New York City residences. In Los Angeles, there was one man who would come up to her doorbell and ring it over and over all night long. Another kicked in her front door, then called her from jail when he was arrested for it.

The tabloids were frenzied with the thought that Cher was spending time away from the spotlight getting plastic surgery done to maintain her youthful looks. She even pursued legal action after one publication claimed she had ribs removed to shrink her frame.

Cher wasn't shy about admitting what procedures she had engaged in during her time in the spotlight. For one, she had gotten her nose done.

The more complicated procedures were the breast augmentation surgeries. It required correction after Cher gave birth to each of her children and again periodically to address scarring.

At the same time that her body was being picked apart, so was her family life. There were tabloid rumours of Cher having trouble in her relationship with Chas. What the public wasn't aware of was the rift between mother and child that came when Chas came out to Cher as a lesbian. Cher had an emotionally-charged reaction, not just because of the news itself. The mom's feelings were also hurt by her discovery that she was the last person close to Chas with whom they had this conversation. It would be some more years before Chas shared news of their sexuality publicly.

Camilletti was also getting more attention. This time, it was relevant, as he was beginning his own acting career. It increased the curiosity audiences had about him. He had been cast in *Loverboy* with Patrick Dempsey and Kate Jackson when he made headlines for a run-in with the paparazzi that got everyone buzzing.

It was late July 1988 when a car accident occurred between Camilletti and a freelance paparazzi photographer outside of Cher's Los Angeles home. Camilletti was driving Cher's Ferrari when he lost control of the car, swerving into her driveway to avoid photographers camped out in wait. Cher recalls the photographers frequently spending time hiding along the long driveway when there weren't police there to remind them it was private property. The paparazzi vehicles would sometimes surround her own, making it hard to get in and out without being photographed.

One photographer – freelancer Peter Brandt, associated with *Star Magazine* at the time – claimed that Camilletti tried to deliberately run him over with the vehicle. Camilletti, in turn, claimed that Brandt and another driver jumped out in front of the Ferrari. He swerved and crashed it while trying to avoid them. Camilletti admitted to going into the photographer's Honda and ripping out the phone in anger. The camera he was using was also damaged in the incident. Cher was shocked to learn that it was her boyfriend who was being arrested and charged with felony assault with a deadly weapon for the incident.

The reason for the fervent media interest at that particular time were rumours that Cher was pregnant and the two were preparing to marry in a secret ceremony. Neither of the two ideas was true, but the former was extracted from Cher being asked by Barbara Walters in an interview during Oscar week if she was open to having more children. Cher said that she would love to add to her family but noted that it might not be possible due to the difficult pregnancies she'd already experienced.

Camilletti was released that same day after Cher posted his £1,500 bail. While she awaited him in the police station, members of the media began to come into the Beverly Hills Police Department and surround her. The artist seemed to disassociate in the moment, solemnly awaiting Camilletti's release before a friend picked them up and drove them back home.

The next day, the couple had a press conference addressing how they felt the media's interest in and scrutiny of their relationship had gotten out of hand. Cher defended Camilletti against accusations he was a 'violent man.' He also spoke for himself, expressing that it was never his intention to harm anyone but only to avoid harm and harassment himself. He was happy to pay to replace the phone and camera that the photographer lost in the mishap and hoped the resolution would be sufficient to end the matter.

The couple also expressed their hopes that the media would understand that they could compel negative situations to occur by not maintaining basic respect for public figures' privacy. It was a subject Cher would revisit anytime she was asked about her relationship with Camilletti in the aftermath of the incident. The Los Angeles City Attorney's office dropped the charges from a felony to a misdemeanour count of reckless driving and damaging the photographer's personal property.

The strain the situation and ones like it were inflicting loomed over the now years-long relationship. Once again, it felt like the connection they'd created when no one knew or cared about their pairing was slipping further away from them with Cher's continued success. Still, the two tried to press forward and hold on to the things about their shared life that they did love.

In August, Cher enjoyed an official launch celebration for Uninhibited's expanded line. The release included a tour of personal appearances at high-end department stores. Not only would Cher appear, but a number of her one-of-a-kind Bob Mackie creations were also put on display for fans to admire. The first stop was New York City's Trump Tower, where Cher showed up in a Bob Mackie-designed, Cleopatra-inspired look, complete with an ornate headdress. Over 10,000 fans showed up, hoping for a glimpse of the star.

She donned the same Cleopatra look to celebrate the fragrance at a Studio 54 Halloween party with an astrology theme. The dress code was 'uninhibited black tie' or costume dress. Later in the night, she changed into a black mini-dress with lacy details. Cher was joined by a ton of celebrities at the event, from Lorne Michaels to Liza Minnelli to Barbara Walters to Billy Crystal. Though so many famous faces came out in support of her, Cher made sure to spend a lot of the night by Camilletti's side. His parents also joined them for the event. The event wasn't the only success. Uninhibited made approximately £11 million in sales in its first year.

In December 1988, Cher said goodbye to her unique, Egyptian-style home. After eight years there, she determined it was time to move on. She sold the seven-bedroom, seven-bathroom home to Eddie Murphy for £4.7 million.

Cher closed out 1988 by quietly beginning work on her nineteenth studio album, *Heart of Stone*. It was her second album on Geffen Records. Many of the contributors to *Cher* would return to work with the artist once again – Jon Bon Jovi, Diane Warren, Desmond Child, and Michael Bolton. The punchy rock tracks were paired with Cher's powerful vocals to deliver a collection of pop-rock hits. Further, they were songs that allowed Cher creative exploration in a way she hadn't felt comfortable exploring in some time.

As she worked on the album in late 1988 and early 1989, fans and culture critics alike were eager to see what Cher would pick as her next film project. The pressure around picking something to follow up her Academy Award-winning performance didn't make Cher eager, however.

At first, she decided to put a pause on making any decisions about movies until after she finished the album.

Not only was there a powerful team behind *Heart of Stone*, but the big names were willing to lend their talents. Bolton and Bonnie Tyler performed some background vocals that made a difference in the richness of those tracks. It was Warren who was responsible for what would be the album's biggest hit and one of the most beloved tracks in her career, 'If I Could Turn Back Time.'

The first single from the album was 'After All,' a duet with Peter Cetera, released in late February 1989. It was also featured in the film *Chances Are*, starring Robert Downey Jr. and Cybill Shepherd, which was released just a few weeks after the single. The album was filled with powerful ballads, so it's no surprise that Cher drew greatly from her relationship with Camilletti, to whom the album was dedicated.

On 18 March 1989, Cher appeared on an HBO special to benefit the homeless, called *Comic Relief III*. The star-studded benefit included Billy Crystal, Whoopi Goldberg, Martin Short, Arsenio Hall, Shelley Long, Gary Shandling, and Robin Williams.

'If I Could Turn Back Time,' was released in June 1989. While audiences were almost instantly enamoured with the song, the same can't be said for Cher. According to Warren, she had to 'beg' the artist to record the song because she didn't think it was a good fit for her. Luckily for everyone, Cher relented.

Cher went all out for the music video for 'If I Could Turn Back Time,' enlisting television director Marty Callner to help her bring her big vision to life. Cher wanted to film the music video aboard the USS Missouri, which would require the Navy's permission. The unlikely agreement came with the thought that the pop culture nod might help enrollment numbers. They filmed the video, which showed the star in her signature daring attire, wearing a Bob Mackie-designed fishnet body stocking with a one-piece ribbon-style bodysuit. There was a very special member of her backing band as well – son Elijah on guitar. Her audience was a crew of Navy officers in ceremonial dress.

The video proved to be very controversial when it first debuted, due in part to how skimpy Cher's outfit was. You could clearly see the singer's backside and the butterfly tattoo on it, causing outrage among viewers. There were immediate calls to ban the music video, with MTV choosing to only allow it to air after 9:00 pm. As a result, a new cut of the video was made that showed less of Cher's more revealing angles. Not only was Cher criticised for the outfit choice, but the Navy was criticised for allowing her to shoot the video aboard their ship and in front of the troops in her chosen attire. Ultimately, no members of the Navy were penalised in association with the music video shoot.

The success of the two singles had Cher thinking about touring for the first time in eight years. While she sought to go on a larger tour, she started with a mini-tour in August 1989. She played eight shows across the Northeast and Midwestern United States, and audiences were obsessed. She quickly raked in over £150,000 a night, inspiring plans for a larger tour across North America.

Before she would embark on that tour, Cher had a film to make. Three years after completing *Moonstruck*, Cher signed on to star in *Mermaids*. The 1960s-era family comedy-drama, based on the 1986 novel by Patty Dann, follows a flighty, fun single mom, Cher's Rachel Flax, as she relocates to a new town with daughters Charlotte, 15, and Kate, 9.

The film began with a bit of casting drama. British actress Emily Lloyd was originally cast in the role of Charlotte Flax. She turned down the lead in *Pretty Woman* in order to take on the role, only to later be fired in favour of Winona Ryder. When news of the move came out in the industry, rumours indicated that Cher demanded Ryder be cast because she looked like she could more plausibly pass as Cher's daughter and that Lloyd was let go as a result. However, the decision belonged to production, not the star, and Cher resented being the scapegoat. Lloyd ultimately sued and later settled with Orion Pictures over the matter. Cher was not involved in the legal matter.

That same month, Cher was set to perform at the MTV Video Music Awards, which aired live from Los Angeles on 6 September. Before she took the stage to perform 'If I Could Turn Back Time,' Andrew Dice Clay was brought out to introduce her. He was given three minutes to do a quick set before Cher came out, during which he let out enough expletives to earn himself a ban from MTV. When she was later asked about how she felt about it, Cher said she wasn't personally offended by the profanity. She pointed out that Elijah was a fan of Clay, and while she didn't love all his material, she understood how his humour appealed to some.

Principal photography on *Moonstruck* began in September 1989. The three-month shoot took place throughout Massachusetts, New Hampshire, and Rhode Island. Cher found that she quickly bonded with both Ryder and Christina Ricci, who was cast as Kate. True to her motherly character, Cher took both the young actresses under her wing.

In the years since, Ricci, in particular, has remembered the filming fondly, explaining that Cher was very patient with her. At 7 years old, she found Cher fascinating and asked a lot of questions about her process as an actress. Rather than get annoyed or bogged down by it, Cher was always happy to take time with her young co-star and answer any questions or concerns she had.

Production on the film was interrupted by Cher's health complications. At one point, she had to take a few days away while she searched for answers to what was happening with her Epstein-Barr diagnosis. While this was going on, the production experienced a shake-up when director Lasse Hallström was replaced by Frank Oz.

Oz's vision for the film was less feel-good quirky family moments and more drama. For example, he suggested the younger daughter character should be killed off to heighten the intensity of emotions. On set, emotions were plenty high. Cher remembers crying throughout filming and struggling as she fought fatigue.

After clashing with both Cher and Winona Ryder, Oz was eventually fired from the film. While the studio was hoping that wouldn't be the case, the contention came down to a place where Cher said if he continued with the film, she would not. Richard Benjamin was brought in to finish off the film.

Cher worried that *Mermaids* would be one of her last films, if not the last film. Between her health struggles and her age, she worried that her opportunities would be limited. She wondered where she fell in the paradigm of on-screen moms. In her mid-forties, she feared it wouldn't be long before the industry wrote her off as 'too old' to play a mom. Off-screen, Chas was in their twenties, and Elijah was navigating his own tenuous teen years.

Once filming concluded on *Mermaids*, Cher could hit the road once again on the Heart of Stone Tour. She rounded out 1989 preparing for the tour, where she would be joined by her 13-year-old son Elijah, who performed as a rhythm guitarist. As she prepared for the tour, her third single, 'Just Like Jesse James,' was released and quickly became a fan-favourite off the album.

She also came to accept that her relationship with Camilletti had come to an end. After the paparazzi run-in at Cher's Los Angeles home, he never felt comfortable living on the West Coast and remained in New York. Though Cher was able to make it work for a time, it became clear that the relationship had come to the end of the road. It was heartbreaking for Cher, who felt that her professional success had cost her a great love. She'd end the decade in an introspective place. While she enjoyed a lot of success, her journey was still continuing. She was finally able to recognise what her dedication cost her in other areas of her life. As determined as ever, she headed into the 90s prepared to do it all, regardless of who stood by her side while she did it.

Chapter Eleven

1990–1994

In January 1990, Cher released the titular single off of *Heart of Stone*. There was also a music video where Cher sang in a dark room with old photos and videos of herself projected on the walls. Once again, the single was well received, making it into the top 20 in the United States and the top 50 in the United Kingdom. With the success of 'Heart of Stone,' Cher became the first female artist to have a Billboard Hot 100 single in four separate decades.

The tour was set to pick back up in early March, but was forced to postpone dates when Cher's rehearsals were interrupted by what she believed to be a bad bout of the flu. The tour's schedule was thrown off, leading it to start toward the end of the month instead.

Once it was up and running, the tour would continue through August 1990. Critics had mixed reviews of the tour. While some enjoyed the fact that the show contained elements of her Vegas act and, in some ways, called back to it, others felt Cher was trying to capitalise on nostalgia instead of moving forward. The set list combined Cher's new big hits with some of her time-honoured favourites. Later in the year, the show would go global.

It was on her 'Heart of Stone' tour that Cher started inviting local chapters of the Children's Craniofacial Association to attend her shows. The kids would get to hang out, play games, eat pizza, and have fun with Cher and her crew. Not only would Cher meet the kids, but she would spend time with their parents and caretakers, listening to them recount the struggles they faced.

Unbeknownst to most, Cher was facing her own health and wellness struggles. She often felt sluggish and like her immune system couldn't keep up with her schedule. Though she'd press on, she was frequently looking for ways to manage the symptoms of the general malaise that she couldn't seem to shake. Cher was always open to different ideologies. In that openness, she tried homeopathic treatments. She also worked with a dietician to fine-tune her nutritional plan to provide her body with as much power as she could.

The speculation about Cher's health, her appearance, and the ever-swirling rumours of plastic surgery led Cher to admit that one of her procedures hadn't gone quite as planned. Her breast surgery was so disastrous that she reportedly had to have two subsequent surgeries to correct what had been done.

Inspired by her health journey and in keeping with the trending interest in celebrity health and fitness, Cher started working on writing *Forever Fit: The Lifetime Plan for Health, Fitness, and Beauty* alongside Dr. Robert Haas. She had starred in different health club commercials throughout the 1980s, but now she was doubling down on her commitment and finding her own way.

During this time, Cher was quietly dating Richie Sambora, whom she'd known from their work on *Cher* together. After catching some Bon Jovi dates, the two got to talking more and started seeing each other. The two enjoyed a special connection but had trouble getting quality time together because of their busy schedule. When they could get together, sparks flew. Though the fling only lasted a few months, the two enjoy a continued friendship and mutual respect for one another that continues to this day.

After finishing the North American leg of the tour, Cher had just over a month before taking the show to Europe for a month, then Australia. While in Australia that November, Cher continued to work with organisations like the Children's Craniofacial Association and the International Craniofacial Foundation to bring those with craniofacial conditions out to her show. Overseas, Cher would discover that there were fewer options for surgical correction than in the United States. As a result, the differences they lived with and the complications that stemmed from them were that much greater.

During her time in Australia, Cher met Marie Jatejic, a 13-year-old girl living with neurofibromatosis. In Australia, the sweet teenage girl would continue to grow up with her differences. Her story and demeanour, in particular, resonated with Cher and made her want to help. Though it wouldn't be immediate, Jatejic's impact on her began in that moment and would later lead to a life-changing moment for the both of them.

In addition to the concert dates on the tour, Cher also performed nearly a full concert at the Adelaide Formula One Grand Prix. In exchange, Cher was celebrated not just by the crowd but by the city as well. Mayor Steve Condous presented her with a key to the city as a thank-you for being the first international music act to perform at the event.

It was during press interviews for *Mermaids* that Cher opened up about one of the ways she was working to improve her health amid continuing struggles – going to therapy. She had quietly undertaken the practice for two years before speaking about it in a November 1990 *Vanity Fair* profile. She revealed it helped her deal with a lot of the more complicated emotions that came with living life in the spotlight.

Cher was also open about drawing a lot of inspiration for the role from her mom, Georgia. She was open about the fact that the two weren't speaking at the time she was making the film, but the parallels between fiction and the reality of the three-woman family growing up were uncanny. Georgia wasn't upset or insulted by the comparison. In fact, she enjoyed the film, which she was able to see ahead of its premiere on 14 December 1990.

A week before the film's premiere, the soundtrack for *Mermaids* was released. Cher contributed two songs to the soundtrack. 'The Shoop Shoop Song (It's In His Kiss),' which was originally recorded by Betty Everett, was by far the breakout hit. It hit number one in the UK and peaked at number 33 on the Billboard Hot 100. For Cher, it was her first UK number one since 'I Got You Babe.' In addition to the catchy, nostalgic tune, there was also a music video that featured Ricci and Ryder as her backup singers. The sweet 60s moment is wrapped up at the end of the video, when it switches from black and white to colour and shows the three in leather jackets, spray painting the wall of an alley. Cher also recorded Barbara Lewis' 'Baby I'm Yours' for the soundtrack. Though that single was released first, it never took off the same way 'The Shoop Shoop Song' did.

In addition to continued press for *Mermaids*, Cher was also working on her twentieth studio album, *Love Hurts*. It would be the last album she'd make with Geffen Records, the completion of her four-year deal. Once again, she would work with John Kalodner, Diane Warren, and Desmond Child. 'The Shoop Shoop Song' would appear on the European release of the album, though it was only on the *Mermaids* soundtrack in the United States.

The album also featured three other covers. Cher took on 'Save Up All Your Tears,' which had been previously recorded by both Bonnie Tyler and Robin Beck. She also sang Kiss's 'A World Without Heroes,' and Judy Collins' 'Fires of Eden.' This collection of songs also saw Cher revisit her own 1975 track, 'Love Hurts,' reimagining it for the sound and vibe of the album, which would hold the same name.

In January 1991, as she worked on the album, she started promoting *Forever Fit*, which was published that month. Cher appeared on the cover of the 21 January 1991 issue of *People Magazine*. Cher was upfront about the fact that making adjustments for a healthier lifestyle was easy for her because there were some accommodations she had already been making for years. She rarely drank and quit smoking. She wasn't interested in drugs. She seldom ate red meat and wasn't into coffee.

Cher admitted her struggles came from her busy lifestyle, where it wasn't always easy to make the best choices for herself. When recording an album or spending hours on a film shoot, for example, she'd fall into the habit of relying on junk food to get a quick bite in amid a chaotic day. She also said her eating habits fluctuated along with her emotional state.

That summer, Cher sat down for an interview with CBS's Steve Kmetko, where he drew parallels between her career foundation and trajectory and Madonna's. Cher wasn't snarky but even-keeled and sincere in her reaction, saying there were things she admired about her fellow singer, but also things she didn't like.

Cher went on to explain that she'd gotten to know Madonna while she was with Sean Penn and that she witnessed her being unkind to people around her on several occasions. Thus began what the public perceived as a feud between the two. In reality, they were pretty indifferent toward each other, with this only coming up from time to time in media-related moments.

On 4 February 1991, CBS aired Cher's live music video, initially titled *Cher…at the Mirage*. The special was made up of footage from Cher's performances at the Mirage Hotel in Las Vegas in 1990.

In the spring, Cher still had Marie Jatejic on her mind. She got the teen's contact information and spoke with her and her mom once again. She was able to get photos of Marie that were then sent to a Texas hospital that specialised in craniofacial surgeries. They made a plan to help Marie out. Cher offered to be by Marie's side during the surgery. At one point, Cher got closer and asked questions about the surgery, why more couldn't be done, and what the plan would be. The doctors were patient in explaining themselves to the star.

Promotional work hit double duty in May when 'Love and Understanding' was released. The music video was kept simple, showing Cher and her band rehearsing the song inter-spliced with a performance of it. It would hit the top 10 in the UK and Austria, landing in the top 20 in the US, Canada, and Germany. Other singles from the album would struggle upon its release on 18 June 1991.

That summer, Cher released *CherFitness: A New Attitude*. It was her first workout video, split into three modular sections depending on the difficulty you're prepared for. The three sections are 'Step Workout,' 'Healthy Back and Abdominals,' and 'Hips, Bottoms, and Thighs.' There was a soundtrack to go along with the workout, which included 'Love and Understanding.' The workout video would sell over 1.5 million worldwide in its first year.

That summer, Cher also shot her cameo in *The Player*, which would be released in April 1992. She did the bit as a favour to Robert Altman, whom she frequently credited as the reason she had a film career at all. She plays herself, walking the red carpet at an event that asks guests to only dress in black and white. In her typical fashion, Cher shows up in a stunning ruby red gown by Bob Mackie with Peter Gallagher on her arm. The only words she can be heard saying are, 'Are we having fun yet?'

In the autumn of 1991, Cher did a number of shows in Atlantic City in celebration of *Love Hurts*. The explosive response encouraged her to take the tour international. She planned tour dates for the rest of the United States and Europe throughout 1992. Thus, the Love Hurts tour was born.

While on the East Coast for those shows, Cher also made a number of other promotional appearances. In late October, Cher appeared on *The Sally Jessy Raphael Show,* giving what would be one of the most memorable interviews in her career. The two women talked frankly about body issues ahead of Cher's demonstration of her workout routine. Cher also opened up about her upbringing, with Georganne and Paulette later joining her on stage. The four women were discussing relationships and Cher's 'type' when Raphael asked, 'Are men important?' to which Cher asked, 'For what?' The audience burst into laughter and commentary.

On Halloween 1991, Cher performed on *The Late Show with David Letterman* in all her big, orange-haired glory. By this point, the artist had gotten a reputation for her memorable appearances on the show, and this one was no different. The two had a particularly flirty banter throughout the appearance, flustering Letterman at times. In addition to their chat, she performed 'Save Up All Your Tears.'

In February 1992, Cher attended the Council of Fashion Designers of America Awards in New York City. She wasn't one of the guests of honour, however. The fashionable artist was there to present the award for Best Accessories Design to Chrome Hearts. During interviews for the event, reporters eagerly pressed to learn the artist's next move, but she remained tight-lipped.

That same month, Cher sat down for an interview with Maury Povich on *The Maury Povich Show.* While the two talked about Cher's headline-making life, the segment focused on Cher's continued work with children with craniofacial differences. During the show, she pledged over £340,000 to the cause.

Cher left the US in March 1992. She arrived in Germany in early April. There, she saw doctors in relation to her continued illness from CFS. She continued to try to balance diet, exercise, and rest to keep her body in optimal shape. She also tried different treatments and medications during her time in Europe, taking advantage of what they offered there that couldn't be found in the US.

Inspired by the success of *CherFitness: A New Attitude*, Cher released a second workout video, *CherFitness: Body Confidence*. Instead of emulating Cher's personal workout, this video was designed to put Cher and participants at home to the test. This time, the workouts focus on dance and resistance bands. The upbeat routine, once again, came with an equally fun soundtrack. This time, Cher used 'If I Could Turn Back Time' for the occasion.

The public was admittedly confused by Cher's turn into the fitness world. What they didn't know was that the star was continuing to experience complications from chronic Epstein-Barr virus, which was renamed Chronic Fatigue Syndrome (CFS). In trying to honour her body's needs, Cher was trying to work less. Still, she needed to make money.

Even though Cher was moving in different spaces, there was no questioning her continued impact. Her life still continued to make headlines left and right. She was referenced frequently in pop culture, like when she was drawn into the popular 1992 animated series *Tiny Toons*.

In June 1992, *Cher...at the Mirage* was released on VHS, this time titled *Cher...at the Mirage*. The timing was perfect, with Cher returning to the US at that time. Her first chunk of performances upon her return were in Las Vegas.

Cher made an unexpected cameo on *Saturday Night Live* on 26 September 1992. The moment came during 'Weekend Update.' Adam Sandler's Opera Man character was performing a recap of all the newsy events they'd missed over the summer break. When he finished his song, Kevin Nealon gave him a standing ovation. The camera then pans into the crowd and shows Cher and Nicolas Cage doing the same.

That same month, Michelle Pfeiffer did an interview with *Rolling Stone* touching on many subjects, one of which is a project in development with Cher. The two wanted to develop a film about an actress, a tabloid editor, and a writer trying to break into entertainment journalism, tentatively titled *Tabloid*. Both had firsthand experiences about the lack of privacy that came with public life and wanted to address it as only they knew how.

Around this time, there were also rumours that Cher was working on another project. It was said that she wanted to transform *The Enchanted Cottage* into a musical for both stage and screen. Cher purchased the rights to the 1945 film in the late 1970s and compared her vision for it to *A Star Is Born* or *Saturday Night Fever*. Sadly, neither *Tabloid* nor the *Enchanted Cottage* remake projects ever came to fruition.

The entertainer enjoyed more time on the East Coast after that. Her remaining tour dates had her in Atlantic City, then New York City, to conclude the 'Heart of Stone' tour. In November in the UK, she released *Greatest Hits: 1965–1992*, a compilation album looking back at her career to that point. The album also included three new releases – a cover of Maxine Brown's 'Oh No Not My Baby,' 'Whenever You're Near,' and a live recording of the cover of Jimmy Cliff's 'Many Rivers to Cross.' It debuted at number one and topped the UK Albums Chart for seven non-consecutive weeks. The collection charted on the top 10 in several different countries across the continent.

In late April 1993, with no fanfare or forewarning, Cher made the decision to travel to Armenia. Over the years, a number of Armenian organisations reached out to Cher about travelling to the area and learning more about her ancestry. Since her Armenian heritage was through her dad, Cher was resistant. She felt almost like a fraud trying to claim a place she had no ties to.

Cher claimed that she was on her way to the Brit Awards when she decided to skip the event and travel to Armenia instead. At the time, the country was in a terrible state. Electricity, gas, and water in the area were limited in the middle of the Nagorno-Karabakh conflict, which had officially begun earlier that year but dated back to differences years in the making. Many people weren't aware of Cher's visit as a result.

Joining her on the trip were Paulette and Robert Camilletti, who had started hanging out with Cher platonically. Though she didn't plan the trip very far in advance, she came with what the area needed in their time of struggle. She travelled on a cargo plane, arranged by the United Armenian Fund, 45 tons of supplies and equipment needed in the area including medical supplies and books, as well as candy and toys for the children suffering. Cher and her team quickly reached out to sponsors to help fill the plane before their hasty departure from London to Armenia.

While there, Cher saw firsthand the vast areas that were littered with tree stumps after families without heat were forced to burn wood from their homes and local trees in order to make it through the harsh cold of winter. She was introduced to different families, children in orphanages, and professionals working in the area, each of whom shared stories of devastation with her. Cher was stricken by the fact that none of these people appeared desperate. Rather, they were openly struggling but pushing through. Their resilience was inspiring to her.

It turns out Cher wasn't entirely detached from her Armenian heritage after all. She learned a few words in the language and educated herself on the international conflict, sharing her opinions in her signature direct way when meeting students at Yerevan State University. When reporters asked about her time in the area, she likened it to Audrey Hepburn's work with UNICEF, in that a celebrity bringing attention to a cause could make a difference. She didn't want to be the face of the matter; however, she was eager to bring others with influence and resources into the fold to make a difference that would be palpable in these people's day-to-day lives.

There was some criticism of the trip, however, from people who questioned what it achieved. Some people thought Cher was just looking for positive press or relevance and wasn't coming from a genuine place. A tremendous amount of photos were taken of the trip, which furthered the idea that it was for some press gain. People pointed to photos of Cher in the courtyard of the Yerevan museum, draped across a decapitated statue of Lenin in a series of shots, as inappropriate and proof she wasn't taking the situation seriously. On the trip itself, Cher told the press her goals weren't political but to bring attention to the area while also helping the people feel a little better and live a little easier, if only for a few days.

Despite some initial hesitance, Cher also agreed to meet with Armenian President Levon Ter-Petrosian before her departure. Cher was concerned her interaction would appear political and didn't believe her feelings and views would align with the leader's. She had a more favourable opinion of him after the meeting than she did going into it, having respect for some of the life experiences he shared during their conversation.

Cher continued to struggle with her health in 1993, finding different ways to make money. One of those opportunities came from her friend Lori Davis, who asked Cher to promote her haircare line. Cher claimed she did use and enjoy the products and agreed on that basis. Her agent wasn't thrilled with the idea of her participating in an infomercial, but Cher didn't feel like she was in a position to be picky about work.

The star agreed to it, not realising how many people would make her the butt of their jokes. She also didn't realise how many times a day the ad would air, which further embarrassed her. People laughed at her and proclaimed her acting career had to be over for her to do that. The late-night hosts, including none other than David Letterman, mocked her mercilessly. On the 8 May 1993 episode of *Saturday Night Live*, Christina Applegate and Chris Farley imitated Cher and Davis in the infomercial practically frame for frame in a skit called 'Focus on Beauty II.'

That October, Cher travelled to Paris Fashion Week for the filming of *Ready to Wear* (aka *Prêt-à-Porter*). Another mutual favour between Cher and Robert Altman, the film featured an ensemble cast who were part filming, part enjoying the actual essence of the week.

In the autumn of 1993, Cher also agreed to an unusual collaboration request. Geffen Records was working on *The Beavis and Butt-Head Experience*, a compilation of songs partially sung by the animated duo. Not only did Cher agree to record a rock version of 'I Got You Babe,' but she agreed to film a music video to commemorate it as well. The music video, released in November 1993, got a lot of airplay on MTV as fans appreciated Cher's ability to laugh at herself.

January 1994 presented Cher with a unique experience she was excited to take on. She was invited by Miles Copeland III, a renowned entertainment executive, to be part of a songwriters' workshop at a castle in France. The workshops took place periodically and were attended by artists including Carole King, Jeff Beck, Jon Bon Jovi, and more. She wrote some poetry there, including a poem about Kurt Cobain that became 'The Fall (Kurt's Blues).

Other poetry Cher worked on, as well as collaborative work with singer/songwriter Bruce Roberts, came together in an album she'd call *Not.com.merical*. She recorded the songs, which had a darker theme, with the help of David Letterman's CBS Orchestra. The album was recorded in New York in just a week's time, but Cher's label at Warner Music wasn't interested in the album. She shelved it, but it wouldn't see the light of day until almost a decade later.

Cher received the honour of being imitated on the 19 March 1994 episode of *Saturday Night Live*. Cast member Sarah Silverman portrayed the artist in the 'Rockers to Help Explain Whitewater' sketch. While some celebrities would get upset about being portrayed on the show, especially if they had appeared on it, Cher was always a good sport about imitations of her, even when they weren't entirely flattering. Her good-natured sense of humour and ability to laugh at herself has earned her a lot of respect in Hollywood circles throughout her career.

Ironically, Cher had been on TV that same day. She performed 'The Shoop Shoop Song' alongside Jools Holland on the UK game show, 'Don't Forget Your Toothbrush.' Cher looked incredible in a white peasant-style babydoll dress paired with thigh-high boots. Her comfort in performing indicated she was trying to see what her limits were as she continued to grapple with chronic fatigue syndrome.

In May 1994, Cher celebrated her 48th birthday and found herself at a crossroads. She was experiencing a bout of feeling unwell because of CFS, combined with menopause. While some people speculated this would be the end of Cher's career, she was in no way giving up. She'd experienced enough times being down to know it was only a matter of time and hard work until she was back on top again, and she was willing to put in both in spades.

While regrouping and figuring out what's next, Cher sold both her Malibu and New York City homes. This time, she hunkered down in Aspen, Colorado, where she felt at peace. On one hand, the slower pace of life during this time frightened Cher, who was used to going nonstop from a young age. On the other hand, it was a welcome period of rest where she got to try new things and appreciate time with the people she cared about.

It wasn't all peace, however. Cher also reignited her 'feud' with Madonna in 1994. In a *Los Angeles Times* interview about the venture, Cher was asked if she thought she would be starting a larger Gothic trend, to which she replied with a barb about Madonna's trendsetter status. People were surprised at the unsolicited stab at Madonna.

Cher spent the summer of 1994 working on a new film. She signed on to Chazz Palminteri's *Faithful* in the leading role of Margaret. The depressed housewife is contemplating ending her own life until she finds out her cheating husband (Ryan O'Neal) has a hit out on her. She befriends her would-be assassin (Palminteri). Filming of the dark comedy took place between New York City and upstate New York from July through late September. The expectation was for the film to come out in early 1995, but that changed when the production company went bankrupt.

In late 1994, Cher released the first in a series of home decor and fashion catalogues. The items featured in *Sanctuary* were by Cher's favourite artisans and designers. All shared a 'spiritual' and 'Gothic' theme that was far from what was popular in the mainstream at that time. Still, it quickly developed a niche following that shows appreciation for the unusual pieces to this day.

The business venture was another way for Cher to bring in money without the gruelling schedule of a tour or film shoot. Those creative impulses weren't dormant in the creator, however. Cher was eager to get back out there and was always planning on the best way to go about it when the time was right.

The end of 1994 was quiet for Cher, but it was a restorative time she needed. Going into the latter half of the decade, Cher would face highs and lows more extreme than any she had up until this point.

Chapter Twelve

1995–1997

After a quieter period in Cher's career, 1995 marked a resurgence. She began the year in the studio, teaming up with Chrissie Hynde, Neneh Cherry, and Eric Clapton for a good cause. In support of Comic Relief and celebration of Red Nose Day, the artists recorded that year's Comic Relief single, a cover of The Judds's 'Love Can Build a Bridge.' The single was released on 6 March 1995 and was well received around the UK, going number one on the UK Singles Chart for a week. It was Cher's second UK number one hit.

The mid-1990s featured numerous rereleases of Cher's previous works on CD. Warrior and Take Me Home were combined into *The Casablanca Years*, released in 1994. In 1995, *Half Breed* had its turn, rereleased early in the year and bringing some of Cher's greatest mid-1970s tracks to new audiences.

After years of resting and recuperating from the impacts of chronic fatigue syndrome on her life, Cher was ready to get back out there. She signed with Warner Music UK's WEA label. Once the deal was done, she began work on her twenty-first studio album, *It's a Man's World*.

Cher spent a good amount of time in the UK while working on the album, which was recorded at Elephant Studios in London. The album was comprised of predominantly tracks traditionally written and sung by men, offering the woman's perspective on them. Like the covers, the original tracks also played with soulful pop, rock, and R&B roots. There, she worked on the second and final edition of her catalogue, *Sanctuary*, appearing on the cover in a full chain-mail outfit and headdress.

Making the album wasn't easy. Cher found herself facing nerves similar to those she had in her early days with Sonny. It had been over five years since her last album, and she had concerns about getting it right. After her experiences with infomercial backlash and battling Chronic Fatigue

Syndrome (CFS), Cher also wanted to make sure she was devoting her energy to the right places. Though she briefly questioned whether music still felt like one of those places, after some time in the studio, she found her stride once again.

In the autumn of 1995, Cher began promotional work for the album. She performed on *Top of the Pops,* channelling Elvis Presley as she performed the first single, 'Walking in Memphis.' The song was released on 13 October in Europe, Australia, and Canada. The performance drew from the music video Cher recorded for the single, where she also dressed as Presley. The song would go gold in the UK, peaking at number eleven on the charts there. It would also chart in other countries throughout Europe, reaching the top twenty in several areas.

On 6 November, *It's a Man's World* was released in Europe, Canada, Oceania, and Japan. Critics in those areas were fans of the album and although it wasn't a massive hit, it was well-received across the board. In the UK, it debuted at number twenty-eight on the Albums Chart.

When Cher wasn't busy with music, she had a new home project. After remodelling and selling 18 different houses, Cher set her sights on a Miami Beach property. Cher's time in Europe was influential to her vision for the home. As always, Cher was willing to get hands-on about the work where needed, putting in countless hours in the weeks leading up to Christmas 1995 to get the house ready so she could celebrate with her family and friends there.

The second and arguably biggest single from the new album, 'One by One,' was released on 6 January 1996 in the UK. Cher co-wrote the song with Anthony Griffiths. Different versions of the song, which was mixed twice, became popular. The UK version of the track was produced by Stephen Lipson, featuring a rock and soul feel. 'One by One' was particularly well-received in the UK, topping the Airplay chart at number two and the Singles chart at number seven.

It's a Man's World wasn't released in the US until 25 June 1996. In the US, the lead-up to the album was marked by the release of 'One by One.' Sam Ward produced a more R&B-aligned track compared to the UK mix. It was released on 21 May. A number of other remixes of the song, many of which were dance-based, would follow and become popular in different areas. The song also entered the top ten on Billboard's US Adult Contemporary, US Dance Club Songs, and US Dance Singles Sales charts.

A day after the US release of *It's a Man's World,* a Dateline NBC interview where Cher sat down with Jane Pauley aired. It would become another truly iconic interview in Cher's career. The two women began by discussing the album and then moved on to relationships. Cher explained that her penchant for younger men isn't intentional. Her experience had been that younger men were less intimidated by everything that came with her being who she was. She also noted that her unpredictable nature made her less appealing to older men, though she'd be open to dating them.

Cher also spoke about her dating philosophy. She talked about her previous comments about finding a male companion to be a 'luxury' rather than a necessity. As before, she clarified that she didn't mean she held disdain for or animosity toward men. She recalled a conversation with Georgia where the well-meaning mom told her, 'You know sweetheart, one day you should settle down and marry a rich man,' to which Cher replied, 'Mom, I am a rich man.' She asserted that perspective made relationships richer because they were a choice rather than a crutch. The quip would be quoted back countless times throughout Cher's career, becoming a favourite media moment.

During the interview, Cher also discussed how chronic fatigue syndrome had affected her career. The piece noted she turned down roles in *Thelma and Louise* and *War of the Roses.* She noted how the infomercials seemed to have wiped out everything she'd done to the point, but she was no stranger to starting over.

Cher released a second single from *It's a Man's World* before the album's US release, 'Not Enough Love in the World.' She would continue to promote the album throughout the year, with two more singles released – 'The Sun Ain't Gonna Shine Anymore' and 'Paradise Is Here.'

In June 1996, Cher would perform 'One by One' during her set at the KIIS and Unite IV concert at the Irvine Meadows Amphitheatre in Irvine, California. Cher looked simple but striking in jeans and a tank top as she performed at the concert, benefiting the Pediatric AIDS Foundation.

That month, Cher also paid a visit to *The Late Show with David Letterman*. Their first interview in five years began with Letterman introducing Cher to perform a track off the album when Howard Stern, dressed as Cher came out and started to perform. Cher herself interrupts the performance and jokes with them both.

The two began by chatting about her time in London before Cher gave Letterman a hard time about not asking her any 'real questions.' They moved on to tattoos and dating, with Letterman in disbelief that Cher wasn't romantically involved with someone. They broke for Cher to perform 'One by One.' At the end of the performance, Cher joked like she was going to kiss Letterman. He turned around and kissed her, then grabbed her butt as the audience gasped. She returned the favour, hysterically laughing as the appearance concluded.

Cher appeared on *The Rosie O'Donnell Show* in July 1996. The two shared many laughs as they browsed items from *Sanctuary*. Cher also talked about her relationships with both David Letterman and Sonny in her signature manner – light-hearted but blunt.

This year also saw Cher shift her focus back to acting as well. In April 1996, *Faithful* finally hit theatres. Though the film wasn't a box office success by any stretch, the dark comedy was received by audiences as a hate-it-or-love-it kind of film.

She also faced a new professional challenge: directing. Demi Moore teamed up with HBO after years of shopping around her three-segment film about abortion. Her team approached Cher, offering a part in *If These Walls Could Talk*. Cher was taken with the concept and wanted to be involved on a deeper level, saying she would act in the film if she could also direct a segment. Moore served as executive producer and Nancy Savoca as director, with Cher ultimately getting her wish to direct a segment.

The film follows three women in the same home, living in different decades and facing unplanned pregnancies. The decisions and options at their disposal were different from 1952 to 1974 to 1996. The goal of the project was to open audiences' eyes to how and why women come to the conclusion abortion, presented without passing judgment.

Cher felt the film was important and took the responsibility of directing very seriously. Her segment featured a woman, played by Anne Heche, who goes to an abortion clinic and finds it surrounded by protestors who don't agree with the practice. Cher played her doctor.

She spoke with concerned actresses Heche and Jada Pinkett, who had reservations about the script. Cher played the middleman, appealing to the studio to make changes and working to find a writer who could get it right. The studio was unsure of her moves at first, but gave her the space to shine, warming up to her approach as they became more familiar with it.

Cher tried to be very hands-on and consider every set experience with a director she'd ever had. In her case, it was a history filled with highs and lows, giving her a lot of modelling of what she did and did not want to do. She focused on the positive, drawing from her relationships with Robert Altman, Norman Jewison, and Mike Nichols. She tried to make decisions from an informed and fair place, which allowed her to form good relationships across the production.

Of course, the subject matter also weighed on her. It was so important to get these stories right. It also had her revisiting her own abortion experience from before her pregnancy with Elijah. The experience was important to the process for Cher, as it always had been in music. She wanted to make sure that she was clear and her actors were comfortable and on the same page.

After nine days of filming, the editing process began. Cher was meticulous in watching every frame of the film. She wanted to make sure that audiences felt the weight of these performances the same way she did, watching them play out, take after take, day after day. She was thrilled to hand in her cut and felt her ego a little bruised when they came back with feedback. She digested it and moved forward, making adjustments while still staying true to her vision.

Cher kept her head down and was busy at work as she celebrated another milestone in 1996 – turning 50. She was asked about the moment in the press for *It's a Man's World* and *If These Walls Could Talk*. Cher was true to her belief that age didn't matter. She was putting in the work to take care of herself, arguably more than at any time in her life before. As a result, she found herself in a place of relative peace. Her relationship with her children, now adults, was stable. She wasn't in a romantic relationship but found work, friendships, and family made it so there was no void to fill.

Audiences first experienced the finished product at the Toronto Film Festival on 18 September 1996. During press for the film that day, Cher told the *Manila Standard* that she was proud of the 'courage' everyone involved with the film had in keeping it true to life.

That same month, Cher was one of the celebrities featured on Kid Rhino's record, *For Our Children Too*. The artists featured on the album sang classic children's songs and nursery rhymes. The group included Elton John, Celine Dion, Natalie Cole, Faith Hill, and more. Cher sang 'A Dream Is A Wish Your Heart Makes' from the beloved *Cinderella*. Profits from the album benefited the Pediatric AIDS Foundation.

Cher took on another project in 1996 that saw her exploring a new territory – video games. In 1996, Cher was one of several artists and musicians who lent their talents to a video game called *9: The Last Resort*. The game was made by Tribeca Interactive, with Robert DeNiro as one of the game's producers. The point-and-click adventure puzzle game has players navigating different musically-related challenges. Characters in the game were voiced by the who's who of Hollywood. James Belushi, Christopher Reeve, Ellen DeGeneres, Anne Heche, Tress MacNeille, Steven Tyler, and Joe Perry all participated. Cher voiced Isadora, the fortune teller who narrated game menus.

On 13 October 1996, *If These Walls Could Talk* premiered on HBO. The film was well-received by both critics and audiences. Viewers and film pros alike were impressed by the balance of care and reality when telling these abortion stories.

That same month, *Architectural Digest* did a feature on her lavish home in Miami Beach, an over 900 sqm home dedicated to her interest in ancient civilisations's styles. By the time the feature was printed, however, the home was no longer hers. Cher had started to enjoy the home earlier in the year, only to discover the home was on the route of a sightseeing boat tour. The lack of privacy led her to sell the property, relocating to another Miami Beach property that was less accessible after the fact.

If These Walls Could Talk was nominated for three Golden Globes. The film itself was nominated for Best Miniseries or Motion Picture Made for Television. Demi Moore was nominated for Best Actress in a Miniseries or Motion Picture Made for Television. Cher was nominated for Best

Supporting Actress in a Miniseries or Motion Picture Made for Television. The ceremony was held on 19 January 1997. Sadly, the film didn't take home awards for any of the three nominations. Still, the legacy of the film's significance has carried farther than any formal accolade could.

The following month, Cher was one of countless celebrities who came out for a special celebration in honour of Elizabeth Taylor's 65th birthday party. *Happy Birthday Elizabeth: A Celebration of Life* was a televised special looking back at the star's many accomplishments on screen and stage. Cher introduced a segment championing Taylor's work on advancing research and resources for those impacted by HIV and AIDS.

Cher made a guest appearance on *The RuPaul Show*, where she continued to promote *It's a Man's World*. The two talked about the album, with her performing 'Paradise is Here.' Cher even performed alongside RuPaul as he performed his best Cher impersonation as he lip-synched 'The Shoop Shoop Song.'

There was another project that had Cher looking both forward and backwards. She began work on a series of autobiographical essays called *The First Time*. It looked back at some of the most pivotal moments in Cher's life and career and all the firsts that brought her to where she was.

In September 1997, Cher was one of the audience guests on *An Audience with Elton John*. She kicked off the question portion of the program. The ease between the two audiences illustrated just how long they've known each other and how comfortable they were with one another.

That same month, Cher appeared as a keynote speaker at the 1997 Parents, Families, and Friends of Lesbians and Gays (PFLAG) National Convention in Orlando, Florida. It had been nearly two years since Chas came out publicly, working in LGBTQ advocacy. Cher was fiercely supportive and also used her platform to further the messaging where she could.

In December 1997, Cher returned to the Met Gala. It was the first time she'd attended since 1985. The year's festivities were tinged with sadness. The year's gala was held in honour of Gianni Versace, who had been gunned down outside his Miami mansion that July.

For the occasion, Cher wore a black, one-shoulder leather Versace evening gown from the F/W 1997 runway collection. The dress had a blue crystal cross emblazoned across half the dress's torso. Cher paired it with a blazer and her hair down for an easy-going look that verged from her flashy roots at the fashion event. It struck the perfect balance between respect and chic needed for the somewhat sombre celebration.

Cher was already friendly with Gianni's sister and right-hand woman, Donatella Versace, at this point. Gianni's murder was a shock to the fashion community, as well as the LGBTQ community. Cher was happy to lend her support, even posing for a photo with Donatella and Madonna, proving once again there was no real heart behind the supposed feud between artists.

There was a quiet close to 1997 for Cher. While she had her mind on her next album, Chas was busy at work on their new job as a consultant on *Ellen*. Elijah was toying around with a musical project. Everyone was preoccupied with what was ahead of them. Little did Cher know that she was gearing up for one of her most transformative periods of all time.

Chapter Thirteen

1998–1999

Cher began 1998 by travelling to London. She was there to work on her album and also for an appearance. She was due to perform at a Harrods location as part of a sales promotion. Known for loving to shop, Cher was happy to take on the gig. It was there that she received a life-changing phone call she was never expecting. On 5 January 1998, Sonny Bono died in a skiing accident that occurred during a family vacation in South Lake Tahoe, California. Sonny was 62 years old.

Bono was with wife Mary and their children, 9-year-old Chesare and 6-year-old Chianna, at the Heavenly Ski Resort. Sonny was skiing with the family when he set off on a route, calling after his son to follow him. Chesare's skis got caught up, and he and Chianna collided a bit. Mary helped them untangle themselves and they lost sight of Sonny.

After a while, Mary and the kids became nervous. They conducted another run to try to locate him and contacted ski patrol, but there was no word of any accidents. He was officially listed as missing hours later. His body was recovered from a wooded area. It was determined that Sonny skied into a tree. His cause of death was determined to be blunt trauma to the head.

Sonny's death came days after Michael Kennedy, son of Robert F. Kennedy, was killed in a similar ski accident. Mary expressed her desire for Sonny to wear a helmet. He told her he'd get one before their next ski trip.

Sonny had been a U.S. Representative for California's 44th District since 1988. He was serving in the One Hundred-Fifth Congress at the time of his death. His death wasn't just a tragedy to those who knew him and loved him. It touched entertainment and politics, making it an almost around-the-clock news story.

Cher received the news from Chas, who called her in London. At first, Cher reacted as she would if she'd heard someone she didn't know well had died. She gave Chas her condolences and asked what had happened. Chas gave her a short description, after which what she was conveying truly began to sink in. Chas had called Georganne to comfort Cher as she tried to get back to Mary and her younger siblings. Once Cher was on the phone with her sister, she crumpled to her knees, sobbing.

Knowing she had to get back to the States, Cher began to prepare herself. She cancelled the Harrods appearance, apologising to Mohamed Al Fayed. Al Fayed was particularly sympathetic to Cher's plight, having lost his son Dodi in the August 1997 car crash in Paris that also took the life of Princess Diana.

Cher knew the trek home would feel like it was taking forever. What she wasn't prepared for was the fact that the media was awaiting her move in this moment. Photographers furiously snapped photos of Cher as she navigated Heathrow Airport with a tissue in hand, dabbing at her eyes. She tried remaining stoic, but the pain was all over her face.

Cher alternated between tears and sleep on her flight back to Los Angeles. She went straight to Sonny and Mary's Palm Springs home. The first face she encountered was Sonny's oldest daughter, Christy. Rather than comfort Christy, Cher was surprised at her stepchild comforting her as she began to weep. The home was full of people who knew Sonny throughout his life, including the part he shared with Cher.

Along with Chas and Elijah, Cher stayed in Palm Springs with the family as they prepared for Sonny's funeral. Cher helped Mary in any way she could. Both of them were there to lend their support to Chas, who had been estranged from Sonny at the time of his death because of their differing political views.

Two days before the funeral, Sonny's close friend, Denis Pregnolato, informed Cher that the whole family decided she should be the one to give Sonny's eulogy. She had her doubts that she was up to the challenge. Not only was she still reeling herself, but she worried about everyone's well-being and the significance of the moment. Pregnolato reassured her it was what everyone felt was best. She knew, for herself and for Sonny, she had to rise to the occasion. She accepted.

Writing the speech would not be easy. Cher had so much she wanted to say about Sonny, but he'd also lived so much and so different a life in the time they'd been apart. She wanted people to know that for all the ribbing and joking, and even the hurtful comments that they traded in the press, she loved and respected Sonny as an intelligent and confident man, whose hard work helped change their lives.

The family had a private wake on Wednesday night ahead of public services. Cher had no intention of going up to the casket and seeing Sonny lying there until Chas decided to do it. Then, Cher wanted to lend her child her support in an incredibly heartbreaking moment. She reluctantly glanced at Sonny and couldn't feel it was Sonny at all. It was her own vision of Sonny in her head that was what she knew and what stayed with her, even after that difficult moment.

Chas would be the one to talk her down when the nerves started getting the best of her ahead of the funeral. Cher noticed the irony in Chas trying to calm her down the way Sonny once would before they'd perform or record.

Sonny's funeral was aired live on CNN and MSNBC on 9 January 1998. Cher had no idea the heartfelt eulogy would be broadcast. Cher was tearful as she began speaking, sharing their story from the very beginning. She shared her happiness that he found joy in a family life with Mary and their kids and even applauded his work in Congress despite their differing political views.

Most striking was the conclusion of the eulogy. Fighting back tears, Cher said, 'So the last thing I want to say is, when I was young, there was this section in the *Reader's Digest*. And it was called "The Most Unforgettable Character I've Ever Met." And for me, that person is Sonny Bono. And no matter how long I live or who I meet in my life, that person will always be Son for me.'

Despite how beautiful and emotional the speech was, it did draw criticism. People questioned whether the family really wanted Cher to speak or if the opportunity was taken from a selfish place. Cher said reading the accusations was particularly difficult for her. Part of her wanted to leave public life for good after she realised people could speak so lowly of her in such a heartbreaking moment of life.

Still, it was hard to deny the genuine bond between Sonny and Cher, visible in the clips played across television stations in the hours and days following his death and in the proximity his family with Mary kept to Cher and Chas.

Cher stuck close to her children following Sonny's death. Elijah even accompanied her to the Academy Awards weeks later, on 23 March 1998. Cher wore a beaded Bob Mackie gown with an unusual headpiece, and while it raised eyebrows, it was a striking look on her. Despite the glow of the dress and accompanying jewellery, there's an obvious sadness visible in Cher in photos from the night.

As the spring came around, Cher headed back to London. She began work on her twenty-second studio album, *Believe*. This time around, Cher's label encouraged her to explore dance music, with the success of dance remixes of some of her older tracks. In particular, New York City's DJ Junior Vasquez remixed 'One by One' into a hit sweeping the big city club scene. She would work with producers Mark Taylor and Brian Rawling to get the sound just right while also bringing in Diane Warren to make sure her songs still felt like they were saying something. Releasing dance music was exactly what Cher was looking to avoid, reluctantly accepting the label's vision for the album.

In keeping with the trends in European dance music, the album featured the use of auto-tune. Cher suggested the effect after hearing it by chance on an independent British artist's album. It was the first time the effect was used as a deliberate creative choice. For a time before it became very popular, it was known as 'The Cher Effect.'

Cher had another special event in April. This time, Chas joined her as she was honoured with the Vanguard Award at the 9th Annual GLAAD (Gay & Lesbian Alliance Against Defamation) Awards. Cher was recognised for lending her support to the gay and lesbian community and promoting their pursuit of equal rights.

Sonny and Cher were honoured with a star on the Hollywood Walk of Fame on 15 May 1998. Mary and the kids joined Cher, Chas, and Elijah for the ceremony. They all posed together as the press took in a special honour. Some thought it was strange that the duo would be honoured together rather than separately. However, Cher had quietly passed on the opportunity for a solo star in 1983.

After the ceremony, they returned to Cher's home. She held a special screening of the CBS documentary special that would air on 20 May, which also happened to be Cher's 52nd birthday.

CBS aired a memorial to Sonny called *Sonny & Me: Cher Remembers*. The special was comprised of clips from throughout their career, interspliced with interviews with Cher and others close to Sonny. Cher talked about Sonny's superstitions in their early career. She says their signature sense of humour was born of resilience, getting through shows where they were being heckled and the band was less than enthusiastic.

Cher made a number of promotional appearances in support of the special. On Jay Leno, she empathised with the fact that Mary was overlooked as a widow by the public, who would always associate Sonny with Cher. She also opened up about going to psychic medium James Van Praagh to try to connect with Sonny. She admitted she wasn't sure what to make of the experience, but said there were things that she was told that were both valid and inexplicable.

Cher returned overseas that summer. Not only did she have to finish work on *Believe*, but she also began shooting her next film, *Tea with Mussolini*. The World War II drama follows a little boy raised by a group of eccentric women growing up in 1930s Florence, Italy, amid Benito Mussolini's dictatorship. She signed on to the film early in the year, a semi-autobiographical story from Franco Zeffirelli. The actress was cast as Elsa, a wealthy American who is all about the glitz and the glam but has a heart beyond her superficial surface.

Cher worked with a formidable cast on the Tuscany filming of the movie – Dame Judi Dench, Dame Maggie Smith, Joan Plowright, and Lily Tomlin. As with so many of her projects, Cher had her doubts going in. She feared she couldn't do the heartfelt story justice and worried about working with actresses of such a high calibre, but those fears were quelled after some time on set. The ladies enjoyed themselves as production unfolded from June to August 1998.

The autumn of 1998 would start a whole new stage in Cher's career. The eponymous single was released on 19 October 1998. It was first released in Europe – in France, followed by the United Kingdom. The single wouldn't be released in the United States until 10 November. The album, which was dedicated to Sonny, was released on 22 October.

Rollout for the single involved several televised performances of the song. In November alone, Cher performed the song on the *Top of the Pops* in the UK and Germany, a talk show in Spain, on *The Rosie O'Donnell Show*, and on *The Late Show with David Letterman*.

'Believe' was a massive success beyond what anyone had expected. It peaked at number one in twenty-three countries around the globe. In the UK, the single debuted at number one, a first in the country for Cher, and remained at number one for seven weeks. It was Cher's most commercially successful single of her career, selling over 11 million copies. To this day, it is the highest-selling single by a solo female artist in the United States. When it hit number one on Dance Club Songs and Hot 100 charts, it set the record for the longest gap between number one singles for an artist. There were thirty-three days and seven months between 'I Got You Babe' and its time at number one, and the same for 'Believe.'

It was a particularly sweet victory for Cher, who almost didn't complete recording the song. She already had reservations about venturing into dance music. As she got to know the song and prepared to record it, she found the same issue the songwriters were having. She loved the chorus but didn't feel strongly about the verses. Cher realised she felt the song was too downcast and depressing. She decided to change the lyrics in the second verse to empower the singer more. She never received a songwriting credit for her changes, however, something she would later regret.

Her suspicions that the song had improved were confirmed when she took the newly completed single home and played it for Elijah. The rocker, with a discerning appetite for music in his own right, was impressed by his mom's take on the dance music craze that was bubbling outside of the US.

Along with the release of the single was the release of the music video directed by Nigel Dick. Cher performs in a lively nightclub while also appearing in a cage where she can't quite reach the rest of the crowd she's singing to. There are several different cuts of the video, which also follow a woman observing her ex at the same club.

The same month *Believe* was released in the US, Cher had another big release. *The First Time* was released on 17 November 1998. The book was full of significant anecdotes from Cher's life. Much of the focus was on her early life and early career with Sonny. The book concludes with Cher tackling her first real loss, opening up about Sonny's death.

Ahead of its release, Cher held a dual signing for *The First Time* and *Believe* in New York City. During her time there, she also appeared on *The Tonight Show with Jay Leno* and *The Rosie O'Donnell Show*.

Cher continued to promote the album in appearances along the East Coast, including one newsworthy one in December. Cher was set to perform at a benefit at the Hammerstein Ballroom. Due to other promotional obligations, she was late, and as a result, Bette Midler's set was also pushed back. This was reportedly annoying to Midler and her team, leading the singer, who had been friendly with Cher up until that point, to make some offhand comments. She went out of her way to make a dig at Cher lip-synching her new, heavily-produced songs, lauding her own live singing instead. The digs allegedly continued offstage, igniting rumours of a feud between the two women.

The whirlwind that was 1998 concluded with Cher on top of the world. The singer was enjoying the success of *Believe* as audiences around the globe took in the album. After one of the hardest moments of her life, things took a turn for the better. Losing Sonny illuminated a lot of what was important to Cher and provided her with a new outlook that would serve her in the next stage of her life.

The hype for 'Believe' continued into January 1999. On 11 January, Cher performed the single at the 26th Annual American Music Awards. The performance mimicked the music video. The nightclub scenes played on a large screen behind her as Cher appeared on stage, in the box just like the video, as other dancers on stage also surrounded her. She comes out of the box in time for the chorus, joining the dancers on stage in the same headpiece she wears in the video.

Cher's newfound popularity afforded her another fun opportunity that January. She was asked to perform the national anthem at Super Bowl XXXIII. While performers often talk about the nerves that come with that big moment, Cher's rendition was well-received. The night was extra special for her because Stevie Wonder, a longtime idol of hers, performed the halftime show.

In February, Cher also performed the song at the 1999 Brit Awards, followed by the 1999 Sanremo Music Festival in Italy. It would also be the month the album's second single, 'Strong Enough,' was released. With so much hype still surrounding 'Believe,' the single was slow-starting at first. It enjoyed success overseas before it took off in the US.

March had Cher busy. Not only was the album rollout continuing, but she was also beginning to promote *Tea with Mussolini*. It premiered first in the UK on 19 March, on which day *Believe* was still charting in the UK. As if the moment wasn't already exciting, it became even more so with the opportunity to meet Prince Charles. He attended the premiere and took some time out to chat with all the stars. While he'd met some of the other stars before, it was his first time meeting Cher.

On 26 March, Cher enjoyed the premiere of *Tea with Mussolini* in Italy. The film was well-received and commercially successful, though Cher wasn't thrilled with how her performance as Elsa came out. She felt the edit on her character was a little heavy, though she admitted she wasn't often satisfied with the final outcome of a movie.

Cher's back catalogue was also celebrated in 1999, when Geffen Records released a compilation album, *If I Could Turn Back Time: Cher's Greatest Hits*. With an entirely new generation falling in love with Cher, the compilation was successful and provided an hour-long look back at Cher's first 30 years in the business.

Cher was invited to sing on the *VH1 Divas Live '99* special that spring. The special gathering, which raised money for the network's Save the Music Foundation, celebrated Cher, Tina Turner, Chaka Khan, and Whitney Houston. The night also featured additional performances by Leann Rimes, Brandy, Mary J. Blige, and Faith Hill. Despite girl power being at the centre of the night's events, Elton John also appeared, performing with Tina Turner and Cher. The special aired live on 13 April, taking place at New York City's Beacon Theatre. Recordings from the night's events would be released as a live concert album later that year.

That same week, Cher appeared on *Larry King Live*. Known as a viewer and sometimes caller on the show, Cher spoke about the resurgence of her career, Sonny's death, and *Tea with Mussolini*. Cher was vulnerable in the interview in the sense that she talked about a few subjects she wouldn't normally. For one, she admitted that tabloid gossip about her, though she tried to avoid it, did hurt her feelings in certain instances where it got back to her. She also noted that for as much surprise as there was about this 'comeback' in her career, she wasn't driven by commercial success. She wanted to make the music and movies that spoke to her and hopefully, would speak to others. How many others and what accolades came along with that were less of a motivating factor for her.

Cher was also candid about the fact that she was equally as surprised by her involvement in Sonny's funeral as the public had been. Sonny's death, being accidental in nature, didn't leave any room for preparation or closure. She simply had her raw feelings and instincts to work off of. Mary, to her credit, was understanding and supportive, though the two would find themselves at odds about other matters regarding Sonny's estate down the line.

On 5 May, Cher sang 'Believe,' as well as 'Strong Enough,' at the 1999 World Music Awards in Monte Carlo. That same month, she sang a rendition of 'The Star-Spangled Banner' on the patriotic compilation album, *Sing America*.

The undeniable power of Cher's career at that moment made one thing clear – it was time to tour. In June 1999, Cher set out on the 'Do You Believe?' tour. The impressive show combined nearly twenty of Cher's greatest tracks with an average of eight costume changes, resulting in quite an entertaining night. Cher truly paid each era of her career its much-earned attention, performing songs that were fan favourites, but didn't quite fit the mould of her newfound dance domain. The first stretch of the tour featured Cyndi Lauper and Wild Orchid as openers. Julio Iglesias Jr. and Michael McDonald also served as openers on the North American leg of the tour.

'All or Nothing' was the third single from *Believe* to be released on 7 June 1999. The dance-pop track found itself in the top forty in the U.S. and hit the top ten in countries around Europe. To promote both the single and the ongoing tour, footage from the tour was inter-spliced with scenes that feature Cher singing in a red wig and silver outfit. There was also a remix video, which was in black and white, that enjoyed some popularity.

That same month, Cher was honoured by the Council of Fashion Designers of America (CFDA). They presented her with their Influence on Fashion Award. In giving Cher this award, they celebrated how she has never been afraid to follow her heart and dress true to herself. Even when her looks have been torn apart by critics, Cher never timidly wears an outfit. She defines it rather than it defining her.

In August 1999, footage from Cher's show at Las Vegas' MGM Grand Garden Arena was filmed and compiled for a live special. *Live in Concert* was released by HBO and showcased Cher playing some of her favourite covers alongside her greatest hits.

The tour moved on to Europe in the autumn. There, Belinda Carlisle opened for Cher as they travelled between the UK, Germany, the Netherlands, Switzerland, Scotland, Italy, Germany, Austria, France, Norway, Sweden, Finland, Denmark, the Czech Republic, Ireland, Belgium, Portugal, and Spain.

That October, 'Dov'e l'amore' was released as the fourth and final single off of *Believe*. The Latin-inspired song featured Spanish elements in the music, despite the fact that the lyrics were in Italian. It was a departure from some of the other material on the album, but had a special appeal in its own right. The song got the attention of Cher's sometimes rumoured rival, Madonna, who was interested in directing the music video for the song. Sadly, the two artists' schedules clashed and they were unable to make it work. Jamie O'Connor would direct the video, which would focus on a man trying to win over a Latina woman in a crowded club as Cher sings in a red flamenco dress with a Chihuahua in tow.

Navigating through Europe took Cher through the end of 1999, which is where that tour was supposed to end. The immense commercial success called for an additional phase to the tour, which Cher was happy to oblige with. Though she did occasionally find life on the road to be challenging, she was also deeply fulfilled in this era of her career and made the most of every opportunity that presented itself while she was well enough and excited enough to do so.

Live in Concert was released on 6 December in the UK and 21 December in the US. Not only did the special air on HBO, but it was also released on CD, VHS, and DVD.

Two days later, Cher appeared at the 1999 Billboard Music Awards, where she was nominated for three different awards: Top Female Artist, Top Hot 100 Song, and Top Female Hot 100 Artist of the Year. 'Believe' won the Top Hot 100 Song.

Cher also made time to team up with Rosie O'Donnell on something special, appearing on O'Donnell's Christmas album, *A Rosie Christmas*. The two sang 'Christmas (Baby Please Come Home).' It was Cher's first-ever Christmas single.

A year that began with a heartbreaking low for Cher turned around. The end of 1999 saw Cher on top of the world, with more success and interest coming. Cher spent the last hours and minutes of 1999 performing in Atlantic City and soaking up her place at the top of the entertainment industry.

Despite a career that spanned three decades and was entering a fourth, Cher was as hot as ever. Furthermore, the success of *Believe* empowered her with the confidence to continue working hard and listening to her gut. It would serve her well entering the new millennium.

Chapter Fourteen

2000–2004

The wild ride that was 1999 continued for Cher into the year 2000. 'Believe' was still completely ubiquitous across global pop culture. You could hear the song anywhere from the supermarket to the hottest club in your city. Cher continued to enjoy the moment while also looking ahead to what her next move would be.

On 23 February 2000, Cher attended the 42nd Annual Grammy Awards in Los Angeles. She had three nominations that night – Best Dance Recording for 'Believe,' as well as Best Pop Album and Record of the Year for *Believe*. She took home the reward for Best Dance Recording, marking her first-ever Grammy win.

Through the first quarter of the year, Cher was getting everything done while continuing to tour on the 'Do You Believe? Tour.' This leg of the tour kept her in North America, with brief stops in Canada amid nearly 20 other US tour dates. The tour was completed on 3 March 2000 in Boston's Fleet Center. Altogether, it's estimated that nearly one million people saw Cher perform throughout the nine-month-long tour.

After the tour, Cher hit the red carpet at the 72nd annual Academy Awards, where she would present 'Best Original Song.' Once again, she dressed for the occasion. In keeping with her Gothic sensibilities, she wore a black velvet gown with a short train. The off-the-shoulder look also included a loosely slung hip chain from which a large and ornate cross hung. Cher wore her black hair up in messy, Medusa-inspired curls. She'd sport a completely different look for the Vanity Fair after-party, with the option for super-bedazzled Dolce & Gabbana jeans, a sequined top, and an oversized denim jacket, paired with slingback heels.

That spring and summer, Cher was busy, but she was considering every possibility that came her way. In an interview that summer, actor Dean Winters revealed Cher was in negotiations to direct an episode of *Oz*.

The opportunity arose after the success of *If These Walls Could Talk*, but unfortunately, it never materialised due to her intensely busy schedule.

In July 2000, Cher's fans and their devotion took things to the next level with CherCon, a fan convention in Chicago, Illinois, where fans gathered to celebrate their love for the artist. In the time leading up to the event, there were rumblings that the large gathering of fans would summon Cher herself to make an appearance. There were even rumours thatweekend, started by people who believed they saw her in the area. While Cher wasn't in attendance, some good did come of the gathering. Attendees raised over £15,000 for the Children's Craniofacial Association.

Cher wasn't in Chicago and didn't appear at the event, she did comment on it the following year during an interview on Swedish talk show *Sen kväll med Luuk*, as a second CherCon was in the works. She explained that she was invited to the Chicago convention but wasn't sure if it would be well-received or negatively affect the mood of the gathering, which celebrated fandom as much as the subject of the fandom. She said that after seeing the photos, it reminded her of Star Trek conventions.

That month, Cher also inadvertently started a rumour she was looking to grow her family. During an interview with *The Sunday Mirror*, Cher discussed friend Sharon Stone's recent adoption of a son at the age of 42. Asked if she would consider doing something similar, the mom of two argued it was a good time of life to raise a child. At that point, Chas was 31, and Elijah was 23, but Cher wasn't closed off to the idea of raising another child. The headlines took it more seriously than she did. While she may have considered the idea for some time, she didn't take any steps to initiate the process.

There was also some bad news in the works for Cher in July 2000. An accountant she had fired in May, Salvatore Sampino, sued the artist, claiming he was wrongfully terminated after warning Cher about her home construction labour violations that occurred during the building of her Malibu home. While he sued the star, he wasn't employed by her. Rather, Sampino was the employee of the contracting company that Cher was using for the project. In his filing, he claimed wrongful termination and retaliation, sexual harassment, defamation, unfair competition, negligence, and unpaid wages, all of which Cher and her team denied the validity of.

Cher got a special opportunity in August 2000. She was invited to perform at the Democratic National Convention. There, she gave an unforgettable performance of 'If I Could Turn Back Time,' to the complete delight of President Bill Clinton, whose successor would be named at that event.

The talent headed to Los Angeles in early September, where she was honoured at the 7th annual Lucy Awards. The Women in Film organisation honoured Cher alongside an impressive group of women, some of whom she had ties to. The other women honoured were Jane Anderson, Anne Heche, I. Marlene King, Nancy Savoca, Sharon Stone, Jennifer Todd, Suzanne Todd, and Michelle Williams.

On 10 September 2000, Cher appeared at the Primetime Emmy Awards. She was nominated for Outstanding Individual Performance in a Variety or Music Program for *Cher— Live in Concert*. Though she didn't take home the win, she got time on stage when she presented the Lead Actress in a Comedy Series award to Patricia Heaton for *Everybody Loves Raymond*. Her look was attention-grabbing, considering she walked the red carpet with her signature long black hair and then appeared in a platinum blond wig. She joked, 'I was so upset about not winning that my hair turned blond.'

Once again, Cher would make an appearance for the Democratic Party. At a campaign event for Al Gore in New Jersey, Cher made an appearance to introduce the candidate to a fired-up audience. Although Cher was one to lend her support based on specific beliefs rather than party, it didn't stop conservative outlets from being less than kind about her appearance.

The artist wasn't much bothered because she was hard at work on her new album. After seeing the success of *Believe*, she wanted to continue to create upbeat dance music. For this album, it seemed like all the talent in the world was available to Cher. She collaborated with both old and new partners.

not.com.mercial was finally released into the world in November 2000. The album, recorded in 1994, was given a modern update. The release was set up so that you could only download the album online for purchase. Cher also emphasised that the music shouldn't be considered a follow-up to *Believe* or the next step in her career. Rather, it was an intimate time capsule from a unique creative period in her life.

The songs, which feature some of the first songs Cher wrote by herself, delve deeply into a lifetime of deeply emotional experiences. Many found the content, which ranges from 'Sisters of Mercy,' drawing on her childhood experience in the Catholic orphanage, to a dedication to Sonny titled 'Classified 1-A,' much darker than anything else Cher has ever released.

The Catholic Church even spoke out against 'Sisters of Mercy,' which they felt was a condemnation of the whole church. Cher later explained that such a statement was not her intention and that she'd had positive experiences with members of the church later in life. She was just speaking about a specific childhood trauma. The misunderstanding might have bothered Cher more at a different time, but her attitude was set. She felt confident in letting those tracks into the world, knowing that they could exist without pressure amid the continued success of *Believe*.

Cher also enjoyed a lighter milestone that month – her first appearance on *Will & Grace*. Despite her immense popularity with the gay community, Cher had never seen the show, which focuses on a group of four friends – two straight women and two gay men.

The season three episode of the hit sitcom 'Gypsies, Tramps and Weed' featured Jack (Sean Hayes) bringing his newest prized possession, a Cher Barbie doll, everywhere with him. In real life, the doll was a work in progress at Mattel. The show was given a £45,000 prototype of the doll, dressed in an outfit designed by none other than Bob Mackie. In carrying it around, he runs into Cher herself. The moment highlighted once again what an icon Cher had become in the LGBTQ community.

Sleazenation, a British lifestyle and fashion magazine, released a controversial yet artful cover for their February 2001 issue. On a bright pink background was a print featuring a classic image of Che Guevara. Instead of Guevara's face, however, it was Cher's. Scott King, the magazine's art director, explained the idea came after hearing a friend pronounce 'Che' with a heavy German accent, which made it sound like 'Cher.' Underneath the image, it read, 'Militant Pop— Do you believe in revolution?'

In May 2001, the same Barbie doll that was used in the episode of *Will & Grace* Cher appeared in aired. Part of the Timeless Treasures collection, the doll featured a lavender criss-cross top with a satin flowing skirt designed by Bob Mackie.

September 2001 was a life-changing time for all citizens of the United States, and Cher was no exception. Cher was among the countless people watching the events of the terrorist attacks that unfolded across the country, feeling helpless. She had special memories of living in New York City and ties to the area, as well as numerous friends and loved ones who called the city home.

Cher was in the midst of a legal headache, her lawsuit with accountant Salvatore Sampino. The case was continuing to trial, a trial Cher would have to appear in for days on end. She was at home, gearing up for another day of trial on 11 September. She woke up early, then dozed off again with her TV on mute. When she woke up, the TV, tuned to BBC, showed the first plane hitting the north tower of the Twin Towers in New York City.

At first, Cher thought it was footage from the 1993 bombing at the World Trade Center. Once she paid closer attention, she was shocked to realise what was unfolding before her very eyes. At home in Los Angeles, she felt helpless at first. It wouldn't be until later that she realised how she could lend her talents to that community.

October 2001 saw Cher begin the next step of her career. She began working on her twenty-fourth studio album, *Living Proof*. It began on 13 October when she appeared on a German TV show called *Wetten, dass…?* There, she debuted 'The Music's No Good Without You,' which would be the first single off the album. She filmed the music video that same month, teaming up with Nigel Dick once again. The music video was designed to appear as if it took place in space, featuring Cher as the queen of a galactic world, yet saddened by the loss of love. She creates a message in a bottle, letting it out into the stars instead of releasing one into the sea.

The single was released on 5 November 2001 everywhere except the United States the following month. Cher was off to *Top of the Pops*, where she performed the track for a lively audience. In the UK, it had risen to number eight on the Singles Chart, making Cher the only female recording artist to have a top 10 hit in the country in every decade of her career. Due to technical difficulties, she ended up having to perform the song twice consecutively. Despite the setback, she brought the same energy and liveliness to the performance. The audience had no choice but to keep up.

The next day, *Living Proof* was released. In the album's liner notes, Cher dedicated 'Song for the Lonely' to 'the courageous people of New York, especially the firefighters, police, Mayor Giuliani, Governor Pataki and my friend Liz.' The latter was a publicity executive at Warner Bros., who worked with both Cher and Madonna.

During one of her UK promotional interviews, Cher was asked about her rumoured friendship with Britney Spears and the idea of a possible collaboration. Cher confirmed that the two were hoping to work together that year, but their similar release dates for their respective albums made it impossible. She shared the desire to work with her, from recording a song to performing together, and hoped they'd try again in 2002.

That month, Cher also attended the Bambi Awards. There, she was honoured as the International Pop Star of the Year after her explosive run with *Believe*.

In December 2001, Cher filmed the music video for 'Song for the Lonely' in New York City. She fell for the concept of the video, which traced New York's history through the years to show how the city's famed skyline evolved over time. The video shows Cher walking the streets of New York as it progresses from sepia-toned shots indicating the eighteenth century, to the black and white nineteenth century, and colour as they came into the twentieth century.

Directed by first-time director Stu Maschwitz, who quickly discovered the power of working for Cher. The filming got special permission from then-Mayor Rudy Giuliani's office for live audio playback in the streets, a practice that has since been made illegal. There were also scenes that required the use of smoke machines. Seeing smoke in the streets so soon after the attacks was understandably startling for some New Yorkers.

A police officer approached the production and informed them that they would have to stop using the smoke machines. There was one more shot Maschwitz needed, so together with the assistant director and Cher, they asked for the chance to film one more shot with the effect. Cher took a Polaroid with the officer and signed it, which got them the time they needed for that final shot. Maschwitz was both impressed with and grateful for Cher's professionalism, doing it all while battling the icy cold of New York City in December.

Cher started off 2002 by being honoured with a special by BBC One, called *Still Cher*. The documentary followed the artist as she began promoting *Living Proof* across Europe. The look back at her life and career featured appearances from both family and friends, including Chas and Elijah, Robert Altman, Peter Fonda, Melanie Griffith, and more.

Next was another trip to the American Music Awards on 8 January. Cher arrived in jeans with black cross appliqués paired with a sheer, gauzy, off-the-shoulder long-sleeve shirt with a bedazzled vest over it. She enjoyed a sweet moment backstage, where she walked into an area where Kiss and *NSYNC were doing an interview together. She greeted Gene Simmons, sweetly nuzzling up close to him without touching his stage makeup.

In a live performance that night, she debuted 'Song for the Lonely.' The song was first introduced to Cher in early 2001, with her recording the song that summer. After the September 11th attacks, Cher saw the song as more than a fun dance anthem. She believed it could be a beacon of hope amid the dark times the country was dealing with.

At that time, Cher was contemplating what her next move would be. She had some movie offers she was considering, but she also wanted to tour and celebrate the upbeat new singles with her fans.

On Valentine's Day 2002, Cher attended the inaugural Love Rocks concert. The benefit, which launched the Entertainment Industry Foundation's National Cardiovascular Research Initiative, honoured U2 frontman Bono and his philanthropic work. At the event, No Doubt and R.E.M. performed. Cher also agreed to perform. In a poignant moment and for the first time ever without Sonny, Cher performed 'I Got You Babe,' accompanied by Michael Stipe.

Cher would later reveal that she had no idea the performance was going to happen ahead of time. Stipe invited her backstage when she arrived, then pitched the idea to her. She was immediately reluctant, but Stipe shared a story he'd heard from Bono. One time, the Irish artist was in a lift, trying to keep a low profile with his head down. The other man inside with them did the same, until he got to his floor. Before exiting, he stopped and turned around and said, 'You know, it's Bon-o.' Bono looked up and realised he'd been in the lift with Sonny. The heartwarming story was enough to convince Cher to go along with the plan.

Later that month, Cher made her return to *The Late Show with David Letterman*. The two fell back into their usual playful quipping back and forth. Once again, she was asked about her dating life. Many people found it hard to believe that Cher wasn't dating, thinking she was just hiding it to avoid ridicule. In truth, Cher was so laser-focused on her career at this point in her life that dating didn't concern her much. She loved love, but she also relished her freedom.

On 1 March, Cher revisited *The Rosie O'Donnell Show*. She talked about the single, her appearance on *Will & Grace* the previous year, and her blond era as she was promoting *Living Proof*. She shared some outrageous stories about her life as she gifted the audience copies of the album.

Ahead of her 56th birthday in May 2002, Cher had a lot going on. *The Guinness Book of World Records* proclaimed her the Oldest Solo Female Artist to Top the Charts in the UK and the Oldest Female Artist to Top the Billboard Hot 100 Chart worldwide.

On 3 May, she took part in *American Bandstand's 50th Anniversary Celebration*, looking back at the cultural phenomenon that was the show. It featured other talents who, like Cher, graced the weekly national broadcast during their rise to the top. Michael Jackson was also there. Though she'd known him since she was a child, Cher found herself uncomfortable with his energy and particularly how he went about protecting his kids, who were also with him at the event.

Cher continued the big month by making a powerful announcement. She announced 'Living Proof: The Farewell Tour,' proclaiming the fifty-city tour, to start that summer, would be the last of her musical career. The original run was slated to go for fifty-nine dates, from June 2002 to September 2002, but it would become a record-breaker in extensions to come.

Many fans wondered why Cher would be considering walking away at the height of her career. On the one hand, many stars want to do just that before their performance quality declines. Cher wasn't like other stars, however. Her idea was to shift from music, where she felt she'd achieved everything she wanted to, to acting in films and on stage.

Next, Cher performed at VH1's *Divas Las Vegas*. She would take the stage alongside Mary J. Blige, Celine Dion, The Chicks, Whitney Houston, Shakira, Stevie Nicks, and Cyndi Lauper. Cher's existing great relationships with many of these talents, combined with her history with Las Vegas throughout her career, made the appearance a no-brainer.

Cher graced the small screen once again that month, making another guest appearance on *Will & Grace*. The episode features Jack (Sean Hayes) being knocked unconscious by boxes falling out of the ceiling. He comes to in a heaven where Cher is God and tells him not to give up on his entertainment dreams. The episode, part of the season four finale, aired on 16 May.

She also sat down for an in-depth interview on *PrimeTime Live* with Cynthia McFadden. There, the topic of dating came up once again. Cher believed that aside from her demanding career, she was an easy person to be in a relationship with. She explains that when she makes an effort to date, it's with the intent to make it a longer commitment. She noted that while it seems glamorous for a woman to marry a famous actor, being the man behind a famous woman didn't hold the same appeal for most balanced.

'Living Proof: The Farewell Tour' kicked off in June in Toronto. Once again, Cher was looking at a twenty-song setlist that mixed fan favourites with deep cuts she adored. To give fans the full Cher effect, she teamed up with Bob Mackie once again for costumes for the tour. This time, Mackie did costumes for the whole production rather than just the star herself.

In June 2002, Cher released a third single in Europe, which would be her final single from the album there. 'Alive Again' was a fun track, but its promotion was disrupted as Cher left Warner Music UK for Warner Bros. A music video was shot for the song, where Cher enjoyed her wig era by wearing multiple different coloured hairdos throughout the video.

July 2002 saw Cher fans gather once again, this time in Las Vegas, for CherCon. Once again, die-hard fans from all eras of her career and all across the country came together. They dressed like Cher. They played games related to Cher. They bought tons of memorabilia celebrating Cher. Members of the Children's Craniofacial Association (CCA) also attended the convention.

The tour was a huge success, and little by little, more dates were added. The autumn of 2002 saw Cher continue to travel through the midwestern US before looping back to the East Coast, dipping into Canada, and going back into the US, heading south before heading back west.

On 11 September, Cher was one of several special guests on *Larry King Live*, looking back at the attacks one year later. During her segment, Cher opened up about how she went from feeling 'Song for the Lonely' was a love song to a song about strength and perseverance after re-listening to the song after that day.

At her 8 November 2002 tour date in Miami, Cher's show was filmed for an NBC television special that wouldn't air until the following spring. The performance was also used for a live concert album, *Live! The Farewell Tour*, which also wasn't released until 2003.

On 9 December, Cher attended the 2002 Billboard Music Awards. There, she was nominated for Dance/Club Play Artist of the Year. She was also presented with an Artist Achievement Award, which was presented to her by Steven Tyler. In her acceptance speech, Cher joked that she wasn't sure which Cher to show up as after decades in the industry. Dressed in Bob Mackie, she acknowledged all of her own hard work and sent a message to the critics who swore her career was on the verge of ending, proclaiming, 'I've had critics for the last 40 years saying that I was on my way out every year.... So fuck 'em. I still have a job and they don't.'

Cher took a break in touring from mid-December 2002 through late January 2003. She closed the year out by announcing the tour's extension, continuing through May.

In February 2003, the *Living Proof: The Farewell Tour* concert special aired on NBC. It covered twenty-two tracks from throughout Cher's four-decade career and also included ten bonus tracks.

She also took a little time out for another project that month. Ever one to joke at her own expense, Cher agreed to be in 2003's *Stuck on You*.

With filming in Miami, it wasn't too hard for Cher to get her scenes done during the latter end of filming.

Cher plays a dramatised version of herself in a situation where she's stuck in a TV contract she doesn't want to fulfil. With no confidence in the material, she hires conjoined twin Walt (Greg Kinnear) as her co-star, thinking he'll help her tank the show. The plan backfired, with Walt helping make the show a resounding hit instead.

The role kicked off with a misunderstanding, with the Farrelly brothers wanting Cher to portray herself while she was looking for cues about her character from them. Once they got on the same page, they found that they worked well together at defining the line between an exaggerated and obviously fictional Cher and the real thing.

Cher's undeniable musical run was celebrated once again in April 2003 with *The Very Best of Cher*, released by Warner Bros, Geffen Records, and MCA. The US release was 21 tracks, while the international edition featured 23 songs. The compilation was very successful,

That same month, NBC introduced *Cher: The Farewell Tour*. The concert special added more buzz to the show, which had been extended at least two different times at that point. By April, the tour was back on the West Coast, snaking back and forth around the country throughout the months that followed. Cher would take a few days here and there, but largely, she kept pushing forward.

In August 2003, the tour dipped back into Canada before beginning its final trek across the US. September 2003 had Cher back in Los Angeles, where she attended the 55th annual Primetime Emmy Awards. She was nominated for Outstanding Variety, Music or Comedy Special for *Cher: The Farewell Tour* on NBC and took home the award.

There was a serious look back at Cher's life in September 2003, when her story was covered on the beloved biographical series *E! True Hollywood Story*. The look back covered the milestone moments that brought Cher to the top of her game.

By October 2003, Cher had brought in nearly £114 million on what was renamed the 'Never Can Say Goodbye Tour.' The final Canadian tour date came on Halloween 2003. That same month, Cher was featured in *Forbes*. The outlet named her the highest-paid female musician of the year. The tour made £110 million to that point, making it the highest-grossing tour by a female artist at that time. To this day, the tour remains in the top 20 highest-grossing tours of all time by women and the third highest-grossing tour by a female artist in the 2000s overall.

Cher was never one to shy away from sharing her opinions on political matters. Her busy schedule didn't keep her from keeping up with current events. That month, she called into C-SPAN during Open Phones to discuss her recent visit to Walter Reed Army Hospital, where she visited with wounded soldiers returning from Iraq. She detailed seeing countless instances of amputations and emphasised how these service members' lives were changed by their time away.

Stuck on You press kicked off in November 2003, with Cher dedicating herself to promoting the film ahead of the premiere the following month. She attended a press conference and a number of events in support of the zany film. Cher also appears on the soundtrack of *Stuck On You*, performing a cover of Flynn's 'Human.'

Audiences appreciated Cher's willingness to laugh at herself, including a few scenes opposite Frankie Muniz, who is her 'young' boyfriend in the film. Cher executed the humour so flawlessly that many assumed the role was written with her in mind. However, the Farrelly brothers hadn't dreamed of getting the icon. Instead, they wrote a more general version with a 'famous actress' in mind. Cher's commitment to the bit made the experience better than expected for all parties involved.

Cher ended the North American leg of the tour in January 2004. She spent the first days of the new year playing her final shows in Las Vegas's MGM Grand Garden Arena. The show was far from over, however, and Cher was far from retired.

Just a few weeks later, Cher announced a European leg to her farewell tour. She was looking forward to getting back on the road and returning to an audience she'd been away from. Cher also found that time living in Europe was always transformational for her, often providing her clarity during trying times.

Cher's break from touring concluded in May 2004, the same month she turned 58. She began the European leg of the 'Never Can Say Goodbye Tour,' which began in Ireland. This segment of the tour was 27 dates, with shows in Ireland, Scotland, England, France, Germany, Austria, Switzerland, Hungary, Germany, Belgium, Denmark, Sweden, Russia, the Netherlands, and Monaco.

In June 2004, *The Very Best of Cher: The Video Hits Collection* was released on both VHS and DVD. The anthology felt like a joyful celebration of Cher's growth and evolution as an artist. It went platinum in both the U.S. and Australia, just as Cher was finishing up her European tour. Once again, that would not be the end of touring, with Cher doing another lap around North America from July 2004 well into the following year.

Aside from her tour, there was something else going on that was important to Cher in 2004 – the US presidential election. When John Kerry became the Democratic front-runner, Cher began to lend her support to him. Some of her messaging was more anti-George W. Bush than pro-Kerry initially, but she came to learn more about his platform and speak to it as the election neared.

Cher was concerned about how LGBTQ rights would be impacted by Republican, conservative leadership. In addition to more partisan support, she made sure to emphasise the importance of voting. She appeared at a number of 'get out the vote' events throughout the course of the year. Of course, the election wouldn't turn out as Cher hoped, but she continues to be vocal about her politics to this day.

Throughout the summer of 2004, Cher was in and out of the US and Canada touring. In August, she announced that the Oceania leg of the tour in spring 2005 would be the end of the tour. She took it easier in October, only performing during a three-night stint in Mexico City. She was back at it in November, at her usual pace, as she continued touring the US up until the holiday season. Cher wrapped up 2004 two years into her farewell tour, nearing a milestone of 300 concert dates. And she still wasn't done yet.

Chapter Fifteen

2005–2009

Cher resumed her Farewell Tour in mid-January 2005 in the US. She wouldn't be stateside much longer, however. In late February, the Oceania leg of the tour began, covering New Zealand and Australia.

On 3 March, Cher appeared on the MTV Australia Awards via satellite from her Sydney tour date. There, she was presented with the VH1 Music First Award in recognition of her storied career. The sweet moment came backstage as she prepared for the show that evening.

Another Cher compilation album was released for fans in March. *Gold* was released by Geffen Records. The two-disc set contained 32 tracks spanning Cher's career. The collection enjoyed decent success in both the US and the UK.

While Cher had said Australia would be the end of the Farewell tour, that didn't prove to be the case. There was one last North American extension through spring 2005. The final thirteen tour dates came in April 2005.

Cher began in Canada, with three dates in Montreal, Ottawa, and London. Then, she returned to the US East Coast and Midwest for four shows. She dipped into Canada for the final three shows in Winnipeg, Regina, and Victoria. The final two shows took place in Los Angeles at the Hollywood Bowl, where she took the stage 40 years prior for the very first time with Sonny, on 29 and 30 April. In all, she visited 48 of the 50 states, with Vermont and Delaware each lacking a sufficiently sized venue for the tour.

Altogether, the tour included a record-breaking 325 dates across 20 different countries. Over three million tickets were sold throughout the course of the three-year tour. The tour grossed over £152 million, and also made a point to give back. Cher donated a portion of her ticket sales to different children's charities, such as UNICEF, World Vision,

Throughout the press, Cher repeated the fact that answered the most asked question – why such a long goodbye? Cher noted that she didn't want to stop touring, making music, or performing in any capacity. When it came to putting on live shows, however, she felt like she was at her physical peak. Faced with the prospect of putting on a lesser show for fans, she decided to call it before the quality of her performance declined. That didn't mean that anything with her desire to perform had changed. The opportunity for just a few more shows while she was already in motion was one she couldn't turn down.

Now, she could rest. Of course, rest didn't look the same for Cher as it did for the average person. She had to stay busy. While she did enjoy having more time to catch up with loved ones and indulge her interests, she still had aspirations in films, both behind the camera and in front of it. There were other industries she considered pursuing, understanding she had an opportunity she'd never had before with the time she was now allotted to focus on other pursuits.

In October 2005, a special celebration of Cher's career was released. *An All-Star Tribute to Cher*. Tiffany, Lisa Loeb, Sheila E., and more covered Cher's biggest hits. The special gathering of artists ranged from people who had worked with Cher before, to those whose careers were inspired by her.

Cher was content to close out 2005 quietly, catching up with family and friends throughout the holiday season. She especially cherished spending time with her all-grown-up children and hearing more about what they loved. Chas continued work as an author and advocate while Elijah dabbled in music.

Many people believed that Cher was working on something in the fashion realm. Though she wasn't dressing to her Bob Mackie showgirl best, she appeared at a number of fashion shows throughout that year. The first was during Mercedes-Benz Fashion Week, at the Agent Provocateur show in March 2006. Some recognised that Cher's toned-down look was unexpected coming off her tour and going into her next chapter, but Cher wasn't shaken or deterred by any chatter.

Part of what Cher wanted to pursue with this next stage of life was using her heightened profile to help advance the causes dear to her. In that, Cher lent her support to Operation Helmet once again. On 28 May 2006, days after turning 60, she called into C-SPAN's *Washington Journal* and read a statement from a service member. She went on to explain that soldiers were sometimes using old, used helmets and noted the amount of head wounds that occur during service. She admitted to being 'emotional' and 'pissed off' and levelled criticisms at President Bush.

Just a few weeks later, on 15 June, Cher accompanied Operation Helmet's team at their meeting with the Tactical Air and Land Forces Subcommittee of the House Armed Services Committee on Capitol Hill. She sat next to Dr. Bob Meaders in her show of support. Cher's appearance wasn't a quiet one, as discussed by the committee members in their statements. It was especially of interest because of two former members of that committee – Sonny and Mary Bono. Sonny's widow, who at that point had engaged in some negative public back and forth with Cher that was ultimately resolved, had successfully been elected to Sonny's vacated seat. At this point in 2006, Mary served on the Energy and Commerce Committee but was given special recognition to participate. Like others speaking that day, she supported the cause. She also thanked Cher and joked about how she was happy she watched C-SPAN, where she first heard about Operation Helmet.

Rep. Solomon Ortiz drew interesting parallels between the two women's experiences of losing Sonny and the struggles of the service members. He pointed to how Sonny, a former member of the committee, had died as the result of a head injury. He recalled listening to Cher's tearful eulogy of Sonny at his funeral. He noted how the two women weren't bonded just by their love of Sonny but by the love all three displayed for the American troops.

While in Washington, Cher did appear alongside Dr. Meaders on C-SPAN's *Washington Journal*. Though she was asked about her politics, Cher tried her best to keep the conversation directed to the cause. She explained that throughout her life and career, she has always tried to stay informed about what's going on in the world, though it may not seem in line with her public persona. Though it was still not the case for much of the country, she also talked about using the internet to keep up-to-date on the news.

Cher also noted her opinion that matters of the troops aren't political. She also disagreed with the notion that the political viewpoints of famous people are discredited as out of touch, as well as the idea that if you don't support the ideas behind a war, then you can't support the troops fighting in it.

Cher spent some time in Paris in July, enjoying Fall/Winter Fashion Week there. She opted for a number of quietly fabulous looks as she took in Polo de Paris, Gaultier, Giorgio Armani, Musee Baccarat, Pelouse de St Cloud, and John Galliano for Christian Dior shows. Cher's prominent place in these shows reminded the public that, though she was considered 'retired' for about a year at that point, she was never too far from the spotlight.

In August 2006, a huge auction was announced, with Cher donating many of her possessions for a charity auction with Sotheby's and Julian's Auctions. As she prepared to let go of her Malibu home, she donated over 700 items spanning her career, from items she curated that inspired *Sanctuary* to the star's Hummer vehicle. As part of the partnership, Cher donated proceeds from the charity to three different charities.

The first was the Children's Craniofacial Association, a longtime beloved cause of hers and one she continues to find new ways of supporting. There was also the Intrepid Fallen Heroes Fund, an organisation dedicated to helping with physical and psychological resources for troops injured in combat. The third organisation was Operation Helmet, which helped supply troops with helmet upgrades that were not available through the military. 'The Cher Collection' was ultimately comprised of 775 items and brought in over £2.6 million when it took place that October.

On 11 September, Cher attended the Los Angeles premiere of *The Ground Truth*, a documentary film. The film showed what it was like coming home for service members who served in Iraq and the challenges they faced after coming home. Cher was there in her continued support of Operation Helmet, toward which ten per cent of the film's proceeds were donated.

In 2007, Cher struggled with her health. Epstein-Barr syndrome reared its head once again. Not only was she battling symptoms and insurmountable fatigue, but a bout of pneumonia worsened her symptoms. Initially, doctors believed she just had bronchitis and prescribed her antibiotics. She continued to work through this time, only to discover her symptoms were getting worse.

As the symptoms progressed, Cher struggled to breathe after the slightest bit of exertion. It became difficult to stand for long periods of time. At one point, Cher believed she might die from the illness. As she had before, she decided to see what medical options were available to her for treatment abroad. Though it took some time, she found success with German medicine and was able to rehabilitate once again. Just as in times before, the time spent unable to work and perform only deepened her desire to return to it. In that, Cher started looking for what was next for her.

That year, Cher was celebrated in doll form once again. This time, Barbie released three different Cher dolls reflecting different eras of the star's career. The Black Label dolls 1970s Cher Bob Mackie Doll, dressed in a Native American headdress and slinky halter and skirt. Next is the 1980s Cher Bob Mackie Doll, which is dressed in the iconic 'If I Could Turn Back Time' music video outfit, albeit a more PG recreation of it. The third doll, released in a more limited quantity, is a millennium-era Cher dressed as a ring leader. The 1980s doll was the first to be released, going on sale in June 2007. The other two dolls hit the market a month later.

2007 was also a year when people who weren't paying close attention to her stardom realised just how much Cher had accomplished in her career. She was awarded the Guinness Book of World Records honour for Highest Grossing Tour by a Female Artist of All Time. She also won a TV Land Award for TV's Greatest Music Moment for her 1987 reunion with Sonny on *Letterman*.

In February 2008, Cher was feeling better and ready to be among her fans again. She announced a residency at The Colosseum at Caesars Palace in Las Vegas. Cher signed on to do nearly 200 shows over a three-year period. While it could seem daunting for some artists, Cher was more than familiar with how Vegas worked and knew she could take on the challenge.

That same month, she made a return to the Grammys. Cher walked the red carpet dressed in a gown by Julia Gerard. She even took the stage. It wasn't to perform, however, but to introduce a dear friend. Cher introduced Beyoncé and Tina Turner as they performed 'Proud Mary' together.

The event also saw Cher catching up with friends old and new. She was seen in conversation with Cyndi Lauper, Jerry Lee Lewis, and Little Richard. She also posed for photos with Miley Cyrus and stopped for a chat with the then-up-and-comer.

The engagement required her to physically build her back up. With that, her creative mind also began to bloom. She was excited to record a new album once the residency was underway. She still had directorial aspirations and felt this was the first step to getting back into the full swing of things.

In getting back to herself, Cher opened herself up to love again. She met Tim Medvetz, an outdoor-loving mountain climber. Medvetz also had a storied life. He was part of the Hells Angels in his younger years before changing his life by centering it on his love for outdoor adventures. The year prior, he'd gained national attention after summiting Mount Everest on his second try, six years after being left paralysed after a motorcycle accident. Additionally, Cher and Medvetz shared a love for the troops. He was co-founder of The Heroes Project, a non-profit organisation that helped veterans handle physical and emotional injuries from service.

The tabloids quickly caught on to the fact that there was an age gap between the two. He was 24 years her junior, though you wouldn't know it from how Cher could keep up with – and even run circles around him from time to time.

Cher's eponymous residency kicked off on 6 May 2008. The show kicked off with a seventeen-song setlist, plus an encore. This, as well as the songs that comprised it, would ebb and flow throughout the residency. The show began in a cadence of four nights a week, every Tuesday, Wednesday, Saturday, and Sunday. It was less vigorous than Cher's last touring stint and also didn't require the same kind of travel, which was a huge upside, especially as she recovered from her medical struggles the year prior.

That same month, Cher appeared on a very special episode of *The Oprah Winfrey Show*. Not only did she agree to a sit-down with the beloved daytime host, but she would do so alongside her longtime friend and fellow diva, Tina Turner. Turner was fresh off of un-retirement, having performed with Beyoncé Knowles at the Grammy Awards the week prior.

Turner and Cher had a genuine connection and maintained a special bond, with their careers often experiencing the same kinds of shifts at the same time. They both found fame in love-based duos that crumbled with their relationships. Though Cher's hardships were nothing like Tina's with ex Ike Turner, she could understand what her friend had been through and support her meteoric transformation in the aftermath.

The interview took place in Las Vegas, where Cher was focused on the residency. The show aired two days after the residency began. The sit-down between the three powerful women who had perseverance in common features laughs and tears as each looked back on their storied journeys. Cher recalled how Tina's quiet power propelled her forward, while Tina laughed at how Cher earned her way by being bold and brazen, even if she was quieter and softer behind the scenes.

The first leg of the tour went from May to June, bringing in packed audiences and millions of dollars in revenue. The show featured 20 costume changes, including a number of Bob Mackie classics. Cher then had time away from Vegas until August 2008, when the show would pick up. Shows went from August through October.

That summer, rumours began to circulate that Cher was in talks to play Catwoman in Christopher Nolan's *Batman* movie. The same batch of casting rumours also talked about Johnny Depp coming on board as The Riddler. Though talk continued publicly through that spring, it wasn't until late summer that the studio shut down both those casting rumours.

Cher also had another film opportunity that she would have to turn down as a result of the tour. Cher was being considered for a role in 2008's *Mamma Mia!*, an opportunity to reunite with her dear friend Meryl Streep. Production schedule conflicted with the touring schedule, though they'd later get to see it through in the film's sequel.

Though she had more of a focus on entertainment, Cher still dedicated a portion of her time and efforts to politics. As the 2008 election approached, she vocalised her support for Hilary Clinton. She showed her support at events in the Miami area, which she was calling home at the time. Not only did she lend her support to the Democratic candidate, but she made a point of denouncing Trump as an inept businessman and disgusting person to platform.

Cher also spent time abroad during her time off from the residency. She travelled to Kathmandu, Nepal, where she engaged in philanthropic work. She spent time with Tibetan children who were students at a school she contributed to having built there. In addition to that contribution, she gathered toys, musical instruments, books, and more to gift the children during her time there. Her commitment to building schools abroad would grow over time, with Cher also building a school in Africa that she visited during this time outside the US.

In February 2009, Cher began the third leg of her Las Vegas residency. It would keep her busy through May of that year. There were some challenges, of course. Cher fell ill a few different times, with her throat struggling with the arid desert environment. Nevertheless, Cher pushed on with the show, splitting much of her time between Los Angeles and Las Vegas. She even celebrated her 63rd birthday on stage. It was business as usual when she performed the residency on the special day.

In June 2009, Cher sued Universal Music Group on behalf of herself and Sonny's heirs, claiming an audit of accounting at the label found that label executives hid earnings from two compilation albums – *Cher: The Greatest Hits* and *The Very Best of Cher*. Cher claimed in doing this, they breached Sonny and Cher's 1972 deal with Kapp Records and her own 1987 deal with the David Geffen Company.

News of the lawsuit was eclipsed by news of Chaz's gender reassignment surgeries. Cher didn't shy away from discussing his transition, admitting she didn't always handle his journey in the LGBTQ community in the best way, but has always had her child's best interest at heart. She'd return to the Las Vegas stage in September 2009, performing through the end of the year.

Towards the end of 2009, Cher also started working on a new film, *Burlesque*. She was approached by filmmaker Steven Antin about the project after casting Christina Aguilera as Ali. Though Queen Latifah and Michelle Pfeiffer were floated for the role of Tess, it was Screen Gems studio president Clint Culpepper who suggested Cher for the role. At the same time, Cher was auditioning for a voice role – Janet the Lioness in *Zookeeper*. She would go ahead to nab both roles to close out the year.

Chapter Sixteen

Chaz

Cher has enjoyed a beautiful, albeit complex, relationship with her oldest child. It began with an unconventional childhood that was full of love but also inconsistency.

The only child of Sonny Bono and Cher was born in 1969. Chastity Sun Bono was the pride and joy of their parents' lives. A child born after a number of losses, everything Chas did lit up the world for both Sonny and Cher. Chas appeared a happy and well-adjusted child, making frequent appearances on their parents' television show. But there was more to life than the few minutes millions of viewers would see on the small screen each week.

Growing up backstage at show venues and on television sets made for unforgettable memories, but Chas did pine for a more 'normal' life at different periods throughout their childhood. That became more difficult to achieve after Sonny and Cher split in 1975, when they were six years old. Splitting time between Sonny and Cher was quite the process as both of them found their way.

Once Sonny left entertainment behind, he was able to provide stability for Chas in a way they hadn't had before. Chas's bond with Sonny was stronger than Cher's in many ways. Sonny would let Chas dress in boys' clothing and treat them like a son, even calling them by their chosen nickname, Fred. Sonny wasn't bothered by any of it.

Cher couldn't help but fall into some of the same dynamics she had with Georgia in her relationship with a younger Chas. As a result, she did have ways of pushing more traditional femininity onto her child. Though Cher was a tomboy in her own youth, she was made uncomfortable by Chas's differences, and could only stay quiet on the subject for so long before making her opinions on the matter known. She was also a fan of compromise, willing to give to Chas's desires in exchange for a bit of the same towards her. It made for complicated feelings about their bond on Chas's end, always feeling like Cher was disappointed with them.

That said, when Chas was adamant about something, Cher would hear her and do her best to respect it. When Chas came home from the second grade one day and told Cher they'd no longer wear dresses, Cher understood Chas was serious and looked to other alternatives when occasions that would call for a dress might arise. The entertainer, at this point, was starting to recognise that she was uncomfortable with her child's gender expression, although she didn't know how to handle the situation to improve things. Sometimes, this would mean distance between the two.

Throughout Chas's childhood, moving was a frequent fact of life. While it was seen by both parents as a fact of life, it was tough as a child. Life changed even more once Chas went from being an only child to an older sibling. When Elijah Blue was born, a new baby nurse was brought in for him, with Chas's longtime nanny being dismissed at the same time. One of the child's closest confidantes, the loss was a tough blow. It became harder still when that nanny was eventually replaced by a harsh one who inflicted a lot of psychological damage on her two charges. It took a long time before Chas was able to tell their parents the extent of the trauma from that time.

There was also another deep trauma in Chas's life at a young age. When Sonny and Cher briefly toured together after their second go at their variety show, Chas and Elijah joined them on the road. Chas required a tutor to stay on top of missed schoolwork. While studying in a hotel room together, the tutor prompted Chas to 'play a game' where the tutor pretended to be a girlfriend and Chas was prompted to be the boyfriend. The tutor would guide the 8-year-old to engage in activity that they were unaware was sexual assault.

While there were dark moments, there was some joy in life on the road. Exploring different parts of the world and seeing how different cultures regarded queerness, though they didn't recognise it as that at the time, was fascinating to Chas. Being around creatives and seeing the wild variety of lifestyles they led showed more possibility than life in any one place.

Puberty would only bring more frustration and complexity to Chas's life. As they began to physically develop, they detested their female attributes. Feeling ashamed of their body, they hid behind oversized clothing, a habit that would continue well into adulthood.

As a teen, Chas started to piece together the ways they felt different and what that meant. After seeing lesbians on screen in *Personal Best*, the movie they saw on their 13th birthday, Chas began to consider whether they might be a lesbian.

As Chas gave more consideration to this possibility, it began to feel like an answer to many questions – why they often felt more masculine than their peers, why they felt uninterested in dating and relationships but gravitated towards friendship with boys. That Christmas, Chas met a friend of Cher's, Joan. Though just a young teen at the time, Chas thought that Joan was fascinating and would later become an important figure in their life.

When Chas returned to living in Los Angeles, Cher encouraged exploring acting. Though initially reluctant, it would become an outlet and a passion they came to appreciate. They began to explore dating while also getting quality time with both Sonny and Cher. Chas lived with Cher that summer, went to acting school, and worked at Bono's restaurant bussing tables. Chas felt like their relationship with both parents improved over that summer, not being bound to a schedule that resulted from either of them touring for the first time.

Chas flourished in the freedom that came with moving to New York City as a teen. They attended Fiorello H. LaGuardia High School of Music & Art and Performing Arts after being accepted at 14. The start of the journey was rocky, with Chas confronted with a rumour that Cher paid their way into the school by donating new equipment for certain programs. There was no truth to it, and Chas dispelled the rumours. They were surprised that in New York's bustling entertainment scene, anyone would care much about Sonny and Cher.

It was during this time they finally began to discover a community where they felt comfortable. They were surrounded by other kids whose level of freedom was similar to their own, which wasn't always the case in Los Angeles. The music scene was bustling with the punk wave of the mid-80s. The corresponding styles gave Chas the opportunity to explore with their look. As they felt increasingly comfortable, they began to come out as a lesbian to friends.

Halfway through their time at the performing arts school, Cher joined them in New York City. The two found themselves living alone together for the first time ever after Elijah decided on boarding school over city life. There was some comfort and direction for the 16-year-old in living with a parent again. Cher also enjoyed the freedom of being able to move freely without being hounded by press. The added ease in both their lives made for a good environment for the pair to reconnect and bond.

The only tension that the two didn't shake during that time was regarding Chas's appearance. Cher regularly commented on disliking their sense of style. At that point, Chas still wasn't out to Cher, who wasn't a fan of their 'sloppy' appearance.

While they weren't out to Cher, there were family members in the know at that point. They came out to Georgia first before starting high school. During their junior year, they came out to Georganne.

For some time, Chas believed they could keep their personal life separate from their relationship with Cher. That changed when Cher walked in on them making out with a date. Though there wasn't a big confrontation, the withheld information hung over the two, creating tension and avoidance between the two.

Chas was also trying to figure themselves out. They even decided to be intimate with a man to rule out the possibility that they were bisexual or just inexperienced. The experience solidified their feeling they were a lesbian. As they became more sure, the prospect of coming out to both parents became more certain.

During their senior year, Chas came out to Sonny. Sonny was supportive and told Chas he'd suspected this might be the case for some time and would be there for her regardless. Still maintaining some distance from Cher, there was a point when Chas was alone in the apartment with Cher's boyfriend, Rob. Knowing Rob was home, Chas still brought home her girlfriend to spend the night. When Cher found out, she asked Sonny, who confirmed the suspicions.

Cher reacted explosively, hurt by the realisation she was the last to know. The hurt and shock of the revelation, which she hadn't considered much prior to that moment, led her to lash out in a way she would later say she was disappointed about but not embarrassed by. She wasn't ashamed, she'd come to explain, because she knew it would have value when she came forth with those feelings, validating many parents who react similarly before coming to a place of acceptance.

A week later, she calmed down and called Chas to apologise and welcome her back, upset by her own reaction. They did try therapy to work through it, with Cher determined to help get the relationship back to a better place. It would take months and even years of work, but the dedication to it meant a lot to Chas.

There was a major relief to Chas in coming out. There was a level of comfortability in their relationships with those closest to them now that the secret was no longer being concealed. That being said, Chas wasn't ready to be out on a more public level. In the summer between high school and college, they got to enjoy travelling to Europe and observing queer culture there. They would go on to study at NYU's acting school for a year before dropping out in pursuit of another creative journey.

Growing up around musical legends filled Chas with an interest in making music and performing. At 19, they started their first band, Ceremony, alongside then-girlfriend Heidi. Chas didn't want to use their parents' connections to rise to the top, determined to grind through the work as countless musicians in the 80s and 90s did in New York City. Rather than looking to benefit from them, they were inspired by both Sonny and Cher and their work ethic. By the summer of 1990, the two had gotten a full band together. The band worked on some demos, shopping them to none other than John Kalodner, then the A&R for Geffen Records.

Chas's sexuality was a private matter for almost three years when that winter, the family learned that would change. Geffen Records was also made aware of a tabloid's plan to out Chas. Their advice was for Chas and Heidi to act as straight as possible. The band, as well as the label, were concerned the outing would be the end of their just budding career.

This forced the pair to withdraw from the LGBTQ community, which was hard for them. They received criticism for this from those they were out to, which was further frustrating. Additionally, they were hounded by the press, losing the privacy they once enjoyed. This put a lot of pressure on the relationship, especially as they navigated a move to Los Angeles to continue working on their album. It was during that time that Chas briefly reconnected with Joan, recognising their crush on her had blossomed into a full-fledged attraction.

Still dedicated to working on things with Heidi, they didn't act on it. Later that year, however, the two had a conversation where they acknowledged how they were growing apart. They didn't agree to a full-fledged breakup, first wanting to complete the album. During that time, Chas began spending more time with Joan. Once the album was completed, after about ten months, while getting ready to promote it live, Chas finally called things off.

It wasn't easy coming to that decision, but the news that Joan's previous bout with cancer was recurring changed their perspective. They worked on promoting the album as Joan went through treatment, which had a promising prognosis at that time. They completed the tour, awaiting a date on their pushed-back album release.

After the initial shock wore off, Cher was dedicated to being a fierce advocate for Chas, as well as being supportive of them in their own personal life. She educated herself on issues facing the LGBTQ community. When Chas became too sick with mono to care for herself and Joan, Cher moved them both in and took care of them until Chas was well enough to bring Joan back home. As 1993 came to a close, Chas was almost exclusively dedicated to caring for Joan, whose condition was worsening. They also dealt with the stress by taking some of Joan's painkillers, the beginning of their addiction struggles.

Joan died from pneumonia contracted during a stem cell transplant that was supposed to save her life in February 1994. It was a true heartbreak for Chas, who would turn 25 the following month. This was deepened when she learned Joan died cancer-free. That same week, Ceremony was dropped from Geffen Records. Chas was back at square one, taking up bartending while trying to figure out their next move. Prescribed

Vicodin for menstrual health issues, their relationship with painkillers also became more concerning.

Chas was courted by *The Advocate* to come out in the publication. While they weren't fond of the idea at first, they were intrigued by the queer publication and reached out for a job. Chas began working there as a writer in January 1995. The following month, they'd grace the cover and publicly come out. They received support from the community and was also propelled into a position to represent them, with multiple opportunities to work with advocacy groups and political campaigns to advance issues important to the community. Between Cher's star power and Sonny's political career, the spotlight was on Chas. Ultimately, Chas made the most of it. They embraced the opportunity and platform they were born into to try to make a difference.

Chas experienced heartbreak at the centre of their world at the sudden death of Sonny. Not only was his death unexpected, but it came at a time when the two were estranged from one another. Politics drove a wedge in the close bond between Sonny and Chas as his views continued to skew more conservative. At that time, they'd tried interviewing him for *The Advocate* and became frustrated that the politician wasn't taking the conversation or the issues seriously. It had been over a year since they'd last spoken at the time of his death.

What's worse, Chas was the one who was tasked with telling Cher the devastating news. Mary Bono had called Chas with the news. Chas then called Cher, who tried to be there for Chas before getting momentarily lost in her own grief. They spent the time between Sonny's death and his funeral surrounded by loved ones who were also grieving. The group would continue to meet periodically and support each other after the initial wave of grief, with Cher often hosting them.

In a sit down with Chas in August 1996 for *The Advocate*, they discussed Chas coming out. Cher admitted she was disappointed in her own reaction, which was emotional rather than rational. It caught the entertainer, who had LGBTQ people around her nearly all her life, by complete surprise, in more ways than one.

Cher also admitted she had a sense Chas could be queer as early as age 11 or 12 and resented that Sonny 'played' into it. They both acknowledged ways that their behaviour led to the situation being what it was and the importance of how far they'd come since that initial explosive incident.

Chas's struggles with prescription medications, which they received more of for migraines that ensued after Sonny's death. They didn't consider themselves a drug addict, rather believing their behaviour stemmed from grief and depression. When they experienced liver failure and an ulcer at the tail end of 1999, they gained clarity on how dire matters were.

In early 2000, Chas decided to get help. They also threw themselves into another relationship in hopes of support staying afloat. Kathy was also sober and introduced them to socializing within that community. The two saw *Boys Don't Cry* together, a movie that allowed Chas to consider that they might be transgender. Chas posed the thoughts to Kathy, who seemed at first unfazed and later uncomfortable by the possibility.

They met with a transgender activist, and in discussing experiences, Chas was stricken by the commonalities and continued to give it real thought, which Kathy was not supportive of. Chas's thoughts of transitioning were sidelined by more medical issues, which led to using prescription medication once again. They still considered themselves sober since it was being recommended to them by a medical professional, but it once again got out of hand. When Kathy broke up with Chas and moved out, she told Cher about Chas's thoughts about being transgender and their pill usage.

Despite Cher's attempts to get them help, Chas wasn't ready to pursue sobriety until March 2004. When they were ready, Cher was there to support them. That included some intensive work for the two in therapy, as Chas worked out some of the issues around their addiction, childhood, and sexuality. As far as gender expression decisions, Chas was advised by their medical team to sideline thinking about that until they had sustained a year of sobriety.

During that time, Chas broached the subject with Cher. The entertainer was initially very supportive and thought it was a good time in their life to move forward with it. She also suggested they talk through it in therapy, where concerns and reservations came to light. Chas also experienced how lesbian women reacted to the idea when dating a woman who was repulsed by the idea, making Chas feel shame.

Chas had their own fears about a physical transition. They wanted to live their truth, but also were aware of the reality they'd have to deal with in their interpersonal relationships, on a public level, and in their advocacy. Getting into a new relationship with partner Jenny, she was also worried about how it would impact their connection.

Despite their mixed experience with life in the spotlight, in 2006, Chas decided to give reality TV a shot. They appeared on *Celebrity Fit Club*, where they served as a team captain and made some serious progress in getting their body into better shape and beginning on a path to a healthier lifestyle. It would also put them in a better position when it came to a possible physical transition.

A healthy lifestyle would also require Chas to take inventory mentally. They felt discomfort in the fact that while they were encouraged to lose weight, they weren't encouraged to build muscle in its place, which they believed would bring them closer to the body they desired.

The professional opportunity also intrigued Chas, who remained interested in public life in some capacity. They hired a publicist to see what other television work could come their way. They had some ideas of their own for a scripted project, but much of the interest they received was in the reality TV space. Their experience with *Celebrity Fit Club* didn't make them want to further work in the genre. They also considered work in the gaming industry, writing a treatment for a role-playing game (RPG) but finding that gaming production companies were only interested in ideas from within.

They felt they had a breakthrough in working with a gay television network on developing a TV movie. Despite working with a longtime friend on the script over time and doing a number of rewrites after the network's interest, the project was shelved in April 2007, bringing Chas back to a depressed state. They once again contemplated transitioning but had extreme anxiety about doing so publicly.

It took over a year of work in therapy and serious consideration before Chas was ready to make that decision. It also took work with Jenny to make sure she understood the changes, physical and emotional, that would come. The two were also continuing to work on their respective sobriety journeys, making for a lot going on. Chas also sought help in group therapy, with Cher sometimes attending with her.

During this time, Chas and Cher were also putting in work on their relationship and in a really good place. This amplified Chas's fear that their mother would reject their physical transition, and it would damage their relationship. Like the other relationships in their life, including that which they shared with the public, they realised they had to let go and make this decision for themselves, knowing they could not control reactions to that decision.

In 2008, Chas was ready to begin a process whose effects would ripple through the rest of their life. Though the conversation with Jenny about that readiness hadn't gone as hoped, they knew they needed to move forward for themselves. They recognised themselves as a transgender man. Chas became Chaz as he began the process of physically transitioning from female to male.

Telling Cher the transition was beginning was a surprisingly calm experience for Chaz, though things would take a turn. After the holidays, Cher wanted to meet with Chas, members of their family, and their therapist to discuss the transition. But when it came time to pick a date, Cher kept evading it. Chaz wouldn't see his mom for months after the admission. Chaz suspected that Cher was struggling with the news and left space there for processing. He kept her posted by text but didn't hear much back. Additionally, Chaz's conversations with Georganne and Elijah made him feel like Cher wasn't the only one who had complicated feelings about the news.

Telling Sonny's widow, Mary, and his younger siblings went better for Chaz and strengthened the relationships there. Chaz would end up sitting down with the therapist and Cher in April, who explained that she thought that Chaz was farther off from starting the process than she initially understood. She also was operating with the knowledge Chaz had told her about feeling transgender years prior and had considered transitioning before but had not gone through with it. The fact the process was starting after so many false starts caught her by surprise. She also shared concerns that the media and the world at large would be cruel to her child. Chaz explained that it was his decision to do it and he couldn't let those factors outweigh the desire to live authentically.

Chaz's transition began at age 40, after many years of consideration and five years of sobriety. The process would take a number of years, but it finally brought Chaz to a place of peace and acceptance. The stillness in their identity would make all the difference. Chaz was preparing to take the news public when outlets picked up on it and threatened to out him. Chaz's publicist worked with TMZ on a statement, but it left just hours for Chaz to share the news with anyone he wanted to hear it personally, rather than in the media. They called Cher for support and got it in spades. She assured him that everyone important who needed to know already knew.

Chaz's transition was met with mixed news from the public. Understanding and tolerance for the transgender community was rising, but not at a high point. While he did get a lot of support, he also got a lot of criticism. It resulted in a lot of press attention, with paparazzi following him and Jenny until the next big story – the death of Michael Jackson – caused them to move on.

Cher would continue to struggle with the transition. After hearing Chaz's voicemail message, the first time she heard his deepened voice, she broke down and admitted she needed some time to wrap her head around it. Though the two didn't speak for months, Chaz didn't take it personally and didn't worry that it was going to be the end of their relationship. He tried to understand that while getting to know Chaz, Cher was also grieving the daughter she welcomed into the world. In tough moments where Chaz would reach out, Cher would do her best to put her own feelings aside and be there for her son.

After recovering from top surgery, Chaz started speaking out about his experience in the media. As he became more comfortable in his own skin, many of his relationships started taking turns for the better. He worked things out with Georganne and Elijah. In time, things with Cher also improved.

The news of Chaz's transition was publicly confirmed in 2009 when he was still amid the process. Chaz also filmed a documentary that followed his transition, *Becoming Chaz*. In doing so, he got more insight into how he was perceived by his loved ones as the transition progressed. He also recognised differences in himself. Chaz also wrote a book, *Transition: Becoming Who I Was Always Meant to Be.*

In speaking with the press, Chaz appeared on *David Letterman, Oprah Winfrey,* and more. Though the questions were often repetitive, Chaz seized on the opportunity to help the average American viewer understand more about what it is to be transgender.

In 2011, Chaz was cast in the fall season of *Dancing With the Stars.* Around the same time, he was filming *Being Chaz,* another documentary special that would show what his life living his truth looked like. The public was getting used to Chaz, and he was happy to speak out on behalf of his community. There were also difficult moments, such as getting death threats for appearing on TV. Chaz also struggled after the end of his six-year relationship with Jenny, which came shortly after *DWTS* concluded.

Chaz tried to focus on his professional life in the subsequent months. He appeared in guest spots on *Degrassi: The Next Generation, The Secret Life of the American Teenager,* and *RuPaul's Drag Race.* Next came roles that required true acting, starting with a short arch on *The Bold and the Beautiful* in 2016.

In 2017, Chaz shifted back to acting, scoring a role on *American Horror Story: Cult.* That same year, Chaz began seeing Shara Mathes. The two hit it off quickly. Chaz was excited to have another chance at love. As of 2024, it's been made public that Shara is now Chaz's fiancée, though neither has discussed the details of their relationship.

Cher appeared alongside Shara, cheering Chaz on at the premiere of the 2024 film in which he starred, *Little Bites.* Though the relationship between the two hasn't always been smooth sailing, Chaz has been in a positive space in his life and Cher has been thrilled to see her oldest thrive.

Chapter Seventeen

2010–2014

In 2010, Cher continued to try to understand Chaz's decision to transition while also continuing on with her bustling career. She started the year by continuing work on *Burlesque*, her return to the big screen.

Cher was excited about the film before being involved, having heard about it through David Geffen. What's more, the opportunity to work with Aguilera sounded like a lot of fun. The filmmakers joked to her that Aguilera was such a fan she'd 'drink her bathwater.'

In on the joke, Aguilera referenced it when she introduced herself to Cher. The two bonded over their fun-loving but no-nonsense attitudes towards life and business. Cher welcomed the opportunity to take Aguilera under her wing in the same way Streep did for her when she went from music to acting. The film also offered Cher an opportunity to sing in a movie. It was something she hadn't gotten to pursue, and the possibility was appealing.

Filming for *Burlesque* concluded in March. Leg 5 of the Las Vegas residency went from April through July. She took a break for just two months before returning to the stage in September through October.

In September, Cher also took the stage at the MTV Video Music Awards (VMAs). She showed up at the event wearing an updated rendition of her iconic 'If I Could Turn Back Time' outfit, a Bob Mackie original. Cher presented Lady Gaga with the award for Video of the Year for 'Bad Romance.' Gaga, accepting the award in her iconic meat dress, found a kindred spirit in the daring singer at that moment. Both women stunned the loudly cheering audience.

During that time, Cher found a new way to connect with her fans – social media. Twitter, in particular, offered her a unique way to connect with her fans. Cher's hilarious and honest tweets, often written with capitalised letters sprinkled throughout and copious emojis, were crafted as it made more sense to her, as a person with dyslexia. She also used the platform to speak out on politics and comment on other current events. In the years that followed, as Twitter became increasingly popular, Cher's popularity on the platform also rose. She's considered one of the most entertaining presences on the platform to this day.

Cher enjoyed a romance during this time also. Late the year prior, she began dating Ron Zimmerman, a TV screenwriter. The two connected in an unlikely manner, connecting on Facebook through a mutual friend. Zimmerman was in disbelief that it was Cher herself until, after a month of chatting online, she called him.

Burlesque debuted in November 2010, with international release dates trickling into the following month. Along with pride for her acting, Cher worked with Diane Warren on her ballad in the film, 'You Haven't Seen the Last of Me.' The parallels between the role and reality were not lost on Cher, moving into another phase in her career.

Chaz accompanied Cher to the premiere. While the two still had a lot of work to get their relationship to a good place, Cher had been better about using her son's preferred pronouns and explaining his journey to others. In this, her own acceptance grew. She realised Chaz was still Chaz in every way that mattered.

The same month, Cher was honoured by having her handprints and footprints added outside the Grauman's Chinese Theatre. Again, Chaz was there for the special moment, as well as Georgia. Not through with the special events, Cher also sat for a lengthy interview with *Vanity Fair*, published in the November 2010 issue.

Reflecting on her career in the interview, Cher compared herself to a bumper car in that, 'If I hit a wall, I'm backing up and going in another direction. And I've hit plenty of fucking walls in my career.'

Cher returned to Las Vegas and her residency after ringing in 2011. This would be the last leg of the residency, continuing through February 2011. The monumental residency, spanning three years, brought in over £73 million in revenue.

After the residency was through, Cher took a well-deserved break. And though she wasn't actively working on any projects, she was still considering her options. She knew she wanted to work on something new, but she also enjoyed her *Burlesque* experience and didn't want to rule out another film.

In January 2012, Cher fans were spooked as the star was the latest in a string of celebrities who had a death hoax purported about them. Cher was very much alive and working on new music. Despite her hesitance to commit, she was working on an album titled *Closer To The Truth*. She hoped for a pop-rock sound but ended up veering more toward dance music as the album's production progressed.

That spring, Cher accompanied Chaz to the 23rd Annual GLAAD Media Awards. There, she presented her son with the Stephen F. Kolzak Award, honouring his prominent place in the LGBTQ community and the entertainment community. Chaz would also take home the award for Outstanding Documentary.

In the early summer of 2012, Gregg Allman came out with a memoir, *My Cross to Bear*. It was there and in promotion of the book that he spoke publicly about his relationship with Cher for the first time. Gregg claimed that he loved Cher for her whimsy but grew to have disdain for her 'militant' ways. Gregg also felt that while he did harm to himself throughout his relationship with Cher, he didn't feel he did anything to ever directly harm her.

During that summer, Cher was out with her mom, Georgia, when the two ran into President Barack Obama. The two women were a bit starstruck, but the politician made a sweet impression on them. Cher tweeted about the encounter and how much it meant to them both.

That same summer, Cher announced that she was working with a team to write a musical about her life and career for Broadway. Cher was honest with her fans about the project being in its early stages and that it would take a long time to come to fruition. She even admitted she wasn't sure it would make it to the finish line. It would end up taking years, but the finished product would be well worth the wait.

In November 2012, Cher began teasing her twenty-fifth studio album, *Closer To The Truth*. After a snippet of her first single, called 'Woman's World,' was leaked online in the autumn of 2012, Cher made the single available for streaming from Thanksgiving Day until its official release on 18 June 2013. Cher's first single in about a decade was met with mixed reviews. Some were apprehensive about her stepping away from the autotune, while others were thrilled with it.

That spring, Cher had her mind on a different project. She worked with P. David Ebserole to create a TV documentary exploring her mom, Georgia, and her storied life. *Dear Mom, Love Cher* premiered on 6 May 2013. Billed as a 'tell-all' that would delve into the family behind the superstar, Cher seized the opportunity to celebrate Georgia alongside Georganne, Chaz, and Elijah, who all appeared in the special.

Cher also had another special opportunity to celebrate Georgia when she released her album, *Honky Tonk Woman*. It was originally recorded by Georgia in the 1980s, working with Elvis Presley's TCB band on the project. The tapes were shoved into storage and re-earthed by Cher, serving as inspiration for the documentary. Included on the album is a mother-daughter duet on a track called 'I'm Just Your Yesterday.'

In August, the music video for 'Woman's World' premiered. Seizing on an opportunity to make some fan dreams come true and raise money for important causes, Cher auctioned off opportunities for walk-on roles in the video to fans, with all proceeds going to GlobalGiving.

Closer To The Truth was released on 20 September 2013. That same month, 'Woman's World' hit number one on the Billboard Dance chart. Cher was proud of the record, which allowed her to explore different genres while still staying true to a sound and a theme. Critics were impressed by Cher's continued way of keeping a pulse on what people wanted.

Another album brought up the question of touring once again. Cher had made a big deal of saying goodbye, but she couldn't resist the call of the road. In September 2013, she announced the 'Dressed to Kill' tour during an appearance on *The Today Show*. Concert dates were set to begin in March 2014. While there, she also introduced the album's second single, her cover of Miley Cyrus' 'I Hope You Find It.' Another track on the album, 'I Walk Alone,' featured background vocals and writing by Pink. The collaborations with younger women in the industry were exciting for Cher, despite the fact that many believed she harboured jealousy toward those she passed her torch to.

The following month, Cher visited Nepal once again. During this trip, she deepened her relationship with Tibetan Buddhism. Neither by her upbringing nor by her lifestyle did Cher ever identify with a particular religion. She was more interested in the ideologies that drove them.

In November, Cher served as a guest judge on *Dancing With The Stars*. Nervous about the stint, Cher did amazing as the contestants danced to different versions of her hits. She gave fair scores and dazzled everyone in the ballroom, even if censors had to catch her letting a profanity slip.

February 2014 featured Cher getting into a public tiff with her record label, Warner Bros. Records, claiming they weren't 'interested' in *Closer To The Truth*. While the album was doing well, Cher believed it had the potential for more, but the highest-ups didn't believe in her or the record.

At the same time, she was preparing for the 'Dressed to Kill' tour. She admitted to finding the tour prep more gruelling than it had been for her in years prior, but she was also dedicated to putting on the best show she could for her fans.

She was also crushed when she found out that due to his own professional obligations, Bob Mackie couldn't provide the costume for the latest tour. While it was billed as a 'professional breakup' at the time, the two not only remain friends to this day but collaborate in big and small ways still.

The 'Dressed to Kill' Tour officially kicked off in March 2014, with Pat Benatar as her opening act. Later, Cyndi Lauper would step in as an opener. Hugh Durrant stepped in to help provide Cher and her team with perfect costumes for the show, bringing his fourteen different designs together in just six weeks' time.

During that tour, Cher would have to fend off rumours about her personal life after being seen with Caitlyn Jenner, who had not yet publicly announced their transition from male to female. Dating rumours about the pair began to circulate. In reality, Jenner was consulting Cher, whom they'd met at a dyslexia event at the White House in the 80s, and Chaz, whom they'd met on *Dancing With The Stars*, about transitioning publicly and advocacy work. Cher was careful to keep Jenner's news to herself when shutting down the rumours.

The singer quietly lent her talents to an unusual project. Under her original stage name, Bonnie Jo Mason, Cher recorded not one, but two songs with the Wu-Tang Clan for their album *Once Upon a Time in Shaolin*…Recording took place in May 2014. The album was famously released with just a single physical copy, purchased by pharmaceutical entrepreneur Martin Shkreli in 2015 in an auction for £1.5 million. However, the album's journey didn't end there. When Shkreli's assets were seized in March 2018, so too was the album. It remained with the United States Department of Justice until it was resold to art collective PleasrDAO for a total of £3 million. Tracks have been leaked in the years since, but there has yet to be a complete, public release.

Touring was a blast for Cher, but it did come with some major downsides. She discovered that the choreography for the tour posed some issues with her existing foot injury, which came from accidentally dropping a weight on it in the gym decades prior. The injury was aggravated by the demanding tour schedule. In mid-June 2014, Cher had to go to the hospital to receive injections to help ease her pain so she could get through tour dates. She talked about her injections on Twitter, saying she had gotten one prior to touring in the early part of the year that made a difference.

Cher concluded the first leg of the 'Dressed to Kill' tour in July 2014. The second leg was set to pick up in the autumn. When it came close to show time, however, Cher was forced to cancel tour dates due to an acute viral infection. Doctors allegedly ordered her to be on bed rest so she could be monitored. Many speculated the infection triggered a resurgence of Cher's Epstein-Barr virus. Later, Cher would classify it as a severe kidney infection. She continued to cancel tour dates throughout September and October. In November, she cancelled all remaining tour dates to focus on her recovery. She was hopeful she'd be able to make up those dates when she recovered, though that would not come to pass. Dates in 2015 were ultimately cancelled.

Chapter Eighteen

Elijah

Elijah Sky Blue Allman was born on July 10, 1976. The only child of Cher and second husband Gregg Allman, Elijah came into a world of creativity and heart but also struggle. Growing up, he always had Cher and formed special connections with several of her significant partners. Gregg, however, was largely absent.

Cher always knew Elijah to be rambunctious, the boisterous counterpart to her quiet Chaz. And though she had an appreciation for his affectionate heart and wild streak, she also struggled to find an effective way of getting through to her son.

One love the two did share was music. Like Chaz, Elijah grew up on the road. Surrounded by musicians, it became clear from an early age that he was among his own. He began experimenting with different instruments as young as 6 years old.

In trying to do the best she could by Elijah and recognising he didn't appreciate or adapt to moving from place to place the same way Chaz did, Cher made an unusual decision. At age 8, she enrolled Elijah in boarding school. Though at the time, he seemed fond of the idea, as an adult, Elijah would say that being away from the rest of his family made him feel 'shunned.'

Though Cher didn't know it, by 11 years old, Elijah was dabbling in drugs. As an adult, he admitted to getting his start with marijuana and ecstasy. Elijah had a distinct awareness of addiction and what it could do, even at that young age. It was, after all, what ultimately drove his parents apart and kept his father at bay.

While away at school, Elijah made tons of friends but struggled with his relationships with his family. He was once very close to Chaz, but the two grew apart. The seven-year age gap, coupled with Chaz's own struggles with sexuality and identity, made it hard for the siblings to connect at that time.

Heroin would ultimately become his drug of choice, one he claimed 'saved' him. Elijah recognised he was using drugs as a means of escape. While he felt like harder drugs kept him from taking his own life, it was also evident to those around him that it kept him from dealing with issues he was trying to outrun.

Having settled on guitar as his chosen instrument, he showed serious talent as he developed the skill. At age 13, he was given his first guitar of his own by Cher's then-beau, Gene Simmons.

Elijah tried to use his budding love of performing music as a basis to reconnect with Gregg. The absentee dad was agreeable to letting his teenage son join him on the road. The environment on Gregg's tours was far different from that on Cher's, giving Elijah unfettered access to whatever drugs piqued his interest. It broke Cher's heart to see her son fall to the same demons that kept her from having the relationship she dreamed of with Gregg. What's worse, she feared for her son's life.

Cher did want to show Elijah that she also had faith in his musical capabilities. That same year, he'd join her band on the 'Heart of Stone' Tour as a rhythm guitarist. He even joined her on stage at the 1988 MTV Video Music Awards.

The relationship between mom and son would only become more complicated as Elijah entered young adulthood and began to experience deeper struggles with addiction. His personal life also made headlines. Growing up, Elijah was friends with a number of famous children, both stars in their own right and the children of celebrities. When he started dating, it was in this pool that he'd explore. Elijah was supposedly once friends with Kourtney Kardashian, though the two never dated. He was romantically linked to Bijou Phillips, Paris Hilton, Nicole Richie, and Heather Graham throughout his late teens and early twenties.

Elijah wanted to and tried to drop out of school on several occasions before turning 18 and graduating from the Hyde School in 1994. Throughout that time, Gregg continued to be consumed by his music career and addiction, in and out of his son's life.

After graduating, Elijah's focus was predominantly on music. He started his band, Deadsy, with a group of friends. One thing was clear from the sound – it wasn't influenced by either of his parents' musical prowess. Deadsy was heavy, recording dark music that Elijah himself described as 'suicide music.' As they developed, they'd incorporate elements of nu-metal. Instead of going by his given name, Elijah would go by P. Exeter Blue.

The band began recording demos in the summer of 1995. The lineup evolved over the next year, when Deadsy would start seeking out a record deal. They were building a solid following, but mainstream success and stability with a record label would prove to be more complicated. The band caught the attention of Sire/Elektra and started working on their debut, self-titled album. When it came time to release and promote the album, however, the two labels split, leaving the record in limbo.

As a result of that deal and the consolidations that came with it, the band ended up at Warner Bros., which offered to let them leave their contract with ownership of their masters. In 1998, they did just that and started working on their next album, *Commencement*.

In 2000, the band signed to Elementree Records. After some more lineup shifts. It took a lot of determination, and at times, the band thought they might never see a project released. They also made important connections – with Korn's Jonathan Davis, who owned their label, and from Limp Bizkit's Fred Durst. In 2001, they hit the road on the Family Values Tour with Korn, Stone Temple Pilots, Linkin Park, and more. The next year, they'd hit the road with Korn and Mindless Self Indulgence.

Life on the road wasn't unfamiliar to Elijah, but it did seem to trigger old habits. While on the road, Elijah started abusing painkillers. Family, friends, and bandmates would encourage him to get help. There were a few attempts at rehab that also impacted the band's ability to keep going.

Additionally, Deadsy would continue to struggle with label woes. Their distribution deal with DreamWorks was taken over by Interscope after a late 2003 merger.

They also started working on *Phantasmagore*. Pieces of the album would come together over the following three years as they tried to find a label to call home. In 2006, they signed with Immortal Records and would release the finished album on that label. With another album came more time on the road. They toured the Family Values Tour once again in 2006, following that up with a co-headlining tour with Deftones. The band even performed at Lollapalooza that year.

In 2007, Elijah shared a brief statement explaining that Deadsy would be taking a hiatus. Other members went on to various projects, with a few commenting that the hiatus was designed for everyone to explore musically. Elijah's exploration was originally going to be through a solo album. He named his solo act Elijah Blue and the Trapezoids in 2008, but there were ultimately never any releases.

That same year, Elijah went back to rehab. Though he'd been there before, this trip changed one big thing for him. It would mark the end of his use of heroin. In getting sober, Elijah was able to open up more about his addiction. He spoke to someone who he believed would understand it intimately – Gregg. The two were able to reconnect and bond over their addiction. At that point, Gregg had seven years of sobriety under his belt. While they could identify with each other, Elijah also knew he didn't want to still be battling these demons into his fifties, as his father did.

In addition to exploring a solo project, Elijah also started to try his hand at visual arts. In the summer of 2010, he debuted his first exhibit, 'Stuff of Legends,' at Malibu's Madison Gallery. The exhibit comments on commercialism, popular art, and celebrity culture through a series of logo-driven imagery.

Cher and Chaz were both in attendance to celebrate Elijah's latest accomplishments. Despite the fact that, like many in his family, Elijah was taken aback by his brother's transition, the initial shock had worn off at that point. Elijah and Chaz were able to reconnect and relate on a different level from that point forward.

Elijah was energised by the work but battling a different issue. He'd started feeling ill a few months before launching the exhibition. The symptoms weren't unfamiliar to him. In fact, they'd recurred over several years, leaving a number of doctors stumped. Tests weren't bringing up anything conclusive. He tried turning to different methods of Eastern medicine and wellness methods to try to remedy the issues he faced.

During that time, Elijah tried a type of body cleanse that his ailing body reacted badly to. It resulted in a weeks-long stay in an intensive care unit, which he's since admitted he didn't think he would make it through. Left without answers or direction, he decided to visit Germany. He'd previously tried pursuing treatment there during an earlier time that he was feeling ill, but didn't feel he made progress.

Cher had previously had a breakthrough in the country in her battle with Epstein-Barr. She hoped her son would find a similar relief, though their relationship continued to have its highs and lows. Elijah would be disappointed by her lack of involvement and more hands-on care about his health. Cher admits that at several points throughout Elijah's life, the two have simply struggled to connect and understand each other in a way that helped their relationship thrive. Of course, she never gave up on her son, even when she did keep her distance or he was keeping his.

He would spend months there getting treatment. It was eventually determined to be Lyme disease, though Elijah acknowledges he'd been tested for the illness before and been told explicitly that wasn't what he was dealing with. During his time in Europe, seeking answers, he met Marieangela King. The two were set up on a blind date in 2013 and ended up travelling Europe together, getting to know one another. At one point, the pair briefly lived with Cher. It was the beginning of over a decade where Cher and King didn't see eye-to-eye. Elijah believed it was because both the women were strong-willed.

King is a musician in her own right, known professionally as 'Queenie,' and appreciated Elijah's unique creative eye. After a few months together, the couple got engaged and decided they would elope in December 2013. While the family wasn't involved in the initial nuptials, the two planned to celebrate later with loved ones back home. The two then took offence to not being invited to celebrate the holidays with Cher.

The following years would be filled with similar little misunderstandings or irritations between Cher and King. Cher continued trying to foster a positive relationship with her daughter-in-law, but their differences always seemed to win out over their similarities. They supported Cher at the premiere of *The Cher Show* on Broadway, but behind the scenes, the three allegedly continued to struggle in their relationship.

Elijah wasn't just caught in the middle in this situation. He was also trying to figure out how to tend to his relationship with an ailing Gregg in his final years. In 2016, the liver cancer he'd previously beaten had returned. He also struggled with cardiac issues, the combination of which led doctors to bar him from touring for his health. After cancelling tour dates in 2016, Gregg shut down rumours he was entering hospice care.

The following year, the cancer spread to one of his lungs. Gregg died in May 2017. For Cher, the loss was also devastating. Though she and Gregg could never work things out, she had a deep love for him. She was honest about his addiction, but loved him despite it all. Just after Gregg's funeral, which she attended with Elijah, she tweeted her final farewell.

Amid the pandemic in April 2020, the couple split. Over a year later, Elijah filed for divorce, citing irreconcilable differences. The two would go on to be on and off throughout the following years. Things between King and Cher came to a head in September 2023 when King made serious allegations against Cher in a filing related to the divorce.

King alleged that she and Elijah were working on their relationship in November 2022. The two were at a hotel together when she claimed that four men came in and 'kidnapped' Elijah from their hotel, with one allegedly specifying it was at Cher's behest. She also claimed that after that, Elijah was put in a rehab facility and that she was being kept from him as he recovered.

Cher denied these claims, though there was immense concern about Elijah behind the scenes. Additionally, there were mental health concerns from all parties involved. Elijah has publicly maintained he has been sober since 2008.

King's filings asked for spousal support, payment of her legal fees, and access to personal items she claimed were being held from her at a home she could no longer access. Further, she accused Cher of helping Elijah hide assets from her in their divorce. She believed the family had an abusive dynamic, accusing both Chaz and some of Elijah's siblings on his Allman side of the family of engaging in emotionally abusive behaviour.

As news of the family legal dust-up started going public, the rumours about Elijah's relapse intensified. In December 2023, Cher made the difficult decision to file for a conservatorship over Elijah. She expressed concern that money he was being paid out of a trust set up for him by Gregg before his death was being wasted on 'self-destructive' behaviours, from drug and alcohol abuse to frivolous spending. In the filing, Cher stated her belief that King was a 'destructive' force in her son's life and didn't have her son's best interest at heart. Further, the on-again, off-again nature of their relationship made it so that King couldn't be trusted to make decisions in Elijah's best interest in the long run.

Elijah wasn't happy with the legal move, which he saw as jeopardising his personal freedoms. In January 2024, Elijah filed to dismiss his divorce from King. The dismissal was granted the following month. He also filed documents in response to the conservatorship request, maintaining his sobriety and capabilities to make decisions with his own best interest at heart.

Cher never wanted the matter of Elijah's health and well-being to be publicly litigated and cause more discontent among the family. After working on the situation among themselves, Cher was satisfied with the results and dropped her bid for conservatorship in September 2024.

In April 2025, King filed for divorce from Elijah, citing irreconcilable differences. As for mother and son, the work on their relationship and the family's dynamic overall continues. Though things have been rocky, Cher is always driven by her instinct to do whatever she can to ensure the best life possible for each of her children.

Chapter Nineteen

2015–2019

Cher was determined to get back to work in 2015. Touring didn't feel like the right move as she continued to recover, so she took the time once again to explore her options.

That spring, Cher received an invitation to an old favourite of an event – the Met Gala. She attended as a guest of Marc Jacobs, wearing a grey, burgundy, and silver dress with three-quarter sleeves and a V-neck. The shimmery outfit was flattering on the star. Cher was lowkey but joyful at the event. There, she posed for a photo with fellow Armenian star Kim Kardashian, who was in attendance in a look inspired by Cher's first Met Gala.

Shortly after the event, it was announced that Cher would be the face of the Marc Jacobs Fall 2015 ad campaign. The star-studded campaign also featured Anthony Kiedis (the Red Hot Chili Peppers frontman who is Sonny's godson), Winona Ryder, Willow Smith, Emily Ratajkowski, Daisy Lowe, and Christy Turlington.

Cher started 2016 by sharing her opinions on the Flint, Michigan, water crisis. Like other causes before it, this one gripped Cher, who appreciated Michigan for its contributions to the music industry. She donated to the cause, as well as speaking about the crisis during a number of television interviews to raise awareness.

In February, Cher sat down for a conversation with Zendaya, who identified her as a 'girl crush' in the *Paper Magazine* feature. Zendaya praised Cher as one of her ultimate role models. Cher, in turn, praised Zendaya's willingness to express herself and be true to her style. Cher admired how Zendaya carried herself and what that would do to help her young fans open up and learn more about themselves.

May marked Cher's 70th birthday. While she never minded a celebration and enjoyed something quiet with friends and family, the moment was a turning point for Cher. The milestone birthday made her think about what she wanted out of the next stage of life.

When the 2016 election came around, Cher was once again eager to lend her voice in support of Democratic candidate Hilary Clinton. Having worked with her husband's campaign with Chaz, Cher was familiar with the Clintons and had a great deal of respect for the then Secretary of State.

Additionally, Cher has been a longtime vocal opponent of Donald Trump. Not only was she disgusted by his behaviour as a public figure, but she didn't have faith in his capabilities. In particular, she feared what his ignorance would mean for the LGBTQ+ community. She warned that she believed he had the capacity to be as dangerous as Hitler or Stalin.

Cher wanted to appeal to young people in her discussion of the issues. In October 2016, she attended the One Young World Summit in Ottawa. Inspired by the vision for a better world that some of these young leaders had, Cher started Free The Wild alongside UK entrepreneur Mark Cowne and South African entertainment professional and conservationist Gina Nelthorpe-Cowne, which aimed to amplify animal conservation efforts while also campaigning for safer containment situations for animals currently living in zoos and other animal-based entertainment establishments.

Embracing how social media was taking on all conversation around the election, Cher often tweeted her opinions. Her tenure as a Twitter personality hadn't slowed down, with fans cherishing her use of capitals and emojis to convey what was on her mind. Her fans were so fond of her political commentary that one fan, designer Anna Niess, made 'I'm With Cher' merchandise for adoring fans, with some of the proceeds going to charity.

In 2017, Cher was prepared to return to touring. She announced Classic Cher, a three-year residency set to go from February 2017 through February 2020. Concerts would take place in Atlantic City, Las Vegas, and Oxon Hill. She did as many as nine shows a month, alternating locations with each leg.

Less than 48 hours after her 71st birthday, Cher took the stage at the Billboard Music Awards. The performance was Cher's first at an award show in 15 years, and yet it seemed like she never missed a beat. She even incorporated an outfit change, going from a look that was EDM meets flapper to her iconic 'If I Could Turn Back Time' look.

The performance went viral when networks blurred out one of Cher's nipples, but the other didn't appear visible, leading many to question whether she had a right nipple. Rather, it seemed one of her pasties was working better for her than the other. She was then honoured with the Billboard Music Artist Achievement Award, presented to her by Gwen Stefani. Cher was not only celebrated for her countless achievements and reinventions throughout her music career, but also for her style and influence on the generation of artists that came after her.

The latter half of the month would be more difficult for Cher. On 27 May 2017, Cher learned of the death of Gregg Allman. Gregg died at the age of 69 as a result of complications from several illnesses. While Cher mourned the man she once loved, she was also concerned for Elijah. The relationship between mother and son was admittedly strained as she didn't see eye to eye with his partner, Marieangela King. Still, she wanted to be there for Elijah during the complicated time. He'd worked on his relationship with Gregg in the years leading up to Gregg's death, with varying results at different points in time. In supporting Elijah, she travelled to Macon, Georgia, for the funeral service.

The second half of the year took a turn for the exciting for Cher. In September, Cher revealed that the musical about her life and career would be moving forward. *The Cher Musical* announced try-outs in Chicago to begin next summer before heading to New York City to prepare for an autumn 2018 premiere.

That autumn also brought Cher back to a movie set. She was cast in *Mamma Mia! Here We Go Again*, a full-circle moment after being unable to work out her schedule to be in the first film a decade prior. Cher plays Ruby Sheridan, mom to Donna, played by Lily James in her younger years and Meryl Streep as she gets older. Ruby shakes things up when she shows up unannounced and ready to make amends with her daughter and get to know her granddaughter, Sophie (Amanda Seyfried).

Cher's casting was announced in October 2017, marking her return to the big screen after a 7-year absence. The role, custom-made for Cher, also allowed the actress the flexibility to choose her own leading man.

She chose Andy Garcia to play Fernando Cienfuegos. She performed ABBA's 'Fernando' in the film, as well as 'Super Trouper,' a full-cast ensemble piece.

The movie, which brought Cher and longtime friend Streep back together on a set, was filmed from August to December 2017. It was filmed across several locations – Vis, Croatia; Bordeaux, France; Stockholm, Sweden; and in the UK, in Oxford and Hampton.

Also that October, Cher made a return to the One Young World summit in Bogotá, Colombia. The gathering of young leaders from over 190 countries around the world featured discussions of many issues that the younger generation is passionate about, with experts from different walks of life providing guidance and inspiration. Cher shared updates about her work on Free The Wild, as well as continuing to share her disdain for the political climate in the United States.

Cher continued her residency in 2018, continuing to wow audiences. She worked through much of January and February of that year, continuing the 'Classic Cher' residency. That was just some of what was up her sleeve for that year, however.

In March, Cher headed to Sydney, Australia, to headline the city's 40th Gay and Lesbian Mardi Gras. She performed 'Believe,' 'Strong Enough,' 'If I Could Turn Back Time,' and 'All or Nothing' to a crowd of adoring fans. Energised by her time there, Cher decided she wanted to tour the area.

A few weeks later, Cher announced an Australian tour that would begin that autumn. Titled the 'Here We Go Again' Tour, there was instantly tons of interest in the performances, adding more dates than originally planned. The tour was then extended into New Zealand.

In April, fans became concerned about Cher after she posted a series of tweets that indicated paranoia, suggesting someone close to her had betrayed her by going to the media about a private matter. She also claimed that doctored text messages between her and her son had been produced. The complications were tied to the ongoing troubles between Cher and Elijah, though she never publicly acknowledged such.

Cher returned to 'Classic Cher' in May. She took some time to start planning the tour before joining the rest of the cast of *Mamma Mia! Here*

We Go Again for the London premiere in July. She posed with Streep, even sharing a kiss during their fun red carpet stroll. The following month, Cher announced an album of ABBA covers, titled *Dancing Queen*, for release in September.

That summer, production was hard at work bringing *The Cher Show* to life. The production would be housed at the Neil Simon Theatre, but began its run in Chicago first. The Chicago run took place from June through July 2018. The production required three different actresses to play Cher during the different eras of her career.

September also marked the beginning of Cher's Oceanic concerts, beginning in Auckland, New Zealand, before heading to Australia. About a week before the tour dates concluded, Cher announced that she would be bringing the concert back to the United States, with tour dates beginning in January 2019.

In December, Cher received yet another special career honour. She was recognised as one of the 2018 Kennedy Center honourees, in recognition of her contributions to the performing arts. Speaking about Cher's illustrious career was Whoopi Goldberg. Cher was then surprised with a special performance by friend and frequent tour mate Cyndi Lauper, as well as Adam Lambert, who brought Cher to tears with his performance of 'Believe.'

That was also the month *The Cher Show* made its Broadway debut after weeks of previews. Stephanie J. Block, Teal Weaks, and Micaela Diamond were the first three actresses to portray Cher. The production also included Jarrod Spector as Sonny, Michael Berresse as Bob Mackie, Michael Campayno as Rob Camilletti, and Matthew Hydzik as Gregg Allman. Of course, Cher was there in the flesh to cheer on the brilliant talent bringing her life's story to the stage. During the show's curtain call, she joined the cast to thunderous applause. Together, they did a special performance of 'If I Could Turn Back Time.' Critics praised the cast for putting their all into performances, even if some of the takes on real events were zany.

Cher spent a lot of time performing in 2019. Like so many others around the globe, she made her plans for the year with no idea of what the following year would entail. Cher began the year with her United

States tour dates for the 'Here We Go Again Tour.' Like many Cher concerts before it, these shows consisted of a twenty-song playlist that showcases her powerhouse vocals, paired with show-stopping visuals.

After performing dates throughout January and February, it was back to Las Vegas for another leg of the 'Classic Cher' residency through the end of March. In April, Tony nominations were announced. *The Cher Show* earned three nominations – Kevin Adams for Best Lighting Design of a Musical, Bob Mackie for Best Costume Design of a Musical, and Stephanie J. Block for Best Performance by a Leading Actress in a Musical.

After a few weeks off, it was back to touring, dipping into Canada at the end of April and continuing concerts around the country until the end of May. Cher also made time for another special performance in May, surprising attendees at the 'camp' themed 2019 Met Gala. Cher went all out with a multi-song performance at the end of the event's dinner, changing costumes to reflect each of her iconic eras.

Aside from her performance, Cher also spoke about what the Met Gala has meant to her in her appearances over the years. Her influence on fashion could be seen throughout the night. Emily Ratajkowski's look was inspired by the artist, as was Kim Kardashian's after-party look for fashion's biggest night. Cher's influence was also celebrated later that month, as she celebrated her 73rd birthday by playing to a sold-out crowd in St. Paul, Missouri.

The Tony Awards show took place in June 2019. While Cher wasn't able to attend, she was watching live and tweeting along. She celebrated emotionally as Mackie and Block took home the awards in their respective categories. It was sweet to see Mackie take home the honour for the first time after decades of costuming and designing throughout the entertainment industry. Cher was proud of Block and touched by her interpretation of her story.

In August, Cher returned to her Las Vegas residency for the last of those shows for the year, concluding on 1 September 2019. Towards the end of that month, it was back to touring, returning to Europe for a string of shows that would continue through November. The tour then returned to the United States, with shows continuing into December.

That month, Cher also debuted her new scent, 'Cher Eau de Couture.' It was her first fragrance since her 1987 scent, 'Cher Uninhibited.' Cher posed for the fragrance's campaign in a sleek black and white photo, complementing the perfume's simple bottle.

Cher surprised fans in an appearance on the *Ellen DeGeneres Show* when Sean Hayes was guest-hosting. After picking her out of the audience, the two sang 'If I Could Turn Back Time' together.

As 2019 closed out, Cher found herself setting another record. She became the first female artist over 90 to gross over £76 million during a concert tour for the 'Here We Go Again' tour.

Chapter Twenty

2020

Though it started without much to note, 2020 would become an unprecedented year for most people around the globe. Cher was no exception. She began the year with plans to continue and complete both her 'Classic Cher' residency in Las Vegas and the 'Here We Go Again Tour,' which had more tour dates planned in the United States throughout the year.

There was also a photo shoot in the middle of downtown Los Angeles alongside Kim Kardashian and Naomi Campbell. They came together for *CR Fashion Book*'s sixteenth issue. In the accompanying interview, Cher talked about having a true 'passion' for fashion and treating finding the right look as she would making the right piece of art. She considers herself an 'emotional' dresser, keeping sentimental pieces and resurfacing them when the time feels right.

She enjoyed another fashion moment that much, starring in DSquared2's Spring-Summer 2020 campaign. The first photo shared shows Cher looking off into the distance as her long, black hair blows back in the wind, showing her sweater that reads 'Icon.'

The election year had Cher's attention early. By February, she was lending her support to Democratic contender Joe Biden. In late February, Cher was due to perform 'Classic Cher' shows in Las Vegas. She performed the first two before finding herself sidelined with an unknown upper respiratory illness. As a result, she cancelled the four remaining dates that month to focus on her recovery, with the intention of rescheduling them.

The following month, Cher would start performing more 'Here We Go Again' tour dates. The politician tweeted his gratitude for her support, joking that he was willing to open for the star in Las Vegas.

Cher performed in Texas and Louisiana on 6, 7, and 10 March. By her 12 March date, she had to make a difficult announcement. Those early days of the month were when many learned about the COVID-19 pandemic, known then as the coronavirus outbreak. She postponed the dates until September, hoping she'd be able to pick up where she left off. Cher was also in talks on two different film projects that she'd have to pump the brakes on. *The Cher Show* also had to pause tour plans after completing its Broadway run and moving onto the show's next stage.

The lockdown was a complete change in lifestyle for so many people, Cher included. She used that time to continue to work on her music while also finding ways to connect with fans and give back to the world at large. During that time, Elijah and Marieangela King were living with Cher, who made a point of keeping in touch with her inner circle though they were apart. This included Chas, a few friends, Georgia, Georganne, and Paulette.

Cher was being careful for a number of reasons. As an asthmatic person, she was concerned that COVID-19 could do serious damage to her body. She was also vigilant about keeping Georgia, 93 that year, safe amid the uncertainty.

She began by recording her first-ever Spanish-language song, a cover of ABBA's 'Chiquita.' She debuted the single on 8 May, with the music video premiering the following day as part of UNICEF's COVID-19 Virtual Special. Cher also created the CherCares Pandemic Resource and Response Initiative (CCPRRI). She got involved in the initiative alongside Dr. Irwin Redlener, the head of Columbia University's Pandemic Resource and Response centre and co-founder of Children's Health Fund.

That same month, Cher's fans organised an effort online to return her 2001 album, *Living Proof*, to the charts, in keeping with similar activities by other fandoms amid global lockdowns. Cher didn't even know such a thing was possible until she was told her fans had gotten it back on the Global iTunes Chart.

That wasn't the only piece of Cher's work to enjoy a resurgence during lockdown. Many people found comfort in revisiting *Moonstruck*, with fans praising it as a perfect comfort watch for the uncertainty of the times.

In June 2020, Cher was once again sharing her feelings on social media as the death of George Floyd gave way to the Black Lives Matter movement. Protests across the country resonated deeply with Cher, who admitted she was too ill to join the crowds on Twitter during that time. Later, she explained she'd been diagnosed with bronchitis, which presented her with more complications as an asthmatic person.

Cher spoke out on many different issues online that summer. She lent support to the UK live music industry, underscoring how instrumental British audiences were to her and Sonny's early success. She highlighted causes that helped small businesses, women and families, and animals. Cher also spoke out about political issues that had taken rise in the US as they navigated the pandemic.

'Here We Go Again' tour dates were pushed back into autumn and winter, but as the pandemic continued, sadly, those too were cancelled. She was able to slowly make a public return as select events began to return that autumn, with many precautions in place. Cher attended the 2020 Billboard Music Awards in October, there to present the Icon Award to Garth Brooks.

Cher also started to get involved with voting efforts across the country as the election drew near. She spoke out in support of early voting and encouraged voters to support Joe Biden and Kamala Harris. She also spoke out about racial injustice, saying she keeps a photo of Trayvon Martin in her home as a reminder of how tragic but common racially motivated violence is.

Cher continued to speak out even after the election. She urged her fans to recognise the crisis in Armenia and Artsakh. She raised awareness about Kavaan, 'the world's loneliest elephant,' who was kept in a zoo where he was being mistreated in Islamabad, Pakistan. Cher campaigned with activists who wanted the elephant moved to a sanctuary. She thanked Prime Minister Imran Khan for the opportunity. The two discussed climate and animal rights issues when they met.

That November, Cher also joined Bryan Adams, Lenny Kravitz, Kylie Minogue, James Morrison, Robbie Williams, and more as part of the BBC's 2020 charity single for BBC Children in Need. The group performed a cover of Oasis' 'Stop Crying Your Heart Out.'

In December, *Bobbleheads: The Movie* premiered, marking Cher's first foray into voice acting since she guest appeared in a *Scooby Doo* episode with Sonny in the 1970s. The movie was put together remotely during the pandemic and didn't get much attention as a result, but for Cher, it was more about the fun of making the project and trying something new than its box-office success.

While many were overwhelmed by a difficult and uncertain year, Cher seemed to flourish in spite of what was happening in the world. She was finding ways to keep herself busy while also staying safe, which proved to be very inspirational for her fans.

Chapter Twenty-One

2021–2025

Cher didn't break her stride heading into 2021. As the world stood somewhere between shut down and reopened, Cher found ways to make her impact be felt.

In late April, *Cher and The Loneliest Elephant* debuted. The Smithsonian Channel documentary followed Cher's trip to Pakistan to see Kavaan along his journey to his new home and how her involvement made a difference.

Cher celebrated her 75th birthday in May 2021. In celebration, she announced that a biopic about her life was in development at Universal Pictures. The project would have Cher work with *Mamma Mia* producers Judy Craymer and Gary Goetzman, with Eric Roth writing the screenplay. Many were curious whether the soundtrack would feature contemporary tunes from throughout the artist's life or be filled with her own hints. Cher was coy about details early on, instead underscoring her excitement about the project.

The following month, proving she's as open to something new as ever, Cher joined TikTok. She introduced herself on the platform in classic Cher fashion – with gratuitous outfit and hair changes as she celebrated Pride Month. The introductory video quickly amassed over 6 million views on the platform. During Pride Month, Miley Cyrus paid homage to both Cher and her impact on the LGBTQ+ community with her take on 'Believe,' performed as part of *Stand By You*, a Pride Month special for Peacock.

Cher also made an appearance on MSNBC, where she talked about vaccines. She explained her desire to help underserved communities in both rural and urban areas around the country. She expressed her joy at having President Joe Biden in office and took the opportunity to continue condemning Donald Trump and the possible danger he could pose to society.

Saweetie also shouted out Cher that month. After the two met for a then-unannounced collaboration, Saweetie rethought her album rollout and decided to delay 'Pretty Bitch Music' to give the record 'feelings' and 'soul.' In a later interview, Saweetie explained that the more she got to know Cher, the more she understood the demeanour needed to move through the industry and get what you want without being trampled upon, especially as a woman.

In July, Cher took some time to travel to Zurich and visit her longtime friend, Tina Turner. At the time, the 'Simply the Best' singer was experiencing various health issues after having battled cancer, survived a stroke, and gotten a kidney transplant. Cher was grateful for the time the two women were able to spend together. She spent more time in Europe throughout the month, photographed in a few different locations as she enjoyed her time abroad.

Cher was back to work in August, posing for rocker and photographer Bryan Adams in a 2022 Pirelli calendar. Cher participated alongside Jennifer Hudson, Iggy Pop, and more.

That October, Cher made headlines for a lawsuit against the trustee of Sonny's estate, Mary Bono. According to the lawsuit, the trustee and the estate were withholding Cher's portion of Sonny and Cher royalties, plus other assets the former spouses shared. Cher alleges that Mary was able to do this by using the Copyright Act to cancel the transfer of copyrights, claiming the Bono Collection Trust sent notices of termination to several music publishers throughout 2016 that also terminated Cher's royalty rights without her consent.

Cher continued with her charitable work in November, appearing as part of a lineup that included Jon Batiste, Norah Jones, Steve Miller Band, Maggie Rogers, and more in a benefit concert for the Ka-Nying Shedrub Ling Monastery and Nagi Nunnery in Nepal. Richard Gere was also in attendance to support the cause. The fundraiser supported the monastery's work, which goes beyond spreading Buddha's teachings and encourages social action in their community and beyond.

In an interview that was published in early 2022, Cher explained that she makes a point of going out of her way to interact with all different types of people. She continued to note that in all her time living the unique life she has; she discovered if she didn't operate intentionally in this way, she could lose track of what was happening in the 'real world,' because so much of working in the entertainment industry involved working and living in a bubble.

Cher and Saweetie's collaboration, starring in a beauty campaign for MAC, 'Challenge Accepted with MAC.' The campaign featured high-energy professionals, from music to sports and more, showing the staying power of the products. When talking about beauty and style in interviews around the campaign, Cher was asked about dying her hair. She commended women who go grey, but said it wasn't for her. She's dedicated to keeping her mane black as long as she can.

There was also Cher's partnership with Ugg that launched that month. Stretching into beauty and fashion this way seemed a no-brainer for the artist, who was known for effortlessly dominating both arenas.

Cher mourned alongside the world when the new year kicked off with the heartbreaking news of Betty White's death. Cher got involved in an NBC special, *Celebrating Betty White: America's Golden Girl*, that honoured White on what would have been her 100th birthday. She performed the theme song to *The Golden Girls*, 'Thank You for Being a Friend,' on the soundstage the beloved sitcom was filmed on.

Cher was uncharacteristically quiet through February and early March, concerning her fans. She later took to Twitter to admit that she was having a hard time and dealing with a lot of hurt in recent years, mentioning family issues in particular. The next day, fans continued to check on Cher, who ensured that she would keep pushing and had a lot in her despite the difficulties she was facing.

In June, Cher teamed up with longtime friend and fellow fashion icon Donatella Versace for a capsule collection celebrating Pride 2022, dubbed 'CHERSACE.' The collection featured the brand's iconic Medusa-head logo made out of rainbow-coloured gems, with the name CHERSACE embellished over it. The design was featured on t-shirts, a hat, and socks. The proceeds from the collection benefited the organisation Gender Spectrum.

That autumn, Cher travelled to Paris for a surprise appearance at Paris Fashion Week. Cher worked with Oliver Rousteing of Balmain to model the brand's new handbag. She also walked in the show's finale in a Balmain bodysuit. It was a major moment, but what happened off the runway would prove to be more impactful.

During her time in Paris for the special event, Cher attended a number of parties. During one, she met Alexander 'AE' Edwards, a Universal Music Group executive and producer. Though he's 41 years Cher's junior, the two hit it off. AE was no stranger to dating in the spotlight, having previously been in a relationship with Amber Rose, with whom he shares son Slash Electric Alexander Edwards.

The two talked and got to know each other for a bit before being spotted out in Los Angeles together that November. The two were spotted going out to dinner at the beloved restaurant to the stars, Craig's, donning matching outfits and holding hands as they walked in. Of course, the relationship garnered a lot of attention. The two seemed to be from completely different worlds, and the age gap was one that the public couldn't ignore. Cher herself has admitted she understands how it can look strange to outsiders. That said, she's stood firm in her belief that her connection with AE is genuine and based in something deeper.

Cher didn't let the conversation around her relationship bother her. That same month, she attended the 2022 CFDA Awards. She attended as the guest of Laurie Lynne Stark, who was one-half of the Chrome Hearts duo receiving the Geoffrey Beene Lifetime Achievement Award at the event. Cher stunned on the red carpet, dressed in a leather Chrome Hearts Dress.

There was another very special event Cher was part of that month, getting the opportunity to present Diane Warren with an honorary Oscar at the Academy of Motion Picture Arts & Sciences' 13th Governors Awards. Other honourees that night included actor Michael J. Fox and directors Peter Weir and Euzhan Palcy. After years of stories and jokes about the making of 'If I Could Turn Back Time,' it was clear that there was no lasting bad blood between the frequent collaborators. Cher even stayed close by as Warren delivered her acceptance speech.

The year had a completely heartbreaking conclusion for Cher. On 11 December 2022, Cher revealed that her mother, Georgia Holt, had died at the age of 96. In the weeks leading up to Georgia's death, Cher made mention of the actress being hospitalised for pneumonia. Mother and daughter had their differences over the years, but their bond was close, and their love was fierce. Cher, along with sister Georganne, were completely crushed by the loss.

At the same time, death wasn't something that Cher's family shied away from discussing. Georgia, like Cher, believed in being celebrated rather than mourned. Cher expressed her desire to celebrate Georgia's life in her favourite place and said she deserved the world for making her into the woman she is. She had a lot of time to ruminate on what this transitional moment in her own life meant, battling the flu through much of the month on top of processing her loss.

AE did his best to lift Cher's spirits, surprising her on Christmas with a beautiful teardrop diamond ring. Excited, Cher shared it on Twitter, only to be met with questions about what the ring meant. A lot of people believed it was an engagement ring and questioned whether his intentions were pure. Cher later clarified that it wasn't an engagement ring, just a gift. Furthermore, she stood up for AE and expressed that he's never done anything that made her question the honesty of his intent.

Cher began 2023 focused on music and her relationship. She shared photos of her joyfully ringing in the new year with AE. She also mused about a new residency and more projects ahead as she kept her loyal Twitter followers posted.

All eyes were on AE and Cher as they attended events together throughout the month. The two were spotted with his son, Slash, having fun together at Disney World. Seeing that the relationship was serious enough for them to be spending time with his son furthered the public conversation about the unusual nature of the relationship. Cher, for her part, just continued doing what made her happy.

Cher also made sure to introduce AE to her sons. Despite rumours indicating her sons were wary of the relationship between her and AE, he came forward himself in an interview, calling the two 'my guys,' as he celebrated how well meeting each other's families had gone. Shortly thereafter, Cher and AE made their red carpet debut at Versace's Fall/ Winter 2023 Fashion Show in Los Angeles. The two were all smiles and looked genuinely enamoured as people continued to try to understand the relationship.

In March, Cher was excited to celebrate one of her favourite collaborators in the industry, longtime friend Carol Burnett. She wore a glittery black Bob Mackie jacket for the event and got to hang out with Mackie at the event. The special aired the following month in celebration of Burnett's 90th birthday. While she didn't perform, she did share some memories of the two from her early career. She thanked Burnett for all the help she gave Cher during her divorce from Sonny as she tried to establish herself as a solo act in television and music.

While doing press for the event, Cher opened up about new music, sharing her excitement to travel to the UK to record not one but two albums. She was excited to work on new music with AE. She also expressed her desire to get back on the road and see fans.

Around her 77th birthday, rumours began to spread alleging Cher and AE had broken up. Just a few days after her birthday, the conversation quickly shifted with the news that her close friend, the icon Tina Turner, died at age 83. Speaking with the press following the news going public, Cher admitted that while Turner had fought hard against various medical ailments, in her final months, she felt 'ready' to die. In fact, she'd felt that way for years prior.

Cher was able to visit Turner close to the end. In various interviews, Cher explained that she tried to get to Zurich to visit as much as possible because she never wanted Turner to feel like her peers had forgotten about her after she retired. During their final visit together, Turner gave Cher a special gift – a pair of her iconic sky-high heels, something the two women shared pride in wearing when they hit stages throughout their careers.

In August 2023, Cher revealed that she was starting over on the biopic project. She declined to explain exactly what didn't work about the original set-up, but emphasised she wouldn't resume work on the project until after the WGA and SAG-AFTRA strikes concluded. It wouldn't be until the following year that Eric Roth opened up about the project in an interview, admitting his screenplay was what ultimately wasn't working for Cher. Despite the decision to professionally part ways, he maintained a friendship with Cher, whom he'd met while working on 1987's *Suspect*.

Cher kicked off the autumn with the announcement that she had a new album, a Christmas album, on the way. She revealed the cover art for *Cher Christmas* on 7 September, clad in jeans and a loose white button-down, standing on a mound of snow with floating red and silver ornaments around her. It was her first featuring original material in over a decade. She also teased special appearances by other artists. Cher was sure to let eager fans know that this was 'not your mama's Christmas album.'

That month, Cher and AE were spotted out and about again, indicating to fans that any previous discord between the two was just temporary. Weeks later, the two popped up together at Paris Fashion Week, where their love story first began. They seemed happy as ever, with Cher changing between three different hairstyles throughout the course of the trip as she smiled on AE's arm.

Cher told *People Magazine* that the two had been an item for over a year and that she was having the time of her life in the relationship. She also opened up about working with AE on her Christmas album, letting him produce one of the tracks, 'Drop Top Sleigh.' She also praised the album for being eclectic, filled with songs she loved making rather than songs that followed a theme more cohesive than the holiday season itself.

On 6 October, Cher released the first single from the album, 'DJ Play a Christmas Song.' She celebrated the release at Paris Fashion Week, dancing along to the track at a club with AE at her side. The song debuted on the Billboard Hot 100, the first of her tracks to do so since 2002's 'Song for the Lonely.' Fans in the UK also came through for Cher, with the song reaching number 18 on the UK Singles Chart. There were also remixes of the song dropped throughout the following month, reimagined as a duet with different partners, including Kelly Clarkson.

The full album, her 27th studio album, was released on 20 October. It featured appearances from Stevie Wonder, Darlene Love, Michael Bublé, Tyga, and Cyndi Lauper. The album marked the beginning of the holiday season for the singer, who would perform in the Macy's Thanksgiving Day Parade just a few weeks later. She also appeared in NBC's *Christmas in Rockefeller Center* days later.

In December, Cher appeared as the headliner for the Royal Variety Performance at London's Royal Albert Hall. It wasn't her only event in the UK. She also appeared for a special event at the Odeon Leicester Square, 'In Conversation.' While she closed out 2023 riding a professional high, Cher continued to struggle in her personal relationships behind the scenes.

In the final days of the year, fans were abuzz with news Cher filed for a conservatorship over 46-year-old son Elijah. Cher expressed concerns for her son's status in recovery, as well as his mental health, amid what she claimed to be erratic financial decisions. With conservatorships as a hot topic in public conversation, the story took off. Cher did speak out on the issue, ultimately saying she was a mother struggling with her child's addiction.

Cher also graced the cover of *PAPER Magazine* that month. In a wide-ranging interview, she talked about how she never made peace with loving her voice, one of the major things that separates her from her legions of fans. She has loved every era of being Cher, however, as evidenced by her continuing strive for more. In fact, she said part of her excitement around 'Believe' was the fact that because of auto-tune, so many people weren't even aware it was a Cher song.

In January, the conversation around Cher and Elijah's relationship picked right back up with the news that her bid for a conservatorship was denied. The singer declined to comment on it publicly, though she continued to explore legal options to protect her son. The legal back and forth between the two would continue throughout most of the year.

A few weeks later, she was in the news for a much more positive reason. Cher was among the first-time nominees for induction to the Rock and Roll Hall of Fame. The timing of the nomination was particularly funny because months prior, during an appearance on *The Kelly Clarkson Show*, Cher went on a quick rant about how she'd never been recognised despite having accolades only the Rolling Stones could measure up to.

With the good news came more family drama, unfortunately. Rumours swirled that Cher was removed from the guest list of Chaz's wedding to fiancée Shara. Ultimately, it was much ado about nothing. To date, Chaz and Shara have not tied the knot.

Another relationship in Cher's life was faring much better. Cher and AE continued to enjoy time together, once again heading to Paris Fashion Week. The two were seated in the front row at the Balmain show, where they first connected a year and a half prior. Shortly thereafter, reporting indicated that despite insinuations to the contrary by the media previously, Cher was getting along well with AE's ex, Amber Rose, as they spent more time with Slash.

In March, it was announced that Cher would be part of the 30th anniversary celebration for amfAR, The Foundation for AIDS Research. Cher was confirmed to be performing at the organisation's annual gala, held at Cannes' Hôtel du Cap-Eden-Roc that spring. Cher, who first got involved with the organisation while getting to know Elizabeth Taylor, was thrilled at the opportunity to raise more awareness for the organisation.

April began with Cher being honoured at the 2024 iHeartRadio Music Awards with the icon award, recognising her career's work. Before Cher took the stage to perform and accept her award, Meryl Streep said a few words about her dear friend, her talent, and her 'giant heart.' A video tribute followed the speech, which gave way to Jennifer Hudson using her powerhouse vocals to perform 'If I Could Turn Back Time.' When she transitioned to 'Believe,' Cher joined her on stage for a special duet. AE was by Cher's side for the special celebration.

Later that month, it was made official that Cher would be inducted into the Rock and Roll Hall of Fame. Joking about her previous snarky comments about the accolade before her nomination, Cher teased that she would still 'accept it as me,' hinting she'd get a few barbs in.

In May, Cher took some time to celebrate one of her favourite people. She attended the premiere of Bob Mackie's documentary, *Bob Mackie: Naked Illusion*. Playing a monumental role in Mackie's storied journey, Cher was happy to lend her support and share some kind thoughts about her dear friend while chatting with reporters.

The same month, Cher turned 78. She celebrated by spending time in Paris with AE. The surprise trip was the kind of gesture that not only made Cher feel special but also assured in their relationship.

The month concluded with Cher winning her lawsuit against Mary Bono. While it wasn't the original amount discussed, Cher was determined to have been shorted approximately £317,000 in unpaid royalties as a result of the unconsented termination.

In June, Cher took some time out to celebrate the LGBTQ community. During a visit to The Abbey in West Hollywood, Cher celebrated with the community amid Pride Month and praised the LGBTQ community for their ardent support throughout her career.

Weeks later, a new ad rolled out featuring Cher singing 'I Got You Babe' in EastEnders' Queen Vic pub. The funny nod to UK television was put together to launch UKTV's U streaming platform. The hilarious spot has Cher superimposed in different locations as she sings, from inside a comedy to a food competition show to an action-packed car chase.

One of Cher's biggest projects finally came one step closer to fruition in July 2024. Cher announced that her memoir *Cher: The Memoir* would be released in two parts. The first part was to be published that November, with part two coming at the same time the following year. The memoir was published by HarperCollins' Dey Street Books.

Following the momentum of looking back at her career, Cher began the month of August by announcing a new greatest hits album, *Forever*. The 21-track album was released just weeks later. A digital-only release, *Forever Fan*, included 40 tracks, featuring Sonny and Cher tracks as well as Cher's solo work.

In September, Cher withdrew her petition for a conservatorship over Elijah, explaining that they'd worked together as a family to reach a place of understanding and that she felt confident in Elijah's ability to make sound decisions for himself. The news was reassuring for fans who were worried for Elijah's safety and rooting for an amicable resolution between mother and son.

That same month, Cher was announced as the headliner as Victoria's Secret brought back their once-beloved fashion show, reimagined to be more inclusive amid a brand overhaul. Tyla also performed at the televised runway event, which took place just weeks later. Cher also attended the inaugural California Crown, among celebrities including Beyoncé, Damson Idris, Allison Janney and more.

Cher was out and about throughout October 2024, from supporting Chaz in his role in *Little Bites* to gearing up the excitement for her memoir. Cher also spoke out amid the rapidly changing U.S. presidential race, backing Kamala Harris and Tim Walz as the Democrats tried once again to fight for a win against Donald Trump.

The most important moment of the month, one that celebrated Cher's monumental career and recognised everything she's achieved within it, came when Cher was inducted as part of the 2024 class into the Rock and Roll Hall of Fame. Cher was introduced by Zendaya. In a heartfelt acceptance speech, Cher recalled falling in love with entertainment, watching Cinderella as a little girl and having a mother who never discouraged her from chasing her dreams. While determination and grit played a role, Cher also acknowledged how much luck played a part in her story. She concluded with celebrating the women in her life and in the world watching who were fighting for a path forward for their dreams. She thanked her family and closest friends as she wrapped up her speech.

The following month, Cher embarked on a book tour that spanned not just the US, but dipped into Europe as well. *Cher: The Memoir*'s first volume was released on 19 November 2024. The next day, the tour began in New York City. Many readers were eager to learn more details about Cher's relationships and her early life. The die-hard fans who knew a lot of Cher's story already appreciated how her voice came through in the telling of them.

Cher enjoyed a lot of adoration for the book, but she also had a scary situation occur at the year's end. Cher was one of over 20,000 people forced to evacuate her Malibu neighbourhood as the Franklin Fire ripped through the area.

In 2025, Cher has been working on new music. Hinting at an album to come at some point of the year and perhaps a tour to accompany it, the ever-talented diva shows no signs of slowing down. She is still active not just in her career but in her closest friendships, her relationship with AE, and her limitless love for her two sons.

Chapter Twenty-Two

Legacy

It's hard to find words to describe Cher and her illustrious career that haven't been spoken countless times before. It's amazing to consider how a young woman who knew she had a love for entertaining would take her would have a life that took twist and turn after twist and turn to bring her to heights beyond her own wildest dreams.

Like so many young people, Cher saw herself in the world around her – from the Disney movies and Broadway plays that established her love of entertainment to the sets that brought her mom closer to stardom in her own right to the streets of Los Angeles, which she finessed to become her training camp for a career that spans decades. Cher took pieces of every experience with her to build a world that made sense to her and became home to countless lost and lonely people who wanted a bigger life.

In her work with Sonny and the decades that followed, Cher created music that spanned genres and generations, finding different ways to connect with audiences while always staying true to herself and her instincts as an artist. Cher honed her voice, though she never gives herself much credit for it, to a distinct tool for which she has become revered by fans around the globe.

Where the world tried to box her in, Cher continued to break out. She proved herself far more than half of a duo, far wider-ranging than just a singer. In her years in the spotlight, Cher became recognised and renowned for her skills as an actress and for her talent in captivating audiences as an all-around performer. She proved herself able to hold her own as a fashion icon, proving to be a model and a muse for different designers throughout her own history. Her partnerships with Bob Mackie made the duo one of the most talked about and referenced in the intersection of pop culture and fashion.

As Cher's star rose, she proved that she doesn't just have talent, but also compassion and true substance. She has been vulnerable about her highs and lows. She doesn't boast about a perfect family, but rather opens up about imperfections, as painful as they've been. She's supported both of her children through monumental life changes, albeit imperfectly, always with her love and concern as a parent at the forefront.

In publicly embracing the LGBTQ community, Cher has made millions of people feel more in tune with themselves. She's also brought her voice to countless other causes dear to her, from animal conservation efforts to helping children with craniofacial differences. In all of her activism, Cher sends the message that she believes in equality among humanity in the truest sense. That feeling of inclusiveness and genuine care has made her a beloved figure to different people from all walks of life.

Whether it's admiration of her talent as an artist and entertainer, her heart as a humanitarian, or her capacity as a public figure, contributing to various areas of art and society, Cher has won the hearts of legions of fans. Her legacy has been, in so many ways, set in stone and yet, it's still being crafted each time she takes a stage, sends a tweet, or writes a new track.

Bibliography

Discography

Solo
Cher. (1965). *All I Really Want To Do* [Album]. Imperial Records, Liberty Records.
Cher. (1966). *The Sonny Side of Chér* [Album]. Imperial Records, Liberty Records.
Cher. (1966). *Chér* [Album]. Imperial Records, Liberty Records.
Cher. (1967). *With Love, Chér* [Album]. Imperial Records, Liberty Records.
Cher. (1968). *Backstage* [Album]. Imperial Records, Liberty Records.
Cher. (1969). *3614 Jackson Highway* [Album]. ATCO Records, Rhino Entertainment Company.
Cher. (1971). *Gypsys, Tramps & Thieves* [Album]. Kapp Records, MCA Records, Universal Music Group.
Cher. (1972). *Foxy Lady* [Album]. Kapp Records, MCA Records.
Cher. (1973). *Bittersweet White Light* [Album]. MCA Records.
Cher. (1973). *Half-Breed* [Album]. MCA Records.
Cher. (1974). *Dark Lady* [Album]. MCA Records.
Cher. (1975). *Stars* [Album]. Warner Bros.
Cher. (1976). *I'd Rather Believe in You* [Album]. Warner Bros.
Cher. (1977). *Cherished* [Album]. Warner Bros.
Cher. (1979). *Take Me Home* [Album]. Casablanca Records, Philips Records.
Cher. (1979). *Prisoner* [Album]. Casablanca Records.
Cher. (1982). *I Paralyze* [Album]. Columbia Records.
Cher. (1987). *Cher* [Album]. Geffen Records.
Cher. (1989). *Heart of Stone* [Album]. Geffen Records.
Cher. (1991). *Love Hurts* [Album]. Geffen Records.
Cher. (1995). *It's a Man's World* [Album]. Warner Music Group, Reprise Records.
Cher. (1998). *Believe* [Album]. Warner Bros.
Cher. (2000). *Not Com.mercial* [Album]. ARTISTdirect.
Cher. (2001). *Living Proof* [Album]. Warner Music Group, Warner Bros.
Cher. (2013). *Closer to the Truth* [Album]. Warner Bros.
Cher. (2018). *Dancing Queen* [Album]. Warner Bros.
Cher. (2023). *Christmas* [Album]. Warner Records.

Collaborative Albums
Sonny and Cher. (1965). *Look at Us* [Album]. Atco Records.
Sonny and Cher. (1966). *The Wonderous World of Sonny & Chér* [Album]. Atco Records.
Sonny and Cher. (1967). *In Case You're in Love* [Album]. Atco Records.
Sonny and Cher. (1972). *All I Ever Need Is You* [Album]. Kapp Records, MCA Records.

Sonny and Cher. (1973). *Mama Was a Rock and Roll Singer, Papa Used to Write All Her Songs* [Album]. MCA Records.
Allman and Woman. (1977). *Two the Hard Way* [Album]. Warner Bros.
Black Rose. (1980). *Black Rose* [Album]. Casablanca Records.

Compilations
Various Artists. (1965). *Baby Don't Go - Sonny & Cher and Friends* [Album]. Reprise Records.
Sonny and Cher. (1967). *The Best of Sonny & Chér* [Album]. Atlantic Records, Atco Records.
Sonny and Cher. (1968). *Sonny & Cher's Greatest Hits* [Album]. Atlantic Records, Atco Records.
Cher. (1968). *Cher's Golden Greats* [Album]. Imperial Records, Liberty Records.
Cher. (1972). *Superpack Vol. 1* [Album]. United Artists Records.
Cher. (1972). *Superpack Vol. 2* [Album]. United Artists Records.
Sonny and Cher. (1972). *The Two of Us* [Album]. Atco Records.
Sonny and Cher. (1974). *Greatest Hits* [Album]. MCA Records.
Cher. (1974). *Greatest Hits* [Album]. MCA Records.
Cher. (1975). *Sings the Hits* [Album]. Springboard International Records.
Sonny and Cher. (1975). *The Greatest Hits* [Album]. Atlantic Records.
Sonny and Cher. (1981). *The Greatest Hits of Sonny & Cher* [Album]. J&B.
Sonny and Cher. (1991). *The Beat Goes On: The Best of Sonny & Cher* [Album]. Atlantic Records, Atco Records.
Cher. (1992). *Greatest Hits: 1965–1992* [Album]. Geffen Records.
Cher. (1999). *If I Could Turn Back Time: Cher's Greatest Hits* [Album]. Geffen Records.
Cher. (1999). *The Greatest Hits* [Album]. WEA Records.
Cher. (2003). *The Very Best of Cher* [Album]. Warner Bros., Warner Strategic Marketing.
Cher. (2005). *Gold* [Album]. Geffen Records.
Cher. (2011). *Icon* [Album]. Geffen Records.
Cher. (2024). *Forever* [Album]. Warner Records.

Live Albums
Sonny and Cher. (1971). *Sonny & Cher Live* [Live Album]. Kapp Records, MCA Records.
Sonny and Cher. (1973). *Live in Las Vegas Vol. 2* [Live Album]. Kapp Records, MCA Records.
Various Artists. (1999). *VH1 Divas 1999* [Live Album]. Arista Records.
Various Artists. (2002). *VH1 Divas Las Vegas* [Live Album]. VH1.
Cher. (2003). *Live! The Farewell Tour* [Live Album]. Warner Bros.

Soundtrack Albums
Sonny and Cher. (1967). *Good Times* [Soundtrack Album]. Atlantic Records, Atco Records.
Cher. (1969). *Chastity* [Soundtrack Album]. Atco Records.
Various Artists. (1990). *Mermaids* [Soundtrack Album]. Geffen Records.
Aguilera, Christina; Cher. (2010) *Burlesque* [Soundtrack Album]. RCA Records.
Various Artists. (2018). *Mamma Mia! Here We Go Again* [Soundtrack Album]. Capitol Records, Polydor Limited.

Video Albums
Cher. (1992). *Extravaganza: Live at the Mirage* [Video Album]. Sony BMG, EV Classics.
Cher. (1993). *The Video Collection* [Video Album]. Geffen Records.
Cher. (1999). *Live in Concert* [Video Album]. HBO Home Video.

Cher. (2003). *The Farewell Tour* [Video Album]. Image Entertainment.
Cher. (2004). *The Very Best of Cher: The Video Hits Collection* [Video Album]. Warner Music Vision.

Filmography

Dexter, Maury, director. *Wild on the Beach*. Twentieth Century Fox, 1965.
Friedkin, William, director. *Good Times*. Columbia Pictures, 1967.
Bono, Sonny. *Chastity*. American International Pictures, 1969.
Bushnell, Scott. *Come Back to the 5 & Dime, Jimmy Dean, Jimmy Dean*. Sandcastle 5 : Viacom Enterprises, 1982.
Nichols, Mike, director. *Silkwood*. ABC Motion Pictures, 1983.
Bogdanovich, Peter, director. *Mask*. Universal Pictures, 1985.
Jewison, Norman, director. *Moonstruck*. Metro-Goldwyn-Mayer Studios, 1987.
Miller, George, director. *The Witches of Eastwick*. Warner Bros, 1987.
Yates, Peter, director. *Suspect*. Tri-Star Pictures, 1987.
Benjamin, Richard, director. *Mermaids*. Orion Pictures, 1990.
Altman, Robert, director. *The Player*. Fine Line Features, 1992.
Altman, Robert, director. *Prêt-À-Porter (Ready to Wear)*. Miramax Films, 1994.
Mazursky, Paul, director. *Faithful*. New Line Cinema, 1996.
Zeffirelli, Franco, director. *Tea with Mussolini*. Universal Pictures, 1999.
Thomas, Bradley. *Stuck On You*. Twentieth Century Fox, 2003.
De Line, Donald. *Burlesque*. Sony Pictures Releasing, 2010.
Coraci, Frank, director. *Zookeeper*. Sony Pictures Releasing, 2011.
Cher. *Edith + Eddie*. 2017.
Parker, Ol, director. *Mamma Mia! Here We Go Again*. Universal Pictures, 2018.
Wise, Kirk, director. *Bobbleheads: The Movie*. Universal 1440 Entertainment, 2020.
Cher. *Little Bites*. RLJE Films, Shudder, 2024.

Television

Bearde, C; Blye, A. [Producers]. (1971–1974). *The Sonny and Cher Comedy Hour* [TV Series].
Geffen, D. [Producer]. (1975–1976). *The Cher Show* [TV Series].
Hahn, P; Vanoff, N. [Producers]. (1976–1977). *The Sonny & Cher Show* [TV Series].
Cher. (1985, 9 April). [Interview by J. Rivers]. In *The Tonight Show*. https://www.youtube.com/watch?v=HiEj5TVdrj4
Cher. (1986, 22 May). Cher Calls Dave an Asshole (D. Letterman, Interviewer) [Interview]. In *The Tonight Show*. https://www.youtube.com/watch?v=k8ZWZw8kykw
Cher, & Bono, S. (1987, 13 November). Sonny & Cher (D. Letterman, Interviewer) [Interview]. In *Late Night with David Letterman*. https://www.youtube.com/watch?v=7msTqzjZ7PU
Cher. (1988, 11 April). Cher (B. Walters, Interviewer) [Interview]. In *Barbara Walters Special*. https://www.youtube.com/watch?v=_pLPg1_c2Zk
Cher. (1991, 31 October). Cher on Letterman (D. Letterman, Interviewer) [Interview]. In *Late Show with David Letterman*. https://www.youtube.com/watch?v=BO68QOgDEw8
Cher. (1991, 30 October). Working Out with Cher (S. J. Raphael, Interviewer) [Interview]. In *The Sally Jessy Raphael Show*. https://www.youtube.com/watch?v=KSrfRbdbnMQ
Weekend Update: Opera Man. (1992, 26 September). *Saturday Night Live*. NBC. https://www.youtube.com/watch?v=kR06f1EET0k
Cher. (1992, October 23). Cher Talks About Craniofacial Association (M. Povich, Interviewer) [Interview]. In *The Maury Povich Show*. https://www.youtube.com/watch?v=PT-ADlgQeDg

Cher. (1995, October). *Top of the Pops*. MTV Persia. https://www.youtube.com/watch?v=VeZ_u2e-Mzo

Cher. (1996, 27 June). Cher and Dave (D. Letterman, Interviewer) [Interview]. In *Late Show with David Letterman*. https://www.youtube.com/watch?v=bL5lqHtByuY

Cher. (1999, 11 January). *American Music Awards* [Award Show]. ABC. https://www.youtube.com/watch?v=uy2-c7KKLoM

Cher . (1999, 3 April). Cher on Larry King Live (L. King, Interviewer) [Interview]. In *Larry King Live*. https://www.youtube.com/watch?v=p6O1uFI1Ahc

Cher. (2001, 9 November). Cher- "Music's No Good Without You" (K. Luuk, Interviewer) [Interview]. In *Sen kväll med Luuk*. https://www.youtube.com/watch?v=mV-4MZudAX8

Staff Author. (2001, 19 October). *Behind the scenes at the Pops*. Bbc.co.uk; BBC News. http://news.bbc.co.uk/2/hi/entertainment/1608247.stm

Cher. (2002, 11 September). CNN Special Edition: September 11: One Year Later (L. King, Interviewer) [Interview]. In *Larry King Live*. https://web.archive.org/web/20030810195003/https://edition.cnn.com/TRANSCRIPTS/0209/11/lkl.00.html

Cher. (2002, 1 March). Cher (R. O'Donnell, Interviewer) [Interview]. In *The Rosie O'Donnell Show*. https://www.youtube.com/watch?v=Ovk0v6XSqMk

Cher. (2002, 20 June). Cher (C. McFadden, Interviewer) [Interview]. In *Primetime*. https://www.youtube.com/watch?v=bRsbalOdy_U

E! (2003, 28 September). *Cher*. E! True Hollywood Story. https://www.facebook.com/share/v/1HvpxM552q/

Cher. (2003, 27 October). [Interview by S. Scully]. In C-*SPAN Washington Journal*. https://www.youtube.com/watch?v=rLSXK4P6SHE

Cher. (2003, 16 December). Cher, The One and Only (H. Smith, Interviewer) [Interview]. In *The Early Show*. https://www.youtube.com/watch?v=npTys0H2IfA

Cook, D. (2004, October 6). My first time with Dylan. *Salon*. https://www.salon.com/2004/10/06/dylan_6/

Cher. (2006, June 14). Operation Helmet (P. Slen, Interviewer) [Interview]. In *C-SPAN Washington Journal*. https://www.c-span.org/program/washington-journal/operation-helmet/159137

Cher. (2019, October 4). Sean Hayes Spots Cher in the Audience (S. Hayes, Interviewer) [Interview]. In *The Ellen Degeneres Show*. https://www.youtube.com/watch?v=vZp7WdgOoO8

Books

Andersen, Hans Christian. *The Ugly Duckling*. Narrated by Cher. Windham Hill Records. (1986). https://www.youtube.com/watch?v=ltLX8BdeMQA

Bono, S. (1991). *And the Beat Goes on* (1st ed.). Pocket Books.

Berman, C. (2001). *Cher*. Chelsea House Publishers.

Bono, C., & Fitzpatrick, B. (2011). *Transition: The Story of How I Became a Man* (1st ed.). Dutton.

Works Written By Cher

Cher, & Haas, R. (1991). *Forever Fit : The Lifetime Plan for Health, Fitness, and Beauty* (1st ed.). Bantam Books.

Cher, & Coplon, J. (1998). *The First Time* (1st ed.). Simon & Schuster.

Cher, C. (2024). *Cher: The Memoir, Part One* (1st ed.). Dey Street Books.

Online resources
UCLA Irv and Xiaoyan Drasnin Communication Archive. (1983). Cher speaking at UCLA 1/19/1983. In *UCLA*. https://www.youtube.com/watch?v=TIACFF_KGiU
Oscars. (1986, March 24). *Jane Fonda Introduces Cher: 1986 Oscars*. YouTube; The Academy of Motion Picture Arts and Sciences. https://www.youtube.com/watch?v=i-ffIC2YnKk
Tactical Air and Land Forces Subcomittee. (2007). Update on the Use of Combat Helmets, Vehicle Armor and Body Armor by Ground Forces in Operation Iraqi Freedom and Operation Enduring Freedom: House Hearing. In *GovInfo*. The Commitee on Armed Services, House of Representatives, 109 Congress, Second Session. https://www.govinfo.gov/content/pkg/CHRG-109hhrg33590/html/
The Bobbie Wygant Archive. (1990, December 8). *Cher, Winona Ryder, & Christina Ricci Interview - "Mermaids."* YouTube; Bobbie Wygant Archive. https://www.youtube.com/watch?v=-pXMRzjBqHY
Oscars. (2009, July 1). *Cher Wins Best Actress | 60th Oscars (1988)*. YouTube. https://www.youtube.com/watch?v=raybaccaAaU
EZCLZIV/SCLUZAY. (2015). *The Work – Once Upon a Time in Shaolin*. SCLUZAY. https://scluzay.com/work
Cher - Trivia. (2025). Notstarring.com. https://www.notstarring.com/actors/cher

Articles
George, W. (1957, 28 October). Elvis Wriggles, Fans Scream at Pan-Pacific. *Los Angeles Times*. https://www.elvispresleymusic.com.au/pictures/1957-pan-pacific-newspaper.html
Twin Cities Music Highlights. (1967, 14 July). *Sonny Without Cher: 1967*. Twin Cities Music Highlights. https://twincitiesmusichighlights.net/event/sonny-without-cher-1967/
Allen, J. (1982, 1 February). Cher and Altman on Broadway. *New York Magazine*. The Stacks Reader. http://www.thestacksreader.com/cher-and-altman-on-broadway/
Zarroli, J. (1985, February 15). *Cher Is "Woman of Year" for Hasty Pudding Club*. Los Angeles Times. https://www.latimes.com/archives/la-xpm-1985-02-15-ca-3404-story.html
United Press International. (1985, May 16). Cher and "Mask" director argue during film festival. *The Ohio State Lantern*, 12. https://osupublicationarchives.osu.edu/?a=d&d=LTN19850516-01.2.48
Cher. (1988, January). Interview: Cher (H. Jacobson, Interviewer) [Interview]. In *Film Comment*. https://www.filmcomment.com/article/interview-cher/
Garties, G. (1988, July 19). Cher and Boyfriend Say Media Spotlight to Blame for Incident. *AP*. https://web.archive.org/web/20230319115414/https://apnews.com/article/7aafc6d44a8470a1409c1191c370115c
Sessums, K. (1990, November). Cher Starred and Feathered. *Vanity Fair*, 162–168; 228–230. https://archive.vanityfair.com/article/1990/11/cher-starred-and-feathered
Heller, Z. (1993, May 8). *Cher: The mercy tour: Cher wasn't sure what sent her to stricken Armenia, land of her fathers, to hand out love and toys. But she was looking for a way to change her life, and this seemed a good place to start | The Independent*. Independent- Culture; The Independent. https://www.the-independent.com/arts-entertainment/cher-the-mercy-tour-cher-wasn-t-sure-what-sent-her-to-stricken-armenia-land-of-her-fathers-to-hand-out-love-and-toys-but-she-was-looking-for-a-way-to-change-her-life-and-this-seemed-a-good-place-to-start-2321930.html
Staff Author. (1994, 30 May). *The Beat Doesn't Go On: Where the Heck is Cher?* Orlando Sentinel; Tribune Publishing. https://www.orlandosentinel.com/1994/05/30/the-beat-doesnt-go-on-where-the-heck-is-cher/
Klein, R. (1996, October). Architectural Digest Visits Cher. *Architectural Digest*. https://archive.architecturaldigest.com/article/1996/10/cher

Allman, E. B., & Hawkey, R. (1997, 1 June). Deadsy (L. Marburger, Interviewer) [Interview]. In *Lollipop Magazine*. https://lollipopmagazine.com/1997/06/deadsy-interview/

Taylor, M., & Rawling, B. (1999, February). Recording Cher's "Believe" (S. Sillitoe, Interviewer) [Interview]. In *Sound on Sound*. https://www.soundonsound.com/techniques/recording-cher-believe

Ladd, M. E. (2000, 15 July). Celebrity Obsession: I Walked the Line. *Ape Culture*. https://www.apeculture.com/music/chercon.htm

The Associated Press. (2001, September 2). *Cher accused of labor violations in home construction*. SouthCoast TODAY; New Bedford Standard-Times. https://www.southcoasttoday.com/story/lifestyle/2001/09/02/cher-accused-labor-violations-in/50426748007/

Ladd, M. E. (2002). Summer of Cher: CherCon 2002 & The Farewell Tour. *Ape Culture*. https://www.apeculture.com/music/summerofcher.htm

Altman, E. B.; et al. (2005, 7 April). The Children of Rock (M. Binelli, Interviewer) [Interview]. In *Rolling Stone*. https://www.rollingstone.com/music/music-news/the-children-of-rock-99823/

Gundersen, E. (2008, February 7). *Spirited Cher goes on and on with the show*. Norwich Bulletin; The Bulletin. https://www.norwichbulletin.com/story/entertainment/local/2008/02/07/spirited-cher-goes-on-on/65031252007/

Millan, M. (2009). *Cher - Cher, Geffen Records, 1987* [Review of *Cher - Cher, Geffen Records, 1987*, by Cher]. https://dailyvault.com/toc.php5?review=6105

Moody, N. M. (2009, 24 February). *Cher lies low when in Sin City*. Spokesman.com; The Spokesman-Review. https://www.spokesman.com/stories/2009/feb/24/cher-lies-low-when-in-sin-city/

Reuters. (2009, 4 June). *Cher sues record label for $6.2 million*. Abc.net.au; ABC News. https://www.abc.net.au/news/2009-06-04/cher-sues-record-label-for-62-million/1703626

Allman, E. B. (2010, 9 July). Celebrity Apocalypse: A Conversation With Artist Elijah Blue (N. Kreiss, Interviewer) [Interview]. In *HuffPost*. https://www.huffpost.com/entry/celebrity-apocalype-a-con_b_638695

Radish, C. (2010, 17 November). *Cher interview- "Burlesque."* Collider; Valnet Publishing Group. https://collider.com/burlesque-cher-interview

Maschwitz, S. (2011, 13 September). A Song For the Lonely. *Prolost*. https://prolost.com/blog/2011/9/13/a-song-for-the-lonely.html

Cooper, L. (2012, 27 January). *Cher subject of internet death hoax*. NME. https://www.nme.com/news/music/cher-1270598

Cordeiro, A. (2013, October 28). Cher in Nepal. *Trinta Dias No Nepal*. https://trintadiasnonepal.wordpress.com/2013/10/28/cher-in-nepal/

Allman, E. B. (2014, February 5). Cher's Son Elijah Blue Felt "Shunned" as a Child (R. Marciano, Interviewer) [Interview]. In *Entertainment Tonight*. https://www.etonline.com/news/143228_Cher_Son_Elijah_Blue_Felt_Shunned_as_a_Child

Page Six Team. (2014, 17 March). *Bob Mackie bows out of Cher's "Dressed to Kill" world tour*. Page Six; New York Post. https://pagesix.com/2014/03/17/bob-mackie-bows-out-of-chers-dressed-to-kill-world-tour/

Nash, A. (2014, August 5). *Music Icon Cher Discusses Identity, Marriage, Motherhood*. AARP Entertainment; AARP. https://www.aarp.org/entertainment/music/info-2014/cher-music-closer-to-truth.html

Bustos, S. (2016, 5 November). *Cher returns to Miami Sunday to campaign for Clinton/Kaine ticket on final day of early voting*. Politico. https://www.politico.com/states/florida/story/2016/11/cher-returns-to-miami-sunday-to-campaign-for-clinton-kaine-ticket-on-final-day-of-early-voting-107125

Craddock, L. (2016, August 2). *Cher Fan Creates "I'm With Cher" Campaign | Billboard.* Billboard; Penske Media Corporation. https://www.billboard.com/music/pop/cher-fan-im-with-cher-campaign-7460894/

Wheway, D. (2016, October 1). WATCH! Cher Attends One Young World Summit. C*her News.* https://chernews.blogspot.com/2016/10/watch-cher-attends-one-young-world.html

Derschowitz, J. (2017, September 28). Cher musical "The Cher Show" to make 2018 Broadway bow. *Entertainment Weekly.* https://ew.com/theater/2017/09/28/cher-musical-broadway-2018/

Sen, M. (2017, 24 February). Cher's Era. *Hazlitt.* https://hazlitt.net/feature/chers-era

Wete, B. (2017, May 22). *Cher Planks Way Better Than You at 71 | Billboard.* Billboard; Penske Media Corporation. https://www.billboard.com/music/awards/cher-proves-she-can-plank-way-better-than-you-at-71-7801280/

Megarry, D. (2018, March 6). *Cher apologises for taking a selfie with Malcolm Turnbull at Mardi Gras.* Gay Times. https://www.gaytimes.com/life/cher-apologises-taking-selfie-malcolm-turnbull-mardi-gras/

McHenry, J. (2018, July 18). *Why "Mamma Mia! Here We Go Again" Cast Cher As Meryl Streep's Mother.* Vulture; New York Magazine. https://www.vulture.com/2018/07/why-mamma-mia-here-we-go-again-cast-cher-as-meryls-mother.html

Hetrick, A. (2018, December 4). *Watch Cher's Surprise Performance at Opening-Night Curtain Call of The Cher Show.* Playbill. https://playbill.com/article/watch-chers-surprise-performance-at-opening-night-curtain-call-of-the-cher-show

JustJared Staff. (2020, February 3). *Cher Stars in DSquared2's Spring Summer Icon Fashion Campaign.* Just Jared. https://www.justjared.com/2020/02/03/cher-stars-in-dsquared2s-spring-summer-icon-fashion-campaign/

Drew, I. (2020, May 4). *How Cher Is Combatting Coronavirus.* Billboard; Penske Media Corporation. https://www.billboard.com/music/music-news/cher-coronavirus-interview-9370577/

Wells, I. (2021, 28 June). The Making of "Moonstruck." *The Walrus.* https://web.archive.org/web/20210628210133/https://thewalrus.ca/the-making-of-moonstruck/

Bennett, J. (2022, March 11). *Cher is "having personal problems," apologizes to fans for being "MIA."* Page Six; New York Post. https://pagesix.com/2022/03/11/cher-is-having-personal-problems-apologizes-to-fans/

Barrett, C. (2022, October 20). The Navy let Cher perform on ship in '89. It's regretted it ever since. *Military Times.* https://www.militarytimes.com/off-duty/military-culture/2022/10/20/the-navy-let-cher-perform-on-ship-in-89-its-regretted-it-ever-since/

Moran, J. (2023, October 26). Cher Just Doesn't Quit. *PAPER Magazine.* https://www.papermag.com/cher-cover#rebelltitem32

Bell, S. (2023, October 27). Cher's Son Estranged Wife Alleges Singer "Continues to Interfere" as Couple Agreed to Work on Marriage amid Divorce. *People Magazine.* https://people.com/cher-accused-interfering-son-elijah-blue-allman-marieangela-king-divorce-8383861

Brew, S. (2024, 1 March). *Cher rejected Eric Roth's biopic script.* Film Stories. https://filmstories.co.uk/news/exclusive-cher-rejects-biopic-script/

Stanton, E. (2024, May 31). *Cher wins years-long legal battle over royalties with Sonny Bono's widow.* Fox Business. https://www.foxbusiness.com/entertainment/cher-wins-years-long-legal-battle-over-royalties-sonny-bonos-widow

Greene, A. (2024, October 19). Cher Proudly Declares "I Changed the Sound of Music Forever" in 2024 Rock Hall Induction Speech. *Rolling Stone.* https://www.rollingstone.com/music/music-news/cher-rock-and-roll-hall-of-fame-2024-speech-1235136176/

Dear Reader,

We hope you have enjoyed this book, but why not share your views on social media? You can also follow our pages to see more about our other products: facebook.com/penandswordbooks or follow us on X @penswordbooks

You can also view our products at www.pen-and-sword.co.uk (UK and ROW) or www.penandswordbooks.com (North America).

To keep up to date with our latest releases and online catalogues, please sign up to our newsletter at: www.pen-and-sword.co.uk/newsletter

If you would like a printed catalogue with our latest books, then please email: enquiries@pen-and-sword.co.uk or telephone: 01226 734555 (UK and ROW) or email: uspen-and-sword@casematepublishers.com or telephone: (610) 853-9131 (North America).

We respect your privacy and we will only use personal information to send you information about our products.

Thank you!